SACRED SPACE

Inspired by one of the most successful spirituality websites around (and for good reason), *Sacred Space* offers readers short but profound meditations on the daily scriptures. Friendly, concise, and consistently thought-provoking, these books are perfect for anyone who would like to pray more and be more connected to God, but may feel too busy to do so. In other words, everyone!

James Martin, S.J.
Author of *My Life with the Saints*

The website Sacred Space has been helping millions to pray for some years. Now Ave Maria Press makes these very helpful and easily usable prayer-helps available in handsome and accessible form, including pocket-sized booklets for the Advent-Christmas and Lenten seasons. What a great service to God's people! I hope millions more will buy the books. God is being well served.

William A. Barry, S.J.
Author of *Paying Attention to God: Discernment in Prayer*

I don't know any other guides to prayer that are so direct, profound, and effective. It's no wonder that right around the world they have proved extraordinarily helpful in leading busy people to stay in touch with the presence of God.

Gerald O'Collins, S.J.
Author of *Jesus: A Portrait*

Sacred Space has provided countless people with a clear and concise resource to pray alone—any time and anywhere—and yet consciously united with numerous others worldwide. This timely, unassuming aid to daily prayer is a gem.

Peter van Breemen, S.J.
Author of *The God Who Won't Let Go*

SACRED SPACE

the prayer book 2009

from the website www.sacredspace.ie

Jesuit Communication Centre, Ireland

ave maria press notre dame, indiana

acknowledgment

The publisher would like to thank Piaras Jackson, S.J., and Alan McGuckian, S.J., for their kind assistance in making this book possible. Piaras Jackson, S.J., can be contacted at feedback@jesuit.ie.

First published in Australia 2008 by
Michelle Anderson Publishing, Pty., Ltd.

Founded in 1865, Ave Maria Press is a ministry of the Indiana Province of Holy Cross.

www.avemariapress.com

ISBN-10: 1-59471-175-5 ISBN-13: 978-1-59471-175-6

Cover and text design by K. H. Coney.

Printed and bound in the United States of America.

how to use this book

We invite you to make a sacred space in your day and spend ten minutes praying here and now, wherever you are, with the help of a prayer guide and scripture chosen specially for each day. Every place is a sacred space, so you may wish to have this book in your desk at work or available to be picked up and read at any time of the day, whilst traveling or on your bedside table, a park bench . . . Remember that God is everywhere, all around us, constantly reaching out to us, even in the most unlikely situations. When we know this, and with a bit of practice, we can pray anywhere.

The following pages will guide you through a session of prayer stages.

Something to think and pray about each day this week
The Presence of God
Freedom
Consciousness
The Word (leads you to the daily scripture and provides help with the text)
Conversation
Conclusion

It is most important to come back to these pages each day of the week as they are an integral part of each day's prayer and lead to the scripture and inspiration points.

Although written in the first person the prayers are for "doing" rather than for reading out. Each stage is a kind of exercise or meditation aimed at helping you to get in touch with god and God's presence in your life.

We hope that you will join the many people around the world praying with us in our sacred space.

Take Time

Take time off each day to think and pray
To care how your life is going.
Give your roots rain.
Take time with a friend to do nothing too important,
But just be together, to enjoy another person.
Give your roots rain.
Take time to write a poem or grow a flower,
To create something that is something of you.
Give your roots rain.
For in your roots you find who you are,
And there too find who God is,
For he has not forced you into his home,
Rather he has made his home in you.

contents

november 30–december 6

Something to think and pray about each day this week:

The Quiet Life

In his classic *The Imitation of Christ*, Thomas à Kempis urges the reader to "enjoy being unknown and regarded as nothing." What he means is the ability to persist through tedium, to survive without the oxygen of recognition, praise, and stroking, to do some good things every day that are seen only by God.

Most of us start life as the center of the universe, being stroked and attended to. Baby's every smile and whimper is responded to and noted. It is an addictive experience, and it is hard to get used to being just one of a family, and later one of a whole class or school, barely noticed.

There are people, like some pop stars, who never recover from the addiction of being the center of attention, never climb out of those infantile lowlands. They find it impossible to survive without notice and applause and spend their energies seeking it. They never fit themselves for the higher ground where the oxygen of appreciation is thinner, and they have to survive, as à Kempis says, unknown and hardly noticed. For all but his last three years, Jesus was happy to live a hidden life. That is where most of the good in this world is accomplished, by parents, caretakers, and all who keep going through the daily offering of their unacknowledged service.

The Presence of God

Lord, help me to be fully alive to your holy presence.
Enfold me in your love.
Let my heart become one with yours.

Freedom

Many countries are at this moment suffering
the agonies of war.
I bow my head in thanksgiving for my freedom.
I pray for all prisoners and captives.

Consciousness

At this moment, Lord, I turn my thoughts to You.
I will leave aside my chores and preoccupations.
I will take rest and refreshment in your presence Lord.

The Word

The word of God comes down to us through the scriptures. May the Holy Spirit enlighten my mind and my heart to respond to the gospel teachings. (Please turn to your scripture on the following pages. Inspiration points are there should you need them. When you are ready, return here to continue.)

Conversation

Sometimes I wonder what I might say
if I were to meet You in person, Lord.
I might say "Thank You, Lord" for always being there for me.
I know with certainty there were times when you carried me.
When through your strength I got through the dark times in my life.

Conclusion

Glory be to the Father, and to the Son, and to the Holy Spirit,
As it was in the beginning, is now and ever shall be,
World without end. Amen

Sunday 30th November,
First Sunday of Advent **Mark 13:33–37**

"Beware, keep alert; for you do not know when the time will come. It is like a man going on a journey, when he leaves home and puts his slaves in charge, each with his work, and commands the doorkeeper to be on the watch. Therefore, keep awake—for you do not know when the master of the house will come, in the evening, or at midnight, or at cockcrow, or at dawn, or else he may find you asleep when he comes suddenly. And what I say to you I say to all: Keep awake."

- Jesus is speaking of his second coming at the end of time. But each of us, before that, can look forward to coming before our Lord. It means that we must so live that it does not matter when he comes.
- Our life becomes a preparation for the vision of happiness.

Monday 1st December **Matthew 8:5–11**

When Jesus entered Capernaum, a centurion came to him, appealing to him and saying, "Lord, my servant is lying at home paralyzed, in terrible distress." And he said to him, "I will come and cure him." The centurion answered, "Lord, I am not worthy to have you come under my roof; but only speak the word, and my servant will be healed. For I also am a man under authority, with soldiers under me; and I say to one, 'Go,' and he goes, and to another, 'Come,' and he comes, and to my slave, 'Do this,' and the slave does it." When Jesus heard him, he was amazed and said to those who followed him, "Truly I tell you, in no one in Israel have I found such faith. I tell you, many will come from east and west and will eat with Abraham and Isaac and Jacob in the kingdom of heaven."

- The centurion was a man with power and status. He was begging a favor from a penniless itinerant teacher and declaring himself unworthy even to entertain Jesus in his house.
- Jesus was amazed, not merely at the trust of the man, but at the fact that his love for his servant led him to cut through all the barriers of rank and race.
- Lord, give me the grace to break with conventions that bind me, listen to my heart, and reach out to those that I can help.

Tuesday 2nd December **Luke 10:21–24**

At that same hour Jesus rejoiced in the Holy Spirit and said, "I thank you, Father, Lord of heaven and earth, because you have hidden these things from the wise and the intelligent and have revealed them to infants; yes, Father, for such was your gracious will. All things have been handed over to me by my Father; and no one knows who the Son is except the Father, or who the Father is except the Son and anyone to whom the Son chooses to reveal him." Then turning to the disciples, Jesus said to them privately, "Blessed are the eyes that see what you see! For I tell you that many prophets and kings desired to see what you see, but did not see it, and to hear what you hear, but did not hear it."

- Thirteen centuries after Jesus, the anonymous author of *The Cloud of Unknowing* urged us in the same way to approach God in love rather than intellectual effort:

> Beat away at this cloud of unknowing between you and God with that sharp dart of longing love. And so I urge you, go after experience rather than knowledge. On account of pride, knowledge may often deceive you, but this gentle, loving affection will not deceive you. Knowledge tends to breed conceit, but love builds.

Wednesday 3rd December,
St. Francis Xavier **Matthew 28:16–20**

Now the eleven disciples went to Galilee, to the mountain to which Jesus had directed them. When they saw him, they worshipped him; but some doubted. And Jesus came and said to them, "All authority in heaven and on earth has been given to me. Go therefore, and make disciples of all nations, baptizing them in the name of the Father and of the Son and of the Holy Spirit, and teaching them to obey everything that I have commanded you. And remember, I am with you always, to the end of the age."

- Lord, you terrify me with this command, "Go, and teach all nations." You were talking to eleven men with little education, money, or influence, in a despised province of the Roman Empire. But they obeyed you because they knew you were with them.
- And today Christians are the largest body of believers on this planet. Today's preaching is different. People are often well educated, but sometimes that makes it harder to make our voice heard than in past days.
- Yet in *Sacred Space* your word goes out potentially to all nations, and you are still with us.

Thursday 4th December **Matthew 7:21, 24–27**

Jesus said to his disciples, "Not everyone who says to me, 'Lord, Lord,' will enter the kingdom of heaven, but only the one who does the will of my Father in heaven. Everyone then who hears these words of mine and acts on them will be like a wise man who built his house on rock. The rain fell, the floods came, and the winds blew and beat on that house, but it did not fall, because it had been founded on rock. And everyone who hears these words of mine and does not act on them will be like a foolish man who built his house on sand. The rain fell, and the floods came, and the winds blew and beat against that house, and it fell—and great was its fall!"

- Lord, you never let me forget that love is shown in deeds, not words or feelings. I could fill notebooks with resolutions and in the end be further from you.
- As William James put it, "A resolution that is a fine flame of feeling allowed to burn itself out without appropriate action, is not merely a lost opportunity, but a bar to future action."

Friday 5th December **Matthew 9:27–31**

As Jesus went on his way, two blind men followed him, crying loudly, "Have mercy on us, Son of David!" When he entered the house, the blind men came to him; and Jesus said to them, "Do you believe that I am able to do this?" They said to him, "Yes, Lord." Then he touched their eyes and said, "According to your faith let it be done to you." And their eyes were opened. Then Jesus sternly ordered them, "See that no one knows of this." But they went away and spread the news about him throughout that district.

- The start of this encounter is in public. Crowds are around Jesus, and the blind men are caught up in the general emotion. They shout at Jesus using a formal title, "Son of David," as though he were a powerful messianic figure dispensing health to crowds.
- Jesus waits until he is in the house, where he can meet the blind men in person and question their faith.

Saturday 6th December **Isaiah 30:19–21**

Truly, O people in Zion, inhabitants of Jerusalem, you shall weep no more. He will surely be gracious to you at the sound of your cry; when he hears it, he will answer you. Though the Lord may give you the bread of adversity and the water of affliction, yet your Teacher will not hide himself any more, but your eyes shall see your Teacher. And when you turn to the right or when you turn to the left, your ears shall hear a word behind you, saying, "This is the way; walk in it."

- "The bread of adversity and the water of affliction" could sound like food, however plain. They do not taste like that when we lose a job, fall ill, lose the affection of friends, or suffer deeply. Then it seems all destructive and wrong.
- But your eyes shall see your Teacher. Your ears shall hear a word behind you, saying, "This is the way; walk in it."

december 7–13

Something to think and pray about each day this week:

Making Preparations

Twice in the year, at Advent and Lent, we spend weeks preparing our souls for a great feast. Try imagining the preparation that Mary made. She spent three months helping her cousin Elizabeth with an unexpected pregnancy. Then she had to face the awful crisis with Joseph, who could not understand how she could be pregnant (Matthew 1:19). Then when things seemed to be on an even course for the birth, she found they had to pull up roots, harness the donkey, and trek up to Bethlehem, where they could find no room in the inn. Mary's main preparation was adjusting to what was unexpected and unwished-for.

The Presence of God

God is with me, but more,
God is within me, giving me existence.
Let me dwell for a moment on God's life-giving presence
in my body, my mind, my heart
and in the whole of my life.

Freedom

God is not foreign to my freedom.
Instead the Spirit breathes life into my most intimate desires,
gently nudging me toward all that is good.
I ask for the grace to let myself be enfolded by the Spirit.

Consciousness

Help me, Lord, to be more conscious of your presence.
Teach me to recognize your presence in others.
Fill my heart with gratitude for the times your love
has been shown to me through the care of others.

The Word

I read the Word of God slowly, a few times over, and I listen to what God is saying to me. (Please turn to your scripture on the following pages. Inspiration points are there should you need them. When you are ready, return here to continue.)

Conversation

How has God's Word moved me? Has it left me cold?
Has it consoled me or moved me to act in a new way?
I imagine Jesus standing or sitting beside me,
I turn and share my feelings with him.

Conclusion

Glory be to the Father, and to the Son, and to the Holy Spirit,
As it was in the beginning, is now and ever shall be,
World without end. Amen

Sunday 7th December,
Second Sunday of Advent **Mark 1:4–6**

John the baptizer appeared in the wilderness, proclaiming a baptism of repentance for the forgiveness of sins. And people from the whole Judean countryside and all the people of Jerusalem were going out to him, and were baptized by him in the river Jordan, confessing their sins. Now John was clothed with camel's hair, with a leather belt around his waist, and he ate locusts and wild honey.

- The attraction of John the Baptist is mysterious. People flocked to him, not to be flattered, but to be told the truth.
- They listened because of what they saw, a man who was indifferent to the world's prizes, a man of minimal needs, who could not be bought by pleasures, comforts, or money, but was passionate about God. They recognized holiness.
- Show me, Lord, what there is about my life that takes from the value of my words and makes me less convincing.

Monday 8th December, The Immaculate
Conception of the Blessed Virgin Mary **Luke 1:26–38**

In the sixth month the angel Gabriel was sent by God to a town in Galilee called Nazareth, to a virgin engaged to a man whose name was Joseph, of the house of David. The virgin's name was Mary. And he came to her and said, "Greetings, favored one! The Lord is with you." But she was much perplexed by his words and pondered what sort of greeting this might be. The angel said to her, "Do not be afraid, Mary, for you have found favor with God. And now, you will conceive in your womb and bear a son, and you will name him Jesus. He will be great, and will be called the Son of the Most High, and the Lord God will give to him the throne of his ancestor David. He will reign over the house of

Jacob forever, and of his kingdom there will be no end." Mary said to the angel, "How can this be, since I am a virgin?" The angel said to her, "The Holy Spirit will come upon you, and the power of the Most High will overshadow you; therefore the child to be born will be holy; he will be called Son of God. And now, your relative Elizabeth in her old age has also conceived a son; and this is the sixth month for her who was said to be barren. For nothing will be impossible with God." Then Mary said, "Here am I, the servant of the Lord; let it be with me according to your word." Then the angel departed from her.

- How does Mary's experience touch me? Am I called to "bear" God in my heart? What issues of surrender and trust arise in my case?
- Can I speak of these things to the Lord?

Tuesday 9th December **Matthew 18:12–14**

Jesus said to his disciples: "What do you think? If a shepherd has a hundred sheep, and one of them has gone astray, does he not leave the ninety-nine on the mountains and go in search of the one that went astray? And if he finds it, truly I tell you, he rejoices over it more than over the ninety-nine that never went astray. So it is not the will of your Father in heaven that one of these little ones should be lost."

- Let us never grow accustomed to this parable. It is the most astonishing suggestion you could imagine. Modern business would focus on the ninety-nine, well behaved and conformist.
- Jesus turns our eyes to that bit of ourselves that wants to do our own thing, go our own way, even when it is self-destructive. As parents have learned, often with pain, it is only love that will save the lost sheep. I cling to that last assurance: "It is not the will of your Father that one of these little ones should be lost."

Wednesday 10th December **Matthew 11:28–30**

Jesus said, "Come to me, all you that are weary and are carrying heavy burdens, and I will give you rest. Take my yoke upon you, and learn from me; for I am gentle and humble in heart, and you will find rest for your souls. For my yoke is easy, and my burden is light."

- I am often weary, Lord, and my burden feels heavy on me. When I look at Christians, some of them indeed seem relaxed and easy in your company. Others appear uptight and driven, not restful people to be near.
- You are a gentle, humble presence. If I feel under pressure in prayer, something is wrong. It is a sign of your presence to me that my soul feels rested.

Thursday 11th December **Matthew 11:11–15**

Truly I tell you, among those born of women no one has arisen greater than John the Baptist; yet the least in the kingdom of heaven is greater than he. From the days of John the Baptist until now the kingdom of heaven has suffered violence, and the violent take it by force. For all the prophets and the law prophesied until John came; and if you are willing to accept it, he is Elijah who is to come. Let anyone with ears listen!

- What was it that placed John the Baptist below "the least in the kingdom of heaven?" He had preached the justice of God and the need for repentance; but he had not lived to see Jesus crucified, and in that, to see the unbelievable extent of God's love for us.

Friday 12th December **Isaiah 48:17–19**

Thus says the Lord, your Redeemer, the Holy One of Israel: I am the Lord your God, who teaches you for your own good, who leads you in the way you should go. O that you had paid attention to my commandments! Then your prosperity would have been like a river, and your success like the waves of the sea; your offspring would have been like the sand, and your descendants like its grains; their name would never be cut off or destroyed from before me.

- "I am the Lord your God, who teaches you for your own good, who leads you in the way you should go."
- Lord, teach me to follow your paths, wherever you lead me.

Saturday 13th December **Matthew 17:10–13**

And the disciples asked him, "Why, then, do the scribes say that Elijah must come first?" He replied, "Elijah is indeed coming and will restore all things; but I tell you that Elijah has already come, and they did not recognize him, but they did to him whatever they pleased. So also the Son of Man is about to suffer at their hands." Then the disciples understood that he was speaking to them about John the Baptist.

- Like John the Baptist, Elijah was a messenger of God. Like other messengers, they were shunned, ridiculed, or even eliminated.
- Advent calls us to this same journey; we risk rejection and dark times, but we are promised a dawn that takes away the darkness.

december 14–20

Something to think and pray about each day this week:

Out of Nowhere

If Jesus were to appear in our world, he would be born unnoticed, to a good, struggling family in Ecuador, Uzbekistan, or some place usually out of the news. People would be puzzled, "Where is that place?" He would not be on television, nor would he occupy a center of power or wealth. He would be pushed around, slandered, and criticized. He would speak simple truths, and some would listen to him and recognize the voice of God. The good news would spread slowly, as it did two thousand years ago. It would graft onto whatever was good in the world. The brokers of power and wealth would not notice it, nor offer their sponsorship. The happy irony of today is that after the first two thousand years, the good news is so widespread that, whether they know it or not, the whole human race is richer for Jesus' birthday.

The Presence of God
What is present to me is what has a hold on my becoming.
I reflect on the presence of God always there in love,
amidst the many things that have a hold on me.
I pause and pray that I may let God
affect my becoming in this precise moment.

Freedom
There are very few people
who realize what God would make of them
if they abandoned themselves into his hands,
and let themselves be formed by his grace. (St Ignatius)
I ask for the grace to trust myself totally to God's love.

Consciousness
In the presence of my loving Creator,
I look honestly at my feelings over the last day,
the highs, the lows, and the level ground.
Can I see where the Lord has been present?

The Word
God speaks to each one of us individually. I need to listen to hear what he is saying to me. Read the text a few times, then listen. (Please turn to your scripture on the following pages. Inspiration points are there should you need them. When you are ready, return here to continue.)

Conversation
What is stirring in me as I pray?
Am I consoled, troubled, left cold?
I imagine Jesus himself standing or sitting at my side,
and share my feelings with him.

Conclusion
Glory be to the Father, and to the Son, and to the Holy Spirit,
As it was in the beginning, is now and ever shall be,
World without end. Amen

Sunday 14th December, Third Sunday of Advent **1 Thessalonians 5:16–19**

Rejoice always, pray without ceasing, give thanks in all circumstances; for this is the will of God in Christ Jesus for you. Do not quench the Spirit.

- Christian joy is not vapid hilarity nor having a laugh, but rather a deep contentment because we are in the hands of a loving God who desires only what is ultimately good for us. This joy goes with gratitude.
- Our proverbial "Thanks be to God" is no idle phrase. It expresses a powerful faith and keeps us in touch with Christian joy.

Monday 15th December **Matthew 21:23–27**

When Jesus entered the temple, the chief priests and the elders of the people came to him as he was teaching, and said, "By what authority are you doing these things, and who gave you this authority?" Jesus said to them, "I will also ask you one question; if you tell me the answer, then I will also tell you by what authority I do these things. Did the baptism of John come from heaven, or was it of human origin?" And they argued with one another, "If we say, 'From heaven,' he will say to us, 'Why then did you not believe him?' But if we say, 'Of human origin,' we are afraid of the crowd; for all regard John as a prophet." So they answered Jesus, "We do not know." And he said to them, "Neither will I tell you by what authority I am doing these things."

- The Chief priests and the elders are motivated by a desire to protect their own position and authority, and by fear—they are afraid of the crowds. Jesus, on the other hand, speaks out fearlessly, regardless of how it might jeopardize his popularity.

- Do I let fear run my life? Do I make decisions on the basis of preserving my position and power? Can I talk to Jesus about this and ask for the grace to be free, as he was?

Tuesday 16th December **Matthew 21:28–32**

Jesus said, "What do you think? A man had two sons; he went to the first and said, 'Son, go and work in the vineyard today.' He answered, 'I will not'; but later he changed his mind and went. The father went to the second and said the same; and he answered, 'I go, sir'; but he did not go. Which of the two did the will of his father?" They said, "The first." Jesus said to them, "Truly I tell you, the tax collectors and the prostitutes are going into the kingdom of God ahead of you. For John came to you in the way of righteousness and you did not believe him, but the tax collectors and the prostitutes believed him; and even after you saw it, you did not change your minds and believe him."

- Well, which am I?
- The first son sounds like a grump, hard to live with. His first reaction tended to be "no." He probably suffered as much as anyone from his own grumpiness. But when the chips were down, you could trust him to help. The second son was the smiling sweet-talker. He liked to be in favor, but when he should have been working, he found something better to do—and probably a plausible excuse afterwards.
- Lord, I would rather be a grumpy but reliable helper than a sweet-talker.

Wednesday 17th December **Matthew 1:1–11**

An account of the genealogy of Jesus the Messiah, the son of David, the son of Abraham. Abraham was the father of Isaac, and Isaac the father of Jacob, and Jacob the father of Judah and his brothers, and Judah the father of Perez and Zerah by Tamar, and Perez the father of Hezron, and Hezron the father of Aram, and Aram the father of Aminadab, and Aminadab the father of Nahshon, and Nahshon the father of Salmon, and Salmon the father of Boaz by Rahab, and Boaz the father of Obed by Ruth, and Obed the father of Jesse, and Jesse the father of King David. And David was the father of Solomon by the wife of Uriah, and Solomon the father of Rehoboam, and Rehoboam the father of Abijah, and Abijah the father of Asaph, and Asaph the father of Jehoshaphat, and Jehoshaphat the father of Joram, and Joram the father of Uzziah, and Uzziah the father of Jotham, and Jotham the father of Ahaz, and Ahaz the father of Hezekiah, and Hezekiah the father of Manasseh, and Manasseh the father of Amos, and Amos the father of Josiah, and Josiah the father of Jechoniah and his brothers, at the time of the deportation to Babylon.

- Today's readings look unsparingly at Jesus' ancestry. Matthew points out that Jesus' forbears included children born of incest (Perez), of mixed races (Boaz), and of adultery (Solomon).
- God entered into our human history with all the episodes that proud people would be ashamed of.

Thursday 18th December **Matthew 1:18–24**

Now the birth of Jesus the Messiah took place in this way. When his mother Mary had been engaged to Joseph, but before they lived together, she was found to be with child from the Holy Spirit. Her husband Joseph, being a righteous man and unwilling to expose her to public disgrace, planned to dismiss her quietly. But just when he had resolved to do this, an angel of the Lord appeared to him in a dream and said, "Joseph, son of David, do not be afraid to take Mary as your wife, for the child conceived in her is from the Holy Spirit. She will bear a son, and you are to name him Jesus, for he will save his people from their sins." All this took place to fulfill what had been spoken by the

Lord through the prophet: "Look, the virgin shall conceive and bear a son, and they shall name him Emmanuel," which means, "God is with us." When Joseph awoke from sleep, he did as the angel of the Lord commanded him; he took her as his wife.

- There is a model here for making decisions and dealing with doubts. Pray about it, carry it as a question, pester God about it. This is the story of Joseph's utterly unique vocation, as foster-father of the Son of God.

Friday 19th December **Luke 1:5–25**

In the days of King Herod of Judea, there was a priest named Zechariah, who belonged to the priestly order of Abijah. His wife was a descendant of Aaron, and her name was Elizabeth. Both of them were righteous before God, living blamelessly according to all the commandments and regulations of the Lord. But they had no children, because Elizabeth was barren, and both were getting on in years. Once when he was serving as priest before God and his section was on duty, he was chosen by lot, according to the custom of the priesthood, to enter the sanctuary of the Lord and offer incense. Now at the time of the incense-offering, the whole assembly of the people was praying outside. Then there appeared to him an angel of the Lord, standing at the right side of the altar of incense. When Zechariah saw him, he was terrified; and fear overwhelmed him. But the angel said to him, "Do not be afraid, Zechariah, for your prayer has been heard. Your wife Elizabeth will bear you a son, and you will name him John. You will have joy and gladness, and many will rejoice at his birth, for he will be great in the sight of the Lord. He must never drink wine or strong drink; even before his birth he will be filled with the Holy Spirit. He will turn many of the people of Israel to the Lord their God. With the spirit and power of Elijah he will go before him, to turn the hearts of parents to their children, and the disobedient to the wisdom of the righteous, to make ready a people prepared for the Lord." Zechariah said to the angel, "How will I know that this is so? For I am an old man, and my wife is getting on in years." The angel replied, "I am Gabriel. I stand in the presence of God, and I have been sent to speak to you and to bring you this good news. But now, because you did not believe my words, which will be fulfilled in their time, you will become mute, unable to speak, until the day these things occur." Meanwhile, the people were waiting for Zechariah, and wondered at his delay in the sanctuary. When he did come out, he could not speak to them, and they realized that he had seen a vision in the sanctuary. He kept motioning to them and remained unable to speak. When his time of service was ended, he went to his home. After those days his wife Elizabeth conceived, and for five months she remained in seclusion. She said, "This is what the Lord has done for me when he looked favorably on me and took away the disgrace I have endured among my people."

- This was a red-letter day for Zechariah: He had been chosen by lot from the hundreds of available priests to offer incense for the Jewish nation. His childlessness, the great grief of his life, would have been on his mind as he prayed. The revelation that he would be the father of a special child was such an answer to prayer as to strike him speechless.
- Lord, before I existed, my parents prayed that I would be born, would live, would have a destiny with you. I thank you for the wonder of my being.

Saturday 20th December **Luke 1:26–38**

In the sixth month the angel Gabriel was sent by God to a town in Galilee called Nazareth, to a virgin engaged to a man whose name was Joseph, of the house of David. The virgin's name was

Mary. And he came to her and said, "Greetings, favored one! The Lord is with you." But she was much perplexed by his words and pondered what sort of greeting this might be. The angel said to her, "Do not be afraid, Mary, for you have found favor with God. And now, you will conceive in your womb and bear a son, and you will name him Jesus. He will be great, and will be called the Son of the Most High, and the Lord God will give to him the throne of his ancestor David. He will reign over the house of Jacob forever, and of his kingdom there will be no end." Mary said to the angel, "How can this be, since I am a virgin?" The angel said to her, "The Holy Spirit will come upon you, and the power of the Most High will overshadow you; therefore the child to be born will be holy; he will be called Son of God. And now, your relative Elizabeth in her old age has also conceived a son; and this is the sixth month for her who was said to be barren. For nothing will be impossible with God." Then Mary said, "Here am I, the servant of the Lord; let it be with me according to your word." Then the angel departed from her.

- I love Mary for her caution. She was perplexed and did not trust visions, so she questioned the message and thought about what the consequences would be. For this, she rose to the greatness which G. M. Hopkins celebrates:

    Mary Immaculate,
    Merely a woman, yet
    Whose presence, power is
    Great as no goddess's
    Was deemèd, dreamed; who
    This one work has to do—
    Let all God's glory through,
    God's glory which would go
    Through her and from her flow
    Off, and no way but so.

december 21–27

Something to think and pray about each day this week:

Turmoil and Joy

The word "push" is charged with meaning and memories for all young mothers. They have all had to push their infant from the warm security of the womb, through a narrow opening, into the cold and dangerous world outside mother. However painful the push, they know that the child is too big to stay and needs to move on and out. Mary knew that experience too, though it is seldom noticed in pious books (most of them written by men who have never suffered in this way). Jesus himself remarked in a parable on the contrast between the pain of childbirth and the mother's later joy that she has brought a child into the world, able to breathe and feed and live outside her body. All that emotional turmoil of pain and anxiety and joy can be read in Mary's face as she cradles baby Jesus.

The Presence of God
God is with me, but more, God is within me.
Let me dwell for a moment on God's life-giving presence
in my body, in my mind, in my heart,
as I sit here, right now.

Freedom
A thick and shapeless tree-trunk would never believe
that it could become a statue, admired as a miracle of sculpture,
and would never submit itself to the chisel of the sculptor,
who sees by her genius what she can make of it. (St Ignatius)
I ask for the grace to let myself be shaped by my loving Creator.

Consciousness
Knowing that God loves me unconditionally,
I can afford to be honest about how I am.
How has the last day been, and how do I feel now?
I share my feelings openly with the Lord.

The Word
I read the Word of God slowly, a few times over, and I listen to what God is saying to me. (Please turn to your scripture on the following pages. Inspiration points are there should you need them. When you are ready, return here to continue.)

Conversation
Do I notice myself reacting as I pray with the Word of God?
Do I feel challenged, comforted, angry?
Imagining Jesus sitting or standing by me,
I speak out my feelings, as one trusted friend to another.

Conclusion
Glory be to the Father, and to the Son, and to the Holy Spirit,
As it was in the beginning, is now and ever shall be,
World without end. Amen

Sunday 21st December,
Fourth Sunday of Advent **Luke 1:26–32**

In the sixth month the angel Gabriel was sent by God to a town in Galilee called Nazareth, to a virgin whose name was Mary. And he came to her and said, "Greetings, favored one! The Lord is with you." But she was much perplexed by his words and pondered what sort of greeting this might be. The angel said to her, "Do not be afraid, Mary, for you have found favor with God. And now, you will conceive in your womb and bear a son, and you will name him Jesus. He will be great, and will be called the Son of the Most High, and the Lord God will give to him the throne of his ancestor David.

- Incarnation: how God enters our world and becomes a creature in time and space. We are still in awe at the mystery of God made man. It has exercised theologians and church councils for centuries.
- Even though we remember it when we see a Christmas crib, God's intervention in human history can never be anything but mind-boggling.

Monday 22nd December **Luke 1:46–56**

And Mary said, "My soul magnifies the Lord, and my spirit rejoices in God my Savior, for he has looked with favor on the lowliness of his servant. Surely, from now on all generations will call me blessed; for the Mighty One has done great things for me, and holy is his name. His mercy is for those who fear him from generation to generation. He has shown strength with his arm; he has scattered the proud in the thoughts of their hearts. He has brought down the powerful from their thrones, and lifted up the lowly; he has filled the hungry with good things, and sent the rich away empty. He has helped his servant Israel, in remembrance of his mercy, according to the promise he made to our ancestors, to Abraham and to his descendants forever." And Mary remained with Elizabeth about three months and then returned to her home.

- Imagine what Mary felt as she received this awesome news. She has questions and voiced them, but she says 'Yes' to God's will for her.
- Then she gives praise to God in the hymn we know as the *Magnificat*—"My soul magnifies the Lord." Can I learn from her example?

Tuesday 23rd December **Luke 1:57–66**

Now the time came for Elizabeth to give birth, and she bore a son. Her neighbors and relatives heard that the Lord had shown his great mercy to her, and they rejoiced with her. On the eighth day they came to circumcise the child, and they were going to name him Zechariah after his father. But his mother said, "No; he is to be called John." They said to her, "None of your relatives has this name." Then they began motioning to his father to find out what name he wanted to give him. He asked for a writing tablet and wrote, "His name is John." And all of them were amazed. Immediately his mouth was opened and his tongue freed, and he began to speak, praising God. Fear came over all their neighbors, and all these things were talked about throughout the entire hill country of Judea. All who heard them pondered them and said, "What then will this child become?" For, indeed, the hand of the Lord was with him.

- It would be good to stop and spend some time watching developments in the house of Elizabeth—once childless—after she has given birth to her "miracle" child.

- How must Elizabeth be feeling? How has it all impacted on old Zechariah? What about the friends and neighbors? What do they make of it?
- And what about my world? Does God break in to my life?

Wednesday 24th December **Luke 1:67–79**

Then his father Zechariah was filled with the Holy Spirit and spoke this prophecy: "Blessed be the Lord God of Israel, for he has looked favorably on his people and redeemed them. He has raised up a mighty savior for us in the house of his servant David, as he spoke through the mouth of his holy prophets from of old, that we would be saved from our enemies and from the hand of all who hate us. Thus he has shown the mercy promised to our ancestors, and has remembered his holy covenant, the oath that he swore to our ancestor Abraham, to grant us that we, being rescued from the hands of our enemies, might serve him without fear, in holiness and righteousness before him all our days. And you, child, will be called the prophet of the Most High; for you will go before the Lord to prepare his ways, to give knowledge of salvation to his people by the forgiveness of their sins. By the tender mercy of our God, the dawn from on high will break upon us, to give light to those who sit in darkness and in the shadow of death, to guide our feet into the way of peace."

- The *Benedictus* is a prayer of prophecy about the coming of the Savior. This "Most High" that Zechariah mentions comes not in a cloud of glory, but as a vulnerable child, with an ordinary family, in a cold stable. That is the kind of God we have.
- This babe in a manger brings light to those in darkness and takes away all my sins, doing away with the power of evil.
- What do I say to him, who loves me beyond all love?

Thursday 25th December,
Feast of the Nativity of the Lord **John 1:1–5**

In the beginning was the Word, and the Word was with God, and the Word was God. He was in the beginning with God. All things came into being through him, and without him not one thing came into being. What has come into being in him was life, and the life was the light of all people. The light shines in the darkness, and the darkness did not overcome it.

- This introduction to John's Gospel probably incorporated an ancient hymn about Christ. It is dense and wonderful. Each phrase can be mined for treasures. "All things were made through him, and without him was not anything made that was made. In him was life, and the life was the light of men. The light shines in the darkness, and the darkness has not overcome it."
- Lord, give me a glimpse of how you infuse all things. Gerald Manley Hopkins, who meditated on these phrases, wrote:

  For Christ plays in ten thousand places,
  Lovely in limbs, and lovely in eyes not his
  To the Father through the features of men's faces.

Friday 26th December,
St. Stephen, the first martyr **Matthew 10:17–22**

Jesus said to his apostles, "Beware of them, for they will hand you over to councils and flog you in their synagogues; and you will be dragged before governors and kings because of me, as a testimony to them and the Gentiles. When they hand you over, do not worry about how you are to speak or what you are to say; for what you are to say will be given to you at that time; for it is not you who speak, but the Spirit of your Father speaking through you. Brother will betray brother to death, and a father his child, and children will rise against parents and have them put to death; and you will be hated by all because of my name. But the one who endures to the end will be saved."

- Lord, I have not been dragged before governors or kings, but there have been social occasions when I felt like a sheep among wolves, and metaphorically flogged for my faith.
- When I am under pressure, do not forget me. See that I am given what I am to say, and help me to be brave enough to say it.

Saturday 27th December,
St. John, Apostle and Evangelist **John 20:2–8**

So Mary Magdalene ran and went to Simon Peter and the other disciple, the one whom Jesus loved, and said to them, "They have taken the Lord out of the tomb, and we do not know where they have laid him." Then Peter and the other disciple set out and went toward the tomb. The two were running together, but the other disciple outran Peter and reached the tomb first. He bent down to look in and saw the linen wrappings lying there, but he did not go in. Then Simon Peter came, following him, and went into the tomb. He saw the linen wrappings lying there, and the cloth that had been on Jesus' head, not lying with the linen wrappings but rolled up in a place by itself. Then the other disciple, who reached the tomb first, also went in, and he saw and believed.

- John recreates the moment when the world was suddenly changed for him. He remembers the baffling message of Mary Magdalene, the frantic Sunday morning race to the tomb, bending down to look into the dark space, seeing the burial clothes doffed and neatly arranged on the stones, allowing Simon Peter to go in first; then the awesome sense that death had met its victor.
- Lord, for me as for John, the belief in your resurrection changes life. I believe that you conquered death, and promise us the same victory. John saw and believed. I have not seen, but I live by that faith.

december 28–january 3

Something to think and pray about each day this week:

Approaching a Friend

We used a word in school to describe any nice thing—it might be a cake, a good game of football, a girl you fancied, or getting off homework. We'd say: It's a gift. It fits what we have this week, a dawning year, 2009. It is God's gift, which is different for each of us. The Lord looks on each of us as he looked on Peter, James, and the others who said: We have left all things and followed you. What about us? We have done the same, and he has a future for us. W. H. Auden put it well: I want to approach the future as a friend, without a wardrobe of excuses.

The Presence of God
As I sit here, the beating of my heart,
the ebb and flow of my breathing, the movements of my mind
are all signs of God's ongoing creation of me.
I pause for a moment, and become aware
of this presence of God within me.

Freedom
I ask for the grace
to let go of my own concerns
and be open to what God is asking of me,
to let myself be guided and formed by my loving Creator.

Consciousness
In the presence of my loving Creator,
I look honestly at my feelings over the last day,
the highs, the lows, and the level ground.
Can I see where the Lord has been present?

The Word
I take my time to read the Word of God, slowly, a few times, allowing myself to dwell on anything that strikes me. (Please turn to your scripture on the following pages. Inspiration points are there should you need them. When you are ready, return here to continue.)

Conversation
Remembering that I am still in God's presence,
I imagine Jesus himself standing or sitting beside me,
and say whatever is on my mind, whatever is in my heart,
speaking as one friend to another.

Conclusion
Glory be to the Father, and to the Son, and to the Holy Spirit,
As it was in the beginning, is now and ever shall be,
World without end. Amen

Sunday 28th December,
Holy Family **Hebrews 11:8, 11–12, 17–19**

By faith Abraham obeyed when he was called to set out for a place that he was to receive as an inheritance; and he set out, not knowing where he was going. By faith he received power of procreation, even though he was too old—and Sarah herself was barren—because he considered him faithful who had promised. Therefore from one person, and this one as good as dead, descendants were born, "as many as the stars of heaven and as the innumerable grains of sand by the seashore." By faith Abraham, when put to the test, offered up Isaac. He who had received the promises was ready to offer up his only son, of whom he had been told, "It is through Isaac that descendants shall be named after you."

- "Descendants were born 'as many as the stars of heaven.'" The faith of Abraham made him the father of many nations. Jews, Christians, and Muslims all revere him as their patriarch.
- At the heart of each strong family and relationship is the union: We stand together with God. We can stray, but we are always welcomed back.

Monday 29th December **Luke 2:25–35**

Now there was a man in Jerusalem whose name was Simeon; this man was righteous and devout, looking forward to the consolation of Israel, and the Holy Spirit rested on him. It had been revealed to him by the Holy Spirit that he would not see death before he had seen the Lord's Messiah. Guided by the Spirit, Simeon came into the temple; and when the parents brought in the child Jesus, to do for him what was customary under the law, Simeon took him in his arms and praised God, saying, "Master, now you are dismissing your servant in peace, according to your word; for my eyes have seen your salvation, which you have prepared in the presence of all peoples, a light for revelation to the Gentiles and for glory to your people Israel." And the child's father and mother were amazed at what was being said about him. Then Simeon blessed them and said to his mother Mary, "This child is destined for the falling and the rising of many in Israel, and to be a sign that will be opposed so that the inner thoughts of many will be revealed—and a sword will pierce your own soul too."

- Simeon waited for the Messiah, not as a conquering warlord, but as God breaking into human history in his own way. Simeon lived a life of constant prayer and quiet watchfulness, and here we have the blessed moment of recognition as he embraces the baby.
- Lord, give me that grace of quiet prayer and of recognizing you when you show yourself to me.

Tuesday 30th December **Luke 2:36–40**

There was also a prophet, Anna the daughter of Phanuel, of the tribe of Asher. She was of a great age, having lived with her husband for seven years after her marriage, then as a widow to the age of eighty-four. She never left the temple, but worshipped there with fasting and prayer night and day. At that moment she came, and began to praise God and to speak about the child to all who were looking for the redemption of Jerusalem. When they had finished everything required by the law of the Lord, they returned to Galilee, to their own town of Nazareth. The child grew and became strong, filled with wisdom; and the favor of God was upon him.

- In this scene, Mary and Joseph are in the Temple with their child performing the rites that a poor Jewish family would.

- Anna, the holy woman who had spent years in prayer and fasting, recognized that salvation had come in this child. What did Anna see? How does she see it? Do I see it?

Wednesday 31st December **John 1:1–13**

In the beginning was the Word, and the Word was with God, and the Word was God. He was in the beginning with God. All things came into being through him, and without him not one thing came into being. What has come into being in him was life, and the life was the light of all people. The light shines in the darkness, and the darkness did not overcome it. There was a man sent from God, whose name was John. He came as a witness to testify to the light, so that all might believe through him. He himself was not the light, but he came to testify to the light. The true light, which enlightens everyone, was coming into the world. He was in the world, and the world came into being through him; yet the world did not know him. He came to what was his own, and his own people did not accept him. But to all who received him, who believed in his name, he gave power to become children of God, who were born, not of blood or of the will of the flesh or of the will of man, but of God.

- In this hymn that introduces the fourth Gospel, John proclaims the faith that marks us as Christian. We believe that Jesus is the Word of God, his perfect expression. "No one has ever seen God. It is God the only Son, who is close to the Father's heart, who has made him known."
- Lord, let me grow in the knowledge of God. May I receive of your fullness, grace upon grace. You took on this mortal flesh for me and lived among us. May this coming year bring me closer to you.

Thursday 1st January,
Solemnity of Mary, Mother of God **Luke 2:16–21**

So they went with haste and found Mary and Joseph, and the child lying in the manger. When they saw this, they made known what had been told them about this child; and all who heard it were amazed at what the shepherds told them. But Mary treasured all these words and pondered them in her heart. The shepherds returned, glorifying and praising God for all they had heard and seen, as it had been told them. After eight days had passed, it was time to circumcise the child; and he was called Jesus, the name given by the angel before he was conceived in the womb.

- We celebrate the most passionate and enduring of all human relationships, that of mother and child. As Mary looked at her baby and gave him her breast, she knew that there was a dimension here beyond her guessing.
- Christians thought about it for four centuries before they dared to consecrate the title, Mother of God. Like Mary, I treasure the words spoken about Jesus, and ponder them in my heart.

Friday 2nd January **John 1:22–28**

Then the priests and Levites said to John, "Who are you? Let us have an answer for those who sent us. What do you say about yourself?" He said, "I am the voice of one crying out in the wilderness, 'Make straight the way of the Lord,'" as the prophet Isaiah said. Now they had been sent from the Pharisees. They asked him, "Why then are you baptizing if you are neither the Messiah, nor Elijah, nor the prophet?" John answered them, "I baptize with water. Among you stands one whom you do not know, the one who is coming after me; I am not worthy to untie the thong of his sandal." This took place in Bethany across the Jordan where John was baptizing.

- John is the last of the great prophets, and he is causing a stir; the authorities are agitated by his baptizing.
- But John leaves them in no doubt about his mission. He is but a "voice" preparing the way; there is another already among them who is "the one." He, John, is not even "worthy to untie the thong of his sandal."
- The time is now.

Saturday 3rd January **John 1:29–34**

The next day John saw Jesus coming toward him and declared, "Here is the Lamb of God who takes away the sin of the world! This is he of whom I said, 'After me comes a man who ranks ahead of me because he was before me.' I myself did not know him; but I came baptizing with water for this reason, that he might be revealed to Israel." And John testified, "I saw the Spirit descending from heaven like a dove, and it remained on him. I myself did not know him, but the one who sent me to baptize with water said to me, 'He on whom you see the Spirit descend and remain is the one who baptizes with the Holy Spirit.' And I myself have seen and have testified that this is the Son of God."

- The Lamb of God—what overtones would that have for John the Baptist? In the story of the Passover, the Angel of Death spared only those houses that were marked with the blood of a slain lamb, the Paschal Lamb. The title recalls Isaiah's picture of one who was led like a lamb to the slaughter, an innocent victim who would endure his sufferings to redeem his people.

- Jesus, Lamb of God, we will never exhaust our knowledge of you with titles. Let me grow steadily in that knowledge, making my picture of you ever richer.

january 4–10

Something to think and pray about each day this week:

God's Revelations

The word "epiphany" originates from the Greek language and it means a "showing" or "manifestation." The feast of the Epiphany of our Lord is linked closely to Christmas as both are feasts of God's manifestations: the first in the form of a helpless, newly-born infant born homeless and in poverty; the second celebrates the same recently born baby in similar circumstances but the material and social surroundings are hardly touched on. On the feast of Epiphany the emphasis is quite different. Here are strangers, foreigners, total outsiders coming to give royal homage to this tiny child. This will be the theme of Matthew's Gospel during the coming year: "Go, therefore, make disciples of all nations." We celebrate a third manifestation, the Baptism of Jesus, next Sunday to close the Christmas celebration of the Incarnation.

Each feast reminds us that Jesus is the revelation of God's unconditional and unending love for each one of us, in every age—not because we "deserve" it in some way, but because God is a God of love.

The Presence of God
I pause for a moment
and reflect on God's life-giving presence
in every part of my body, in everything around me,
in the whole of my life.

Freedom
Many countries are at this moment suffering
the agonies of war.
I bow my head in thanksgiving for my freedom.
I pray for all prisoners and captives.

Consciousness
Knowing that God loves me unconditionally,
I look honestly over the last day, its events and my feelings.
Do I have something to be grateful for? Then I give thanks.
Is there something I am sorry for? Then I ask forgiveness.

The Word
God speaks to each one of us individually. I need to listen to hear what he is saying to me. Read the text a few times, then listen. (Please turn to your scripture on the following pages. Inspiration points are there should you need them. When you are ready, return here to continue.)

Conversation
How has God's Word moved me? Has it left me cold?
Has it consoled me or moved me to act in a new way?
I imagine Jesus standing or sitting beside me,
I turn and share my feelings with him.

Conclusion
Glory be to the Father, and to the Son, and to the Holy Spirit,
As it was in the beginning, is now and ever shall be,
World without end. Amen

Sunday 4th January,
The Epiphany of the Lord **Matthew 2:1–2, 7–12**

In the time of King Herod, after Jesus was born in Bethlehem of Judea, wise men from the East came to Jerusalem, asking, "Where is the child who has been born king of the Jews? For we observed his star at its rising, and have come to pay him homage." . . . Then Herod secretly called for the wise men and learned from them the exact time when the star had appeared. Then he sent them to Bethlehem, saying, "Go and search diligently for the child; and when you have found him, bring me word so that I may also go and pay him homage." When they had heard the king, they set out; and there, ahead of them, went the star that they had seen at its rising, until it stopped over the place where the child was. When they saw that the star had stopped, they were overwhelmed with joy. On entering the house, they saw the child with Mary his mother; and they knelt down and paid him homage. Then, opening their treasure chests, they offered him gifts of gold, frankincense, and myrrh. And having been warned in a dream not to return to Herod, they left for their own country by another road.

- I love the Bavarian custom of chalking "G M B" for Gaspar, Melchior, and Balthasar on the wall of each room of the house on Epiphany morning. These are the names that tradition assigns to the Magi, representing all the nations of the world.
- As more and more people move to our shores and come into our neighborhoods and homes, do they discover you there, Lord? If justice and love are to be found in my home, then visitors, like the Magi, will be overwhelmed with joy and pay you homage.

Monday 5th January **Matthew 4:12–17**

Now when Jesus heard that John had been arrested, he withdrew to Galilee. He left Nazareth and made his home in

Capernaum by the lake, in the territory of Zebulun and Naphtali, so that what had been spoken through the prophet Isaiah might be fulfilled: "Land of Zebulun, land of Naphtali, on the road by the sea, across the Jordan, Galilee of the Gentiles—the people who sat in darkness have seen a great light, and for those who sat in the region and shadow of death light has dawned." From that time Jesus began to proclaim, "Repent, for the kingdom of heaven has come near."

- Over the past few weeks we have been watching the gradual unfolding of God's plans in the Word made flesh.
- Now we see Jesus come of age and realize that the plans have a purpose.
- How does this purpose affect me?

Tuesday 6th January **1 John 4:7–10**

Beloved, let us love one another, because love is from God; everyone who loves is born of God and knows God. Whoever does not love does not know God, for God is love. God's love was revealed among us in this way: God sent his only Son into the world so that we might live through him. In this is love, not that we loved God but that he loved us and sent his Son to be the atoning sacrifice for our sins.

- Religious practice and shared beliefs may help sustain a faith community, but the measure of my Christian commitment is not my adherence to these. The measure is: Do I love?
- Love can be expressed in many ways. It is in what we say, what we do, and how we treat other people that love is made real, just as God's love for us was expressed most clearly by what Jesus did.
- Let me think of the people I have encountered in the last few days and am likely to encounter today and tomorrow.

Wednesday 7th January **1 John 4:11–16**

Beloved, since God loved us so much, we also ought to love one another. No one has ever seen God; if we love one another, God lives in us, and his love is perfected in us. By this we know that we abide in him and he in us, because he has given us of his Spirit. And we have seen and do testify that the Father has sent his Son as the Savior of the world. God abides in those who confess that Jesus is the Son of God, and they abide in God. So we have known and believe the love that God has for us. God is love, and those who abide in love abide in God, and God abides in them.

- John seems to be writing from his personal experience of living in community in Ephesus.
- Can I imagine their relationships, built on love, that left them convinced that God lived among them?
- Is there something here for me?

Thursday 8th January **Luke 4:16–21**

When Jesus came to Nazareth, where he had been brought up, he went to the synagogue on the sabbath day, as was his custom. He stood up to read, and the scroll of the prophet Isaiah was given to him. He unrolled the scroll and found the place where it was written: "The Spirit of the Lord is upon me, because he has anointed me to bring good news to the poor. He has sent me to proclaim release to the captives and recovery of sight to the blind, to let the oppressed go free, to proclaim the year of the Lord's favor." And he rolled up the scroll, gave it back to the attendant, and sat down. The eyes of all in the synagogue were fixed on him. Then he began to say to them, "Today this scripture has been fulfilled in your hearing."

- The "local boy" is speaking in public to his neighbors for the first time. How does he feel?

- He has a mission. How does this affect me? This beginning is full of drama. Where will it end?

Friday 9th January **Luke 5:12–14**

Once, when Jesus was in one of the cities, there was a man covered with leprosy. When he saw Jesus, he bowed with his face to the ground and begged him, "Lord, if you choose, you can make me clean." Then Jesus stretched out his hand, touched him, and said, "I do choose. Be made clean." Immediately the leprosy left him. And he ordered him to tell no one. "Go," he said, "and show yourself to the priest, and, as Moses commanded, make an offering for your cleansing, for a testimony to them."

- Can I let myself be touched by this poor, broken man, in desperation at the feet of Jesus?
- What do they say to each other? What happens?

Saturday 10th January **John 3:25–30**

Now a discussion about purification arose between John's disciples and a Jew. They came to John and said to him, "Rabbi, the one who was with you across the Jordan, to whom you testified, here he is baptizing, and all are going to him." John answered, "No one can receive anything except what has been given from heaven. You yourselves are my witnesses that I said, 'I am not the Messiah, but I have been sent ahead of him.' He who has the bride is the bridegroom. The friend of the bridegroom, who stands and hears him, rejoices greatly at the bridegroom's voice. For this reason my joy has been fulfilled. He must increase, but I must decrease."

- The rise in Jesus' popularity was seen as a threat by John the Baptist's followers. Is John himself threatened?
- What is the source of this joy that John feels?

january 11–17

Something to think and pray about each day this week:

Saying Yes

Each of us tends to be either a yes-sayer or a no-sayer. Other things being equal, when asked to do something, some find reasons not to do it, others instinctively say "yes." Many of us think of God as a no-sayer, someone who is never quite satisfied. Paul (II Cor 1:18–20) gives a different picture: In God, the answer is always "yes."

Jesus is shown to be an affirmer as well, the one who gives life, frees us for action, and says "yes" to us. Look back for a moment. His first miracle is turning water into wine so that the party can go on. The individuals who come to him often feel awful, guilty, ashamed. Magdalene kneels silent at his feet. Jesus says "You have loved much, you're okay." A leper comes before him seeking cure. Jesus touches the leprosy and says "Yes, you're okay." The woman taken in adultery, or the Samaritan woman who had five husbands, or the noisy children who annoy the apostles, appear before him not knowing what he will say. He says "Yes, go in peace, you're okay." Peter has betrayed him, and meets him after the resurrection, unsure how he will be received. Jesus says "I know you love me, feed my sheep, you're okay."

The Presence of God
The world is charged with the grandeur of God (Gerard Manley Hopkins).
I dwell for a moment on the presence of God
around me, in every part of my body,
and deep within my being.

Freedom
In these days, God taught me
as a schoolteacher teaches a pupil (St Ignatius).
I remind myself that there are things God has to teach me yet,
and ask for the grace to hear them and let them change me.

Consciousness
How do I find myself today?
Where am I with God? With others?
Do I have something to be grateful for? Then I give thanks.
Is there something I am sorry for? Then I ask forgiveness.

The Word
I read the Word of God slowly, a few times over, and I listen to what God is saying to me. (Please turn to your scripture on the following pages. Inspiration points are there should you need them. When you are ready, return here to continue.)

Conversation
Sometimes I wonder what I might say
if I were to meet You in person, Lord.
I might say "Thank You, Lord" for always being there for me.
I know with certainty there were times when you carried me,
when through your strength I got through the dark times in my life.

Conclusion
Glory be to the Father, and to the Son, and to the Holy Spirit,
As it was in the beginning, is now and ever shall be,
World without end. Amen

Sunday 11th January,
The Baptism of the Lord **Mark 1:7–11**

John proclaimed, "The one who is more powerful than I is coming after me; I am not worthy to stoop down and untie the thong of his sandals. I have baptized you with water; but he will baptize you with the Holy Spirit." In those days Jesus came from Nazareth of Galilee and was baptized by John in the Jordan. And just as he was coming up out of the water, he saw the heavens torn apart and the Spirit descending like a dove on him. And a voice came from heaven, "You are my Son, the Beloved; with you I am well pleased."

- Imagine yourself there, perhaps standing in the shallows, the water flowing around your ankles. Allow the scene to unfold.
- The young man from Nazareth joins the queue waiting for John's baptism: a symbol of purifying, but also of birth—coming up out of the waters of the womb into a new life as God's beloved child.
- Lord, when I realize that you love me and are well pleased with me, it is like the start of a new life. As I hear your voice, I know that I have a purpose and a destiny.

Monday 12th January **Mark 1:14–20**

Now after John was arrested, Jesus came to Galilee, proclaiming the good news of God, and saying, "The time is fulfilled, and the kingdom of God has come near; repent, and believe in the good news." As Jesus passed along the Sea of Galilee, he saw Simon and his brother Andrew casting a net into the sea—for they were fishermen. And Jesus said to them, "Follow me, and I will make you fish for people." And immediately they left their nets and followed him. As he went a little farther, he saw James son of Zebedee and his brother John, who were in their boat mending the nets. Immediately he called them; and they left their father Zebedee in the boat with the hired men, and followed him.

- There is no shortlist of candidates for these jobs, no recruiters or interviews. Jesus moves along the lakeshore, meets dozens of fishermen, and finally Simon, Andrew, James, and John. He calls them to a global mission.
- Jesus' call is simple: "Follow me." Today his followers form the largest body of believers on the planet. Let me never lose a sense of how extraordinary this moment is.

Tuesday 13th January **Mark 1:21–28**

They went to Capernaum; and when the sabbath came, Jesus entered the synagogue and taught. They were astounded at his teaching, for he taught them as one having authority, and not as the scribes. Just then there was in their synagogue a man with an unclean spirit, and he cried out, "What have you to do with us, Jesus of Nazareth? Have you come to destroy us? I know who you are, the Holy One of God." But Jesus rebuked him, saying, "Be silent, and come out of him!" And the unclean spirit, convulsing him and crying with a loud voice, came out of him. They were all amazed, and they kept on asking one another, "What is this? A new teaching—with authority! He commands even the unclean spirits, and they obey him." At once his fame began to spread throughout the surrounding region of Galilee.

- Jesus taught with authority; and the authority came from his person. There we see what it can mean to be fully human: compassionate, fearless, loving, with a passion for justice and awareness of what is in the human heart.
- It is by watching him and pondering his words and behavior that I too will learn what it is to be human.

Wednesday 14th January **Mark 1:29–31**

As soon as they left the synagogue, they entered the house of Simon and Andrew, with James and John. Now Simon's mother-in-law was in bed with a fever, and they told him about her at once. He came and took her by the hand and lifted her up. Then the fever left her, and she began to serve them.

- There is a moment of truth in the cure of Simon's mother-in-law. When we are cured from a sickness by whatever means, it is tempting to sit back and accept people's good wishes and congratulations. This sick woman felt her temperature drop, and energy return to her limbs, "and she began to serve them."
- Lord, thank you for my health, not something to luxuriate in, but the means by which I can serve others.

Thursday 15th January **Mark 1:40–45**

A leper came to Jesus begging him, and kneeling he said to him, "If you choose, you can make me clean." Moved with pity, Jesus stretched out his hand and touched him, and said to him, "I do choose. Be made clean!" Immediately the leprosy left him, and he was made clean. After sternly warning him he sent him away at once, saying to him, "See that you say nothing to anyone; but go, show yourself to the priest, and offer for your cleansing what Moses commanded, as a testimony to them." But he went out and began to proclaim it freely, and to spread the word, so that Jesus could no longer go into a town openly, but stayed out in the country; and people came to him from every quarter.

- The leper was breaking the law that ordered lepers to stay at a distance from people. Jesus not only listened to the law-breaker, but touched him, touched the dreaded sores that disfigured the leper. This was not charity at a distance, but an intimate cure.

- Lord, I am tempted to keep my distance from offensive suffering. That is not your way.

Friday 16th January **Mark 2:1–5**

When Jesus returned to Capernaum after some days, it was reported that he was at home. So many gathered around that there was no longer room for them, not even in front of the door; and he was speaking the word to them. Then some people came, bringing to him a paralyzed man, carried by four of them. And when they could not bring him to Jesus because of the crowd, they removed the roof above him; and after having dug through it, they let down the mat on which the paralytic lay. When Jesus saw their faith, he said to the paralytic, "Son, your sins are forgiven."

- Lord, I have felt paralyzed at times, without the courage to act because of some failure or criticism that took the heart out of me.
- Then I relied on the help of good friends, like the four stretcher-bearers, to bring me to the point where I could hear you say: "Get up and walk." Suddenly, as W. H. Auden put it, I was able to approach the future as a friend, without a wardrobe of excuses.

Saturday 17th January **Mark 2:13–17**

Jesus went out again beside the sea; the whole crowd gathered around him, and he taught them. As he was walking along, he saw Levi son of Alphaeus sitting at the tax booth, and he said to him, "Follow me." And he got up and followed him. And as he sat at dinner in Levi's house, many tax collectors and sinners were also sitting with Jesus and his disciples—for there were many who followed him. When the scribes of the Pharisees saw that he was eating with sinners and tax collectors, they said to his disciples, "Why does he eat with tax collectors and sinners?" When Jesus heard this, he said to them, "Those who are well have no need of a physician, but those who are sick; I have come to call not the righteous but sinners."

- Who would be your chosen companions today, Lord? Not the tax collectors, but maybe the pedophiles, the addicts, and others at the very bottom of society's barrel.
- May I too have time for the sick and the outcast.

january 18–24

Something to think and pray about each day this week:

One, in God's Name

We are in the week of prayer for Christian unity. Jesus called his message good news, and so it is, a way of living that celebrates life and gives a meaning to suffering and death. If there is a better one, please let me know. The message is simple, but it is muddled by the multiplicity of religions and persuasions and churches. We echo Jesus' prayer: That they may be one including Moslems, Jews, and all varieties of Christians. It is a long, slow journey toward unity, but praying together and banking on the things we have in common will hasten that journey. Men make divisions, Christ unites. The true history of the church is not in the institutions or doctrines, in the councils and reformations and sects. The true history of the church is in the believers who pray to God our Father through the mediation of Christ his son. Where two or three or thousands are gathered in God's name, he is there.

The Presence of God
As I sit here, God is present,
breathing life into me and into everything around me.
For a few moments, I sit silently,
and become aware of God's loving presence.

Freedom
If God were trying to tell me something, would I know?
If God were reassuring me or challenging me, would I notice?
I ask for the grace to be free of my own preoccupations
and open to what God may be saying to me.

Consciousness
In God's loving presence I unwind the past day,
starting from now and looking back, moment by moment.
I gather in all the goodness and light, in gratitude.
I attend to the shadows and what they say to me,
seeking healing, courage, forgiveness.

The Word
I take my time to read the Word of God, slowly, a few times, allowing myself to dwell on anything that strikes me. (Please turn to your scripture on the following pages. Inspiration points are there should you need them. When you are ready, return here to continue.)

Conversation
What is stirring in me as I pray?
Am I consoled, troubled, left cold?
I imagine Jesus himself standing or sitting at my side,
and share my feelings with him.

Conclusion
Glory be to the Father, and to the Son, and to the Holy Spirit,
As it was in the beginning, is now and ever shall be,
World without end. Amen

Sunday 18th January,
Second Sunday in Ordinary Time **John 1:35–42**

The next day John again was standing with two of his disciples, and as he watched Jesus walk by, he exclaimed, "Look, here is the Lamb of God!" The two disciples heard him say this, and they followed Jesus. When Jesus turned and saw them following, he said to them, "What are you looking for?" They said to him, "Rabbi" (which translated means Teacher), "where are you staying?" He said to them, "Come and see." They came and saw where he was staying, and they remained with him that day. It was about four o'clock in the afternoon. One of the two who heard John speak and followed him was Andrew, Simon Peter's brother. He first found his brother Simon and said to him, "We have found the Messiah" (which is translated Anointed). He brought Simon to Jesus, who looked at him and said, "You are Simon son of John. You are to be called Cephas" (which is translated Peter).

- Such a searching question that is: What are you looking for? Many would say: I'm not looking for anything. I am just trying to survive. But in sober moments we realize that we would like our lives to amount to more than just getting and spending, eating and sleeping.
- Lord, I want you to look at me as you looked at Simon. Invite me to see where you are to be found and to remain with you.

Monday 19th January **Mark 2:18–22**

Now John's disciples and the Pharisees were fasting; and people came and said to him, "Why do John's disciples and the disciples of the Pharisees fast, but your disciples do not fast?" Jesus said to them, "The wedding-guests cannot fast while the bridegroom is with them, can they? As long as they have the bridegroom with them, they cannot fast. The days will come when the bridegroom is taken away from them, and then they will fast on that day. No one sews a piece of unshrunk cloth on an old cloak; otherwise, the patch pulls away from it, the new from the old, and a worse tear is made. And no one puts new wine into old wineskins; otherwise, the wine will burst the skins, and the wine is lost, and so are the skins; but one puts new wine into fresh wineskins."

- That is how you were seen, Lord, as somebody always ready for a party, somebody who enjoyed life and lived it to the fullest.
- Here you are warning me against being hung up on the negatives, on rules and restrictions. You have come with good news, that we may have life and have it in more abundance.

Tuesday 20th January **Mark 2:23–28**

One sabbath Jesus was going through the grain fields; and as they made their way his disciples began to pluck heads of grain. The Pharisees said to him, "Look, why are they doing what is not lawful on the sabbath?" And he said to them, "Have you never read what David did when he and his companions were hungry and in need of food? He entered the house of God, when Abiathar was high priest, and ate the bread of the Presence, which it is not lawful for any but the priests to eat, and he gave some to his companions." Then he said to them, "The sabbath was made for humankind, and not humankind for the sabbath; so the Son of Man is lord even of the sabbath."

- Lord, when human need was crying out to you, the law took second place. It seems so obvious that the sabbath, and law, are made for humankind, not vice versa. It took courage as well as clarity of mind to state the obvious.

Wednesday 21st January **Mark 3:1–6**

Again he entered the synagogue, and a man was there who had a withered hand. They watched him to see whether he would cure him on the sabbath, so that they might accuse him. And he said to the man who had the withered hand, "Come forward." Then he said to them, "Is it lawful to do good or to do harm on the sabbath, to save life or to kill?" But they were silent. He looked around at them with anger; he was grieved at their hardness of heart and said to the man, "Stretch out your hand." He stretched it out, and his hand was restored. The Pharisees went out and immediately conspired with the Herodians against him, how to destroy him.

- "He was grieved at their hardness of heart." It is sometimes a fine balance between being a person with strong convictions and being one who is rigid and stubborn.
- How do I find myself responding? Am I set in my ways? Can the Lord disturb them?

Thursday 22nd January **Mark 3:7–12**

Jesus departed with his disciples to the sea, and a great multitude from Galilee followed him; hearing all that he was doing, they came to him in great numbers from Judea, Jerusalem, Idumea, beyond the Jordan, and the region around Tyre and Sidon. He told his disciples to have a boat ready for him because of the crowd, so that they would not crush him; for he had cured many, so that all who had diseases pressed upon him to touch him. Whenever the unclean spirits saw him, they fell down before him and shouted, "You are the Son of God!" But he sternly ordered them not to make him known.

- In one sentence Mark indicates the enormous draw of Jesus. To listen to him and feel his healing touch, people walked one hundred

miles from Jerusalem and further south, from the lands east of the Jordan and the Mediterranean cities of Tyre and Sidon.
- In this time of prayer for church unity, we sense the convergence of millions who love Jesus and pray through him to the Father. Let us touch him, and hear him, but never claim to own him.

Friday 23rd January **Mark 3:13–19**

He went up the mountain and called to him those whom he wanted, and they came to him. And he appointed twelve, whom he also named apostles, to be with him, and to be sent out to proclaim the message, and to have authority to cast out demons. So he appointed the twelve: Simon (to whom he gave the name Peter); James son of Zebedee and John the brother of James (to whom he gave the name Boanerges, that is, Sons of Thunder); and Andrew, and Philip, and Bartholomew, and Matthew, and Thomas, and James son of Alphaeus, and Thaddaeus, and Simon the Cananaean, and Judas Iscariot, who betrayed him.

- Jesus took risks in his selection. Tax collector Matthew was an agent of the colonial power of Rome and seen by Jews as a traitor. His colleague Simon the Cananaean was so nationalistic he was nicknamed the Zealot.
- From the start, Christians were a very diverse lot, able to live and work together because of their love of Jesus.

Saturday 24th January, St. Francis de Sales **John 15:9–17**

"As the Father has loved me, so I have loved you; abide in my love. If you keep my commandments, you will abide in my love, just as I have kept my Father's commandments and abide in his love. I have said these things to you so that my joy may be in you, and that your joy may be complete. This is my commandment, that you love one another as I have loved you. No one has greater love than this, to lay down one's life for one's friends. You are my friends if you do what I command you. I do not call you servants any longer, because the servant does not know what the master is doing; but I have called you friends, because I have made known to you everything that I have heard from my Father. You did not choose me, but I chose you. And I appointed you to go and bear fruit, fruit that will last, so that the Father will give you whatever you ask him in my name. I am giving you these commands so that you may love one another."

- Francis de Sales is the patron saint of journalists and has left us what we would call sound-bites: "Ask for nothing and refuse nothing . . ."
- Consider all the past as nothing and say, like David: Now I begin to love my God.

january 25–31

Something to think and pray about each day this week:

Walking Out Into the Deep

Four fishermen are called: "Follow me and I will make you fishers of people." At once, we are told, Peter and Andrew left their nets and their occupation behind, and followed after Jesus. Just as quickly, leaving their father Zebedee and his hired men, James and John also went after him.

It was a complete act of trust and a total surrender of themselves. To what? Actually, they had no idea; no idea of where they were going or of what the future held. This was the extent of their great trust in this man who came suddenly into their lives, challenging them to leave behind their security and to walk away with him. They would, in fact, go through many unexpected experiences, some of them joyful, some of them full of pain.

The call is still going out to each one of us. Am I ready to answer? To follow? What limits my freedom to follow? What are the nets that still entangle me? What personal relationships are blocking my way? What anxieties? What self-centered ambitions?

The Presence of God
As I sit here with my book, God is here
around me, in my sensations, in my thoughts, and deep within me.
I pause for a moment and become aware
of God's life-giving presence.

Freedom
I need to close out the noise, to rise above the noise;
The noise that interrupts, that separates,
The noise that isolates.
I need to listen to God again.

Consciousness
I remind myself that I am in the presence of the Lord.
I will take refuge in His loving heart.
He is my strength in times of weakness.
He is my comforter in times of sorrow.

The Word
God speaks to each one of us individually. I need to listen to what he is saying to me. (Please turn to your scripture on the following pages. Inspiration points are there should you need them. When you are ready, return here to continue.)

Conversation
Do I notice myself reacting as I pray with the Word of God?
Do I feel challenged, comforted, angry?
Imagining Jesus sitting or standing by me,
I speak out my feelings, as one trusted friend to another.

Conclusion
Glory be to the Father, and to the Son, and to the Holy Spirit,
As it was in the beginning, is now and ever shall be,
World without end. Amen

Sunday 25th January,
Third Sunday in Ordinary Time **Mark 1:14–20**

Now after John was arrested, Jesus came to Galilee, proclaiming the good news of God, and saying, "The time is fulfilled, and the kingdom of God has come near; repent, and believe in the good news." As Jesus passed along the Sea of Galilee, he saw Simon and his brother Andrew casting a net into the sea—for they were fishermen. And Jesus said to them, "Follow me, and I will make you fish for people." And immediately they left their nets and followed him. As he went a little farther, he saw James son of Zebedee and his brother John, who were in their boat mending the nets. Immediately he called them; and they left their father Zebedee in the boat with the hired men, and followed him.

- Jesus moves slowly toward Simon and Andrew, conscious that he is disturbing their work, but calling them to another task. When he speaks that incredible "Follow me," they felt his attraction and knew: This is somebody you can take a risk with.
- You look at me, Lord, and I look at you as you ask me to work for a kingdom of justice and love.

Monday 26th January **Mark 3:22–30**

And the scribes who came down from Jerusalem said, "He has Beelzebul, and by the ruler of the demons he casts out demons." And he called them to him, and spoke to them in parables, "How can Satan cast out Satan? If a kingdom is divided against itself, that kingdom cannot stand. And if a house is divided against itself, that house will not be able to stand. And if Satan has risen up against himself and is divided, he cannot stand, but his end has come. But no one can enter a strong man's house and plunder his property without first tying up the strong man; then indeed the house can be plundered. Truly I tell you, people will be forgiven for their sins and whatever blasphemies they utter; but whoever blasphemes against the Holy Spirit can never have forgiveness, but is guilty of an eternal sin"—for they had said, "He has an unclean spirit."

- Jesus opens us up here to a global mission, the fight against evil, which is recognized by the human mind, whether in the form of hatred, sickness, or injustice, or the sort of barbarisms that we hear of daily.
- Those who struggle against such evil are on the side of Jesus, whatever they call themselves.

Tuesday 27th January **Mark 3:31–35**

Then the mother and brothers of Jesus came; and standing outside, they sent to him and called him. A crowd was sitting around him; and they said to him, "Your mother and your brothers and sisters are outside, asking for you." And he replied, "Who are my mother and my brothers?" And looking at those who sat around him, he said, "Here are my mother and my brothers! Whoever does the will of God is my brother and sister and mother."

- Lord, I hear a gentleness in your voice. You blessed Mary not for the bond of blood with you, but because she was the handmaid of the Lord whose response to God's angel led to the Incarnation.
- In a culture where blood relationships really counted, you were pointing to deeper relationships, like the one that I have with you.

Wednesday 28th January,
St. Thomas Aquinas **Matthew 23:8–12**

Jesus said to the crowds, "But you are not to be called rabbi, for you have one teacher, and you are all students. And call no one your father on earth, for you have one Father—the one in heaven. Nor are you to be called instructors, for you have one instructor, the Messiah. The greatest among you will be your servant. All who exalt themselves will be humbled, and all who humble themselves will be exalted."

- The best teachers and parents are those who do not rely on their status or insist on respect. Instead, they earn it through humble service and devotion to those in their care.
- Have you ever met anyone like that? A teacher, or someone else in authority who had no regard for their office or rank and would just try to help wherever they could?
- Can I ask the Lord for that grace?

Thursday 29th January **Mark 4:21–25**

He said to them, "Is a lamp brought in to be put under the bushel basket, or under the bed, and not on the lampstand? For there is nothing hidden, except to be disclosed; nor is anything secret, except to come to light. Let anyone with ears to hear listen!" And he said to them, "Pay attention to what you hear; the measure you give will be the measure you get, and still more will be given you. For to those who have, more will be given; and from those who have nothing, even what they have will be taken away."

- When Christians are under fire, for instance over clerical sex abuse, it is tempting to hide our light under a bushel for fear of provoking further attacks.

- Jesus' words ring so true: Nothing is hidden that will not be disclosed. There is a grace in this disgrace. The fact that priests committed crimes and were sometimes protected by their superiors does not lift our responsibility to preach the gospel.

Friday 30th January **Mark 4:30–34**

Jesus said to the crowd, "With what can we compare the kingdom of God, or what parable will we use for it? It is like a mustard seed, which, when sown upon the ground, is the smallest of all the seeds on earth; yet when it is sown it grows up and becomes the greatest of all shrubs, and puts forth large branches so that the birds of the air can make nests in its shade." With many such parables he spoke the word to them, as they were able to hear it; he did not speak to them except in parables, but he explained everything in private to his disciples.

- Lord, your images of the kingdom are alive and organic. It has its own pattern of growth, a tiny plant that grows into a massive tree with room for every creature.
- Let me never imagine that I am the architect or builder of your kingdom. Enough for me to be patient, a seed growing slowly, animated by your spirit.

Saturday 31st January, St. John Bosco **Matthew 18:1–5**

At that time the disciples came to Jesus and asked, "Who is the greatest in the kingdom of heaven?" He called a child, whom he put among them, and said, "Truly I tell you, unless you change and become like children, you will never enter the kingdom of heaven. Whoever becomes humble like this child is the greatest in the kingdom of heaven. Whoever welcomes one such child in my name welcomes me."

- Jesus told the disciples to change and become humble like children. How? We cannot regain our youth, inexperience, or innocence. But we can learn to put our ego in its place, to stop pushing ourselves forward, hogging the conversation.
- We can learn to be happy in the background, no longer the center of attention or striving to be the greatest. To be comfortable in that role is a huge grace.

february 1–7

Something to think and pray about each day this week:

Coming Toward God

Describing progress toward God, Von Hügel writes of an institutional stage, followed by a critical stage, and culminating in what he calls a mystical stage. This does not mean magic or heavenly voices, but rather this: We oldies have seen it all and know that good and evil, like the wheat and cockle of the parable coexist not merely in countries and institutions, but in each of us. Pitch darkness and pure light are seldom the order of the day. We learn to live with both, light out of darkness. We do the best we can, and are ready to renounce the seductions of having the perfect formulation of reality or the perfect formula for everyone's life.

In the mystical phase we still carry with us the institutional phase: We still love the sights and sounds of worship carried out well, and the sense of participating in a great body of believers. We have not left the critical phase behind, but carry it with us: We use our heads about our religion and have no illusions about the weaknesses of Jesus' followers—after all, Peter, the first pope, had to live with the memory of denying the Lord publicly, again and again. But when we have argued about all the great questions of human existence, especially the mystery of evil, we realize that we rely more on the gift of faith than on clear-cut reason.

The Presence of God

At any time of the day or night we can call on Jesus.
He is always waiting, listening for our call.
What a wonderful blessing.
No phone needed, no emails, just a whisper.

Freedom

I will ask God's help,
to be free from my own preoccupations,
to be open to God in this time of prayer,
to come to love and serve him more.

Consciousness

How am I really feeling? Light-hearted? Heavy-hearted?
I may be very much at peace, happy to be here.
Equally, I may be frustrated, worried, or angry.
I acknowledge how I really am.
It is the real me that the Lord loves.

The Word

I read the Word of God slowly, a few times over, and I listen to what God is saying to me. (Please turn to your scripture on the following pages. Inspiration points are there should you need them. When you are ready, return here to continue.)

Conversation

Remembering that I am still in God's presence,
I imagine Jesus himself standing or sitting beside me,
and say whatever is on my mind, whatever is in my heart,
speaking as one friend to another.

Conclusion

Glory be to the Father, and to the Son, and to the Holy Spirit,
As it was in the beginning, is now and ever shall be,
World without end. Amen

Sunday 1st February,
Fourth Sunday in Ordinary Time **Mark 1:21–28**

Then they came to Capernaum, and on the sabbath Jesus entered the synagogue and taught. They were astounded at his teaching, for he taught them as one having authority, and not as the scribes. Just then there was in their synagogue a man with an unclean spirit, and he cried out, "What have you to do with us, Jesus of Nazareth? Have you come to destroy us? I know who you are, the Holy One of God." But Jesus rebuked him, saying, "Be silent, and come out of him!" And the unclean spirit, convulsing him and crying with a loud voice, came out of him. They were all amazed, and they kept on asking one another, "What is this? A new teaching—with authority! He commands even the unclean spirits, and they obey him." At once his fame began to spread throughout the surrounding region of Galilee.

- When the Jewish scribes spoke in the synagogue, they would begin: "There is a teaching that . . ." and would go on to quote old traditions. When Jesus spoke, it was from his personal authority, as one who knows God. The impact was immediate and powerful.
- Thank you, Lord, for opening the door into the knowledge of God. May I enter and keep learning.

Monday 2nd February,
The Presentation of the Lord **Luke 2:25–33**

Now there was a man in Jerusalem whose name was Simeon; this man was righteous and devout, looking forward to the consolation of Israel, and the Holy Spirit rested on him. It had been revealed to him by the Holy Spirit that he would not see death before he had seen the Lord's Messiah. Guided by the Spirit, Simeon came into the temple; and when the parents brought in the child Jesus, to do for him what was customary under the law, Simeon took him in his arms and praised God, saying, "Master, now you are dismissing your servant in peace, according to your word; for my eyes have seen your salvation, which you have prepared in the presence of all peoples, a light for revelation to the Gentiles and for glory to your people Israel." And the child's father and mother were amazed at what was being said about him.

- Simeon believed in a life of constant watchfulness and prayer until God should come. There is a double surprise here: the delight of Simeon at being able to welcome the Promised One, and the astonishment of Mary and Joseph at what was being said about their boy.
- Lord, may I too open my eyes in grateful amazement when I see your interventions in my life.

Tuesday 3rd February **Mark 5:25–30**

Now there was a woman who had been suffering from hemorrhages for twelve years. She had endured much under many physicians, and had spent all that she had; and she was no better, but rather grew worse. She had heard about Jesus, and came up behind him in the crowd and touched his cloak, for she said, "If I but touch his clothes, I will be made well." Immediately her hemorrhage stopped; and she felt in her body that she was healed of her disease. Immediately aware that power had gone forth from him, Jesus turned about in the crowd and said, "Who touched my clothes?"

- This bleeding woman is the patron saint of medical patients: She had endured much under many physicians and had spent all that she had; and she was no better, but rather grew worse.
- Finally, we turn to the Lord and find help, maybe not in a cure, but in peace.

Wednesday 4th February **Mark 6:1–6**

Jesus went on to his hometown, and his disciples followed him. On the sabbath he began to teach in the synagogue, and many who heard him were astounded. They said, "Where did this man get all this? What is this wisdom that has been given to him? What deeds of power are being done by his hands! Is not this the carpenter, the son of Mary and brother of James and Joses and Judas and Simon, and are not his sisters here with us?" And they took offense at him. Then Jesus said to them, "Prophets are not without honor, except in their hometown, and among their own kin, and in their own house." And he could do no deed of power there, except that he laid his hands on a few sick people and cured them. And he was amazed at their unbelief. Then he went about among the villages teaching.

- Francois Mauriac wrote in his life of Jesus: "It is baffling to record that, for a period of thirty years, the Son of Man did not appear to be anything other than a man. Those who lived with him thought they knew him. He fixed their tables and chairs. They ate and drank with his extended family. When he stepped outside the role they had fixed for him, they put him down as just a workman."
- Lord, there are depths in each of us that only you can glimpse. A put-down tells more about the speaker than about the victim. Save me, Lord, from such folly.

Thursday 5th February **Mark 6:7–13**

Jesus called the twelve and began to send them out two by two and gave them authority over the unclean spirits. He ordered them to take nothing for their journey except a staff; no bread, no bag, no money in their belts; but to wear sandals and not to put on two tunics. He said to them, "Wherever you enter a house, stay there until you leave the place. If any place will not welcome you and they refuse to hear you, as you leave, shake off the dust that is on your feet as a testimony against them." So they went out and proclaimed that all should repent. They cast out many demons and anointed with oil many who were sick and cured them.

- These instructions indicate how the disciples carried out their work. Communication of the good news had to be by word of mouth and depended on the traveling missioners. Many listeners could not read, and Jesus stressed not so much the message as the medium, i.e. the lifestyle of the preachers.
- Forgive me, Lord, when my lifestyle distorts your gospel.

Friday 6th February **Hebrews 13:1–8**

Let mutual love continue. Do not neglect to show hospitality to strangers, for by doing that some have entertained angels without knowing it. Remember those who are in prison, as though you were in prison with them; those who are being tortured, as though you yourselves were being tortured. Let marriage be held in honor by all, and let the marriage bed be kept undefiled; for God will judge fornicators and adulterers. Keep your lives free from the love of money, and be content with what you have; for he has said, "I will never leave you or forsake you." So we can say with confidence, "The Lord is my helper; I will not be afraid. What can anyone do to me?" Remember your leaders, those who spoke the word of God to you; consider the outcome of their way of life, and imitate their faith. Jesus Christ is the same yesterday and today and for ever.

- "Remember those who are in prison as though you were in prison with them," says the letter to the Hebrews. Today's reading from Mark tells the sordid story of the final hours of John the Baptist, beheaded for a frivolous promise of Herod.

- Lord, you spent your last night before your crucifixion in prison. Bring comfort to the thousands of good people who are languishing behind bars. They are my sisters and brothers. There but for the grace of God I would be too.

Saturday 7th February **Mark 6:30–34**

The apostles gathered around Jesus, and told him all that they had done and taught. He said to them, "Come away to a deserted place all by yourselves and rest a while." For many were coming and going, and they had no leisure even to eat. And they went away in the boat to a deserted place by themselves. Now many saw them going and recognized them, and they hurried there on foot from all the towns and arrived ahead of them. As he went ashore, he saw a great crowd; and he had compassion for them, because they were like sheep without a shepherd; and he began to teach them many things.

- Here is a phrase to ponder: "He had compassion on the crowd because they were like sheep without a shepherd." Jesus, Son of the eternal Father, sees the crowd as his sisters and brothers.
- His gaze spans the millennia of humankind, sees our need for direction, for compassion, and for seeking some meaning in existence.

february 8–14

Something to think and pray about each day this week:

Signs and Wonders

February 11 is the feast of our Lady of Lourdes, perhaps the most famous of Catholic private revelations. The spirit is speaking in many places, wherever you see good being done. This still leaves us the responsibility to test the spirits, as St. Paul puts it. Our Lord himself was wary of those who wanted signs and wonders. He discouraged his disciples from speculating about when the end of the world would be. This has not deterred later would-be prophets from foretelling doomsday or offering private revelations. The Church has always said: Be skeptical. Revelation ended with the death of the last apostle. Believing in private revelations is not part of our faith, but an optional extra, to be treated with caution. Look to the quality of the prophet's life, the absence of ego, greed, or self-seeking. Judged in that way, Bernadette of Lourdes, and the spirit of prayer and service that pervades the shrine, measure up well.

The Presence of God

I pause for a moment
and think of the love and the grace that God showers on me,
creating me in his image and likeness, making me his temple.

Freedom

Lord, grant me the grace to be free from the excesses of this life.
Let me not get caught up with the desire for wealth.
Keep my heart and mind free to love and serve you.

Consciousness

In the presence of my loving Creator,
I look honestly at my feelings over the last day,
the highs, the lows, and the level ground.
Can I see where the Lord has been present?

The Word

God speaks to each one of us individually. I need to listen to what he is saying to me. (Please turn to your scripture on the following pages. Inspiration points are there should you need them. When you are ready, return here to continue.)

Conversation

Sometimes I wonder what I might say
if I were to meet You in person, Lord.
I might say "Thank You, Lord" for always being there for me.
I know with certainty there were times when you carried me,
when through your strength I got through the dark times in my life.

Conclusion

Glory be to the Father, and to the Son, and to the Holy Spirit,
As it was in the beginning, is now and ever shall be,
World without end. Amen

Sunday 8th February,
Fifth Sunday in Ordinary Time **Mark 1:29–31**

As soon as they left the synagogue, they entered the house of Simon and Andrew, with James and John. Now Simon's mother-in-law was in bed with a fever, and they told Jesus about her at once. He came and took her by the hand and lifted her up. Then the fever left her, and she began to serve them.

- Jesus liked physical contact. He lifted the sick woman by the hand. He put his fingers into the ears of the deaf mute and touched his tongue with spittle. He touched lepers. Jairus begged him: Lay your hand on my daughter to make her better.
- Lord, let me not fear to touch, to bless, and to come close to others as you did.

Monday 9th February **Mark 6:53–56**

When Jesus and the disciples had crossed over, they came to land at Gennesaret and moored the boat. When they got out of the boat, people at once recognized him, and rushed about that whole region and began to bring the sick on mats to wherever they heard he was. And wherever he went, into villages or cities or farms, they laid the sick in the marketplaces and begged him that they might touch even the fringe of his cloak; and all who touched it were healed.

- Is there some sickness or distress that I want Jesus to heal me of? Can I put myself among those in this scene who need healing?
- Jesus is offering that healing. Can I accept it from him?

Tuesday 10th February **Mark 7:1–2, 5–8**

Now when the Pharisees and some of the scribes who had come from Jerusalem gathered around him, they noticed that some of his disciples were eating with defiled hands, that is, without washing them. So the Pharisees and the scribes asked him, "Why do your disciples not live according to the tradition of the elders, but eat with defiled hands?" He said to them, "Isaiah prophesied rightly about you hypocrites, as it is written, 'This people honors me with their lips, but their hearts are far from me; in vain do they worship me, teaching human precepts as doctrines.' You abandon the commandment of God and hold to human tradition."

- Jesus and his uneducated disciples are mixing with sophisticated Pharisees from Jerusalem, men who have mastered the intricate rules about ritual purity and look down on those who are ignorant of them.
- As Christians we can set up our own norms of what is god-fearing and respectable and forget that it is the heart that matters. Jesus always sees through the externals of behavior to the love and goodness that may lie beneath.

Wednesday 11th February **Mark 7:14–23**

Then he called the crowd again and said to them, "Listen to me, all of you, and understand: there is nothing outside a person that by going in can defile, but the things that come out are what defile." When he had left the crowd and entered the house, his disciples asked him about the parable. He said to them, "Then do you also fail to understand? Do you not see that whatever goes into a person from outside cannot defile, since it enters, not the heart but the stomach, and goes out into the sewer?" (Thus he declared all foods clean.) And he said, "It is what comes out of a person that defiles. For it is from within, from the human heart, that evil intentions come: fornication, theft, murder, adultery, avarice, wickedness, deceit, licentiousness, envy, slander, pride, folly. All these evil things come from within, and they defile a person."

- Jesus called the crowd again. This lesson about the heart has to be repeated and stressed. Good manners and proper behavior vary from group to group, but the underlying goodness or badness crosses all social divides. That is what we look to.

Thursday 12th February **Mark 7:24–30**

From there Jesus set out and went away to the region of Tyre. He entered a house and did not want anyone to know he was there. Yet he could not escape notice, but a woman whose little daughter had an unclean spirit immediately heard about him, and she came and bowed down at his feet. Now the woman was a Gentile, of Syrophoenician origin. She begged him to cast the demon out of her daughter. He said to her, "Let the children be fed first, for it is not fair to take the children's food and throw it to the dogs." But she answered him, "Sir, even the dogs under the table eat the children's crumbs." Then he said to her, "For saying that, you may go—the demon has left your daughter." So she went home, found the child lying on the bed, and the demon gone.

- In the absence of napkins, Jewish diners would wipe their dirty hands on chunks of bread that they then threw under the table for the dogs to eat.
- Mark sees here a symbol of Jesus' message, the bread of heaven, which the Gentile world seized on after the Jews had rejected it.

Friday 13th February **Mark 7:31–37**

Then Jesus returned from the region of Tyre, and went by way of Sidon towards the Sea of Galilee, in the region of the Decapolis. They brought to him a deaf man who had an impediment in his speech; and they begged him to lay his hand on him. He took him aside in private, away from the crowd, and put his fingers into his ears, and he spat and touched his tongue. Then looking up to heaven, he sighed and said to him, "*Ephphatha*," that is, "Be opened." And immediately his ears were opened, his tongue was released, and he spoke plainly. Then Jesus ordered them to tell no one; but the more he ordered them, the more zealously they proclaimed it. They were astounded beyond measure, saying, "He has done everything well; he even makes the deaf to hear and the mute to speak."

- "Be opened!" That was your key message. Do not shut yourself off, but treasure the senses that open you to the world of other people.
- O Lord, you are not a God of dead but of living people. We ask you who have made us, to bless us and keep us alive. Receive us when we die, renew us when we grow old, make us open if we become closed to you, for the sake of Jesus Christ your Son.

Saturday 14th February,
Sts. Cyril and Methodius **Luke 10:1–6**

After this the Lord appointed seventy others and sent them on ahead of him in pairs to every town and place where he himself intended to go. He said to them, "The harvest is plentiful, but the laborers are few; therefore ask the Lord of the harvest to send out laborers into his harvest. Go on your way. See, I am sending you out like lambs into the midst of wolves. Carry no purse, no bag, no sandals; and greet no one on the road. Whatever house you enter, first say, 'Peace to this house!' And if anyone is there who shares in peace, your peace will rest on that person; but if not, it will return to you."

- "Peace to this house!" You send us like lambs, Lord, vulnerable, unthreatening, with no weapons, no resources, offering simply the gifts of peace and of healing. But my temptation is always to look for more resources, more courses, more back-up.
- Yours is a hard lesson to learn. I must come back to it again and again.

february 15–21

Something to think and pray about each day this week:

Learning from Silence

There is a story from the desert fathers. A certain brother came to the abbot Moses seeking a word from him. The old man said, "Go and sit in your cell, and your cell will teach you everything." The ability to sit still, in silence, with nothing except the silence (not even a mobile phone or the sound of music), really does frighten people. As St. Anthony explained, "The one who sits in solitude and quiet has escaped from three wars: hearing, speaking and seeing; yet against one thing shall he continually battle: that is, his own heart." More than a thousand years later Pascal was of the same mind: "The sole cause of man's unhappiness is that he does not know how to stay quietly in his room."

The Presence of God

As I sit here with my book, God is here.
Around me, in my sensations, in my thoughts, and deep within me.
I pause for a moment and become aware
of God's life-giving presence.

Freedom

A thick and shapeless tree-trunk would never believe
that it could become a statue, admired as a miracle of sculpture,
and would never submit itself to the chisel of the sculptor,
who sees by her genius what she can make of it. (St Ignatius)
I ask for the grace to let myself be shaped by my loving Creator.

Consciousness

How am I really feeling? Light-hearted? Heavy-hearted?
I may be very much at peace, happy to be here.
Equally, I may be frustrated, worried, or angry.
I acknowledge how I really am. It is the real me that the Lord loves.

The Word

God speaks to each one of us individually. I need to listen to what he is saying to me. (Please turn to your scripture on the following pages. Inspiration points are there should you need them. When you are ready, return here to continue.)

Conversation

Do I notice myself reacting as I pray with the Word of God?
Do I feel challenged, comforted, angry?
Imagining Jesus sitting or standing by me,
I speak out my feelings, as one trusted friend to another.

Conclusion

Glory be to the Father, and to the Son, and to the Holy Spirit,
As it was in the beginning, is now and ever shall be,
World without end. Amen

Sunday 15th February,
Sixth Sunday in Ordinary Time **Mark 1:40–45**

A leper came to Jesus begging him, and kneeling he said to him, "If you choose, you can make me clean." Moved with pity, Jesus stretched out his hand and touched him, and said to him, "I do choose. Be made clean!" Immediately the leprosy left him, and he was made clean. After sternly warning him he sent him away at once, saying to him, "See that you say nothing to anyone; but go, show yourself to the priest, and offer for your cleansing what Moses commanded, as a testimony to them." But he went out and began to proclaim it freely, and to spread the word, so that Jesus could no longer go into a town openly, but stayed out in the country; and people came to him from every quarter.

- Lord, you warned the leper to keep your mission a secret. What mattered for you was your inner sending, your contact through prayer with the Father.
- Preserve me, Lord, from the cult of image and from wanting to publish what I am about. I want to be like you, drawing inner strength rather from prayer and my link with God.

Monday 16th February **Genesis 4:6–7**

The Lord said to Cain, "Why are you angry, and why has your countenance fallen? If you do well, will you not be accepted? And if you do not do well, sin is lurking at the door; its desire is for you, but you must master it."

- In the story of the first murder (Cain killing Abel), scripture imagines sin lurking at the door and calls on us to master it.
- There are times when it would be wrong to "go with the flow." I have to face down the unruly passions in myself and master them.

Tuesday 17th February **Mark 8:14–17**

Now the disciples had forgotten to bring any bread; and they had only one loaf with them in the boat. And he cautioned them, saying, "Watch out—beware of the yeast of the Pharisees and the yeast of Herod." They said to one another, "It is because we have no bread." And becoming aware of it, Jesus said to them, "Why are you talking about having no bread? Do you still not perceive or understand?"

- The disciples are worried about having too little bread, and Jesus is saying: Surely you have learned that you do not need to worry about that when you are with me?
- I need to learn from experience too, Lord. The worries that seem huge in a moment of crisis seem trivial a week later. I survive sickness, temptation, and failure and bounce back. Help me to keep my spirits up.

Wednesday 18th February **Mark 8:22–25**

They came to Bethsaida. Some people brought a blind man to Jesus and begged him to touch him. He took the blind man by the hand and led him out of the village; and when he had put saliva on his eyes and laid his hands on him, he asked him, "Can you see anything?" And the man looked up and said, "I can see people, but they look like trees, walking." Then Jesus laid his hands on his eyes again; and he looked intently and his sight was restored, and he saw everything clearly.

- This is a scene to relish step by step. Villagers lead the blind man to Jesus: Please touch him! Jesus takes him by the hand and takes him away from the crowd, and with an intimately personal gesture he puts saliva on the blind eyes and talks him through his recovery of sight.

- It is a tender, intense encounter—one that the blind man must have treasured all his life. Contemplate it slowly.

Thursday 19th February **Mark 8:27–33**

Jesus went on with his disciples to the villages of Caesarea Philippi; and on the way he asked his disciples, "Who do people say that I am?" And they answered him, "John the Baptist; and others, Elijah; and still others, one of the prophets." He asked them, "But who do you say that I am?" Peter answered him, "You are the Messiah." And he sternly ordered them not to tell anyone about him. Then he began to teach them that the Son of Man must undergo great suffering, and be rejected by the elders, the chief priests, and the scribes, and be killed, and after three days rise again. He said all this quite openly. And Peter took him aside and began to rebuke him. But turning and looking at his disciples, he rebuked Peter and said, "Get behind me, Satan! For you are setting your mind not on divine things but on human things."

- I can feel with Peter: His beloved leader, for whom he has left his family and livelihood, is now saying that he is going to fail. Peter is voicing the temptation that will assail Jesus in Gethsemini, on the eve of his passion; hence the vehemence of Jesus' rebuke.
- Lord, when I forget about the cross, I am forgetting you.

Friday 20th February **Mark 8:34**

Jesus called the crowd with his disciples, and said to them, "If any want to become my followers, let them deny themselves and take up their cross and follow me."

- "Let them deny themselves." At one time I thought I had to go out seeking opportunities for self-denial. Now I know that the biggest challenges to my ego come unbidden and unwanted. My cross often comes to me on two legs.

- I find my peace in your will, Lord, not in the comforts I plan for myself.

Saturday 21st February **Mark 9:2–8**

Six days later, Jesus took with him Peter and James and John, and led them up a high mountain apart, by themselves. And he was transfigured before them, and his clothes became dazzling white, such as no one on earth could bleach them. And there appeared to them Elijah with Moses, who were talking with Jesus. Then Peter said to Jesus, "Rabbi, it is good for us to be here; let us make three dwellings, one for you, one for Moses, and one for Elijah." He did not know what to say, for they were terrified. Then a cloud overshadowed them, and from the cloud there came a voice, "This is my Son, the Beloved; listen to him!" Suddenly when they looked around, they saw no one with them any more, but only Jesus.

- The story captures the vivid, trembling memory of Peter as he recounted it to Mark: the whiteness of Jesus' clothes, the sudden drop from awe-inspiring visions to seeing no one any more, but only Jesus.
- It is in your friendship, Lord Jesus, that I find the bridge linking me to the awful majesty of God.

february 22–28

Something to think and pray about each day this week:

In God's Presence

The prayers said at baptism often include phrases about exorcism and turning away from evil. Good parents are often uneasy with this language. They cannot see this precious mite, their baby, as sinful or in the power of the devil. On the other hand, they treasure the rite of baptism as a re-birth. Little Deirdre has been born in the flesh, and now she is reborn in the Spirit. She is a born-again Christian. The phrase is often used in a narrow sense to denote fanatical fundamentalists. Deirdre is born in the spirit in the sense that her new life reaches beyond this world. She is not made for death but for a life in God's church, the Christian community, in this world, and in the enjoyment of God's presence in the next.

The Presence of God

Jesus waits silent and unseen to come into my heart.
I will respond to His call.
He comes with His infinite power and love.
May I be filled with joy in His presence.

Freedom

I ask for the grace
to let go of my own concerns
and be open to what God is asking of me,
to let myself be guided and formed by my loving Creator.

Consciousness

Knowing that God loves me unconditionally,
I can afford to be honest about how I am.
How has the last day been, and how do I feel now?
I share my feelings openly with the Lord.

The Word

I read the Word of God slowly a few times over, and I listen to what God is saying to me. (Please turn to your scripture on the following pages. Inspiration points are there should you need them. When you are ready, return here to continue.)

Conversation

Remembering that I am still in God's presence,
I imagine Jesus himself standing or sitting beside me
and say whatever is on my mind, whatever is in my heart,
speaking as one friend to another.

Conclusion

Glory be to the Father, and to the Son, and to the Holy Spirit,
As it was in the beginning, is now and ever shall be,
World without end. Amen

Sunday 22nd February,
Seventh Sunday in Ordinary Time **Mark 2:1–5**

When he returned to Capernaum after some days, it was reported that he was at home. So many gathered around that there was no longer room for them, not even in front of the door; and he was speaking the word to them. Then some people came, bringing to him a paralyzed man, carried by four of them. And when they could not bring him to Jesus because of the crowd, they removed the roof above him; and after having dug through it, they let down the mat on which the paralytic lay. When Jesus saw their faith, he said to the paralytic, "Son, your sins are forgiven."

- There is goodness and ingenuity in this scene. The four friends of the paralytic were ready to take enormous trouble over him, to make sure he had contact with Jesus.
- I can imagine the curiosity of the crowd, I can imagine Jesus smiling, and then surprising everyone by tackling the man's inner sickness.
- I can imagine the joy all around as the man obeys Jesus' word, picks up his mat and walks away on his own feet.

Monday 23rd February **Mark 9:17–24**

Someone from the crowd answered Jesus, "Teacher, I brought you my son; he has a spirit that makes him unable to speak; and whenever it seizes him, it dashes him down; and he foams and grinds his teeth and becomes rigid; and I asked your disciples to cast it out, but they could not do so." He answered them, "You faithless generation, how much longer must I be among you? How much longer must I put up with you? Bring him to me." And they brought the boy to him. When the spirit saw him, immediately it convulsed the boy, and he fell on the ground and rolled about, foaming at the mouth. Jesus asked the father, "How long has this been happening to him?" And he said, "From childhood. It has often cast him into the fire and into the water, to destroy him; but if you are able to do anything, have pity on us and help us." Jesus said to him, "If you are able! All things can be done for the one who believes." Immediately the father of the child cried out, "I believe; help my unbelief!"

- In this dramatic cure, the phrase that stays with me is the father's cry: "I believe; help my unbelief!" It describes the mix of light and darkness that together make up our faith. There must be some light, some hope.
- Jesus makes that a condition of cure. When we are near despair, there is always some small task we can tackle that will get us moving and show that we hope for a way out.
- Lord, the brightest light in my darkness is you. I trust in you.

Tuesday 24th February **Mark 9:33–37**

They came to Capernaum; and when he was in the house he asked them, "What were you arguing about on the way?" But they were silent, for on the way they had argued with one another who was the greatest. He sat down, called the twelve, and said to them, "Whoever wants to be first must be last of all and servant of all." Then he took a little child and put it among them; and taking it in his arms, he said to them, "Whoever welcomes one such child in my name welcomes me, and whoever welcomes me welcomes not me but the one who sent me."

- Do you want to kill ambition in me, Lord? I don't think so: rather that when I want to be first, I need to realize that all authority should be a form of service, not of ego-massage.

Wednesday 25th February,
Ash Wednesday **Psalm 50(51):1–10**

Have mercy on me, O God, according to your steadfast love; according to your abundant mercy blot out my transgressions. Wash me thoroughly from my iniquity, and cleanse me from my sin. For I know my transgressions, and my sin is ever before me. Against you, you alone, have I sinned, and done what is evil in your sight, so that you are justified in your sentence and blameless when you pass judgment. Indeed, I was born guilty, a sinner when my mother conceived me. You desire truth in the inward being; therefore teach me wisdom in my secret heart. Purge me with hyssop, and I shall be clean; wash me, and I shall be whiter than snow. Let me hear joy and gladness; let the bones that you have crushed rejoice. Hide your face from my sins, and blot out all my iniquities. Create in me a clean heart, O God, and put a new and right spirit within me.

- "Put a new and right spirit within me." Have I the courage to trust myself to this profound, Godly love that would take my broken sinfulness and recreate me with a clean heart?
- How does this affect me as I begin my Lenten journey?

Thursday 26th February **Luke 9:22–25**

Jesus said to his disciples: "The Son of Man must undergo great suffering, and be rejected by the elders, chief priests, and scribes, and be killed, and on the third day be raised." Then he said to them all, "If any want to become my followers, let them deny themselves and take up their cross daily and follow me. For those who want to save their life will lose it, and those who lose their life for my sake will save it. What does it profit them if they gain the whole world, but lose or forfeit themselves?"

- Jesus gives advice that is both spiritually and psychologically sound. We hold in high esteem those who give their lives for a worthy cause, even to the point of losing their own.
- Am I spending most of my time winning what is unimportant—position, status, wealth—while turning a deaf ear to those around me? Am I "existing" or "living"?

Friday 27th February **Matthew 9:14–15**

Then the disciples of John came to him, saying, "Why do we and the Pharisees fast often, but your disciples do not fast?" And Jesus said to them, "The wedding guests cannot mourn as long as the bridegroom is with them, can they? The days will come when the bridegroom is taken away from them, and then they will fast."

- Lord, you used a lovely image for your time with us: a honeymoon period, a week when the bride and groom kept open house and relished the joy of new love.
- To be with you then was to know that the world is young and full of hope, while realizing that the honeymoon joy will not last forever.

Saturday 28th February **Luke 5:27–32**

After this he went out and saw a tax collector named Levi, sitting at the tax booth; and he said to him, "Follow me." And he got up, left everything, and followed him. Then Levi gave a great banquet for him in his house; and there was a large crowd of tax collectors and others sitting at the table with them. The Pharisees and their scribes were complaining to his disciples, saying, "Why do you eat and drink with tax collectors and sinners?" Jesus answered, "Those who are well have no need of a physician, but those who are sick; I have come to call not the righteous but sinners to repentance."

- Who today would be in Matthew's position, hated and despised by the public? Not the tax collectors: It is quite respectable now to work for Internal Revenue. The media parades different hate-objects for us today: drug dealers, rapists, pedophiles.
- You would sit with them, Lord. They too need your grace.

march 1–7

Something to think and pray about each day this week:

The Invitation to Freedom

We are at the start of Lent, the time of the year when the church invites us to test our freedom and to question the notion: I can take it or leave it alone. Try that with grumbling, drunkenness, talking about yourself, stealing, gambling, or other habits that diminish our freedom. What habits make you hard to live with? Lent is about regaining control of our own lives, especially in those areas that damage other people. We don't admire those whose appetites or habits lead them by the nose. Nearly all of us have habits, or even addictions, that keep us from God and harm both ourselves and others. These seven weeks before Easter help us to focus our energy on improving.

The Presence of God

For a few moments, I think of God's veiled presence in things:
in the elements, giving them existence;
in plants, giving them life; in animals, giving them sensation;
and finally, in me, giving me all this and more,
making me a temple, a dwelling-place of the Spirit.

Freedom

God is not foreign to my freedom.
Instead the Spirit breathes life into my most intimate desires,
gently nudging me toward all that is good.
I ask for the grace to let myself be enfolded by the Spirit.

Consciousness

Knowing that God loves me unconditionally,
I can afford to be honest about how I am.
How has the last day been, and how do I feel now?
I share my feelings openly with the Lord.

The Word

The Word of God comes down to us through the scriptures. May the Holy Spirit enlighten my mind and my heart to respond to the gospel teachings. (Please turn to your scripture on the following pages. Inspiration points are there should you need them. When you are ready, return here to continue.)

Conversation

How has God's Word moved me? Has it left me cold?
Has it consoled me or moved me to act in a new way?
I imagine Jesus standing or sitting beside me,
I turn and share my feelings with him.

Conclusion

Glory be to the Father, and to the Son, and to the Holy Spirit,
As it was in the beginning, is now and ever shall be,
World without end. Amen

Sunday 1st March,
First Sunday of Lent **Mark 1:12–15**

And the Spirit immediately drove him out into the wilderness. He was in the wilderness forty days, tempted by Satan; and he was with the wild beasts; and the angels waited on him. Now after John was arrested, Jesus came to Galilee, proclaiming the good news of God, and saying, "The time is fulfilled, and the kingdom of God has come near; repent, and believe in the good news."

- I, too, have known times of temptation when I felt on my own except for the wild beasts, the irrational forces that were messing up my life.
- Lord, you felt the influence of evil and were tested. You were purified as you came through a difficult time. When I was in the middle of such a time, it did not feel like God's hand, but like desolation and despair. When I look back, I can see how God was shaping me.

Monday 2nd March **Matthew 25:31–40**

"When the Son of Man comes in his glory, and all the angels with him, then he will sit on the throne of his glory. All the nations will be gathered before him, and he will separate people one from another as a shepherd separates the sheep from the goats, and he will put the sheep at his right hand and the goats at the left. Then the king will say to those at his right hand, 'Come, you that are blessed by my Father, inherit the kingdom prepared for you from the foundation of the world; for I was hungry and you gave me food, I was thirsty and you gave me something to drink, I was a stranger and you welcomed me, I was naked and you gave me clothing, I was sick and you took care of me, I was in prison and you visited me.' Then the righteous will answer him, 'Lord, when was it that we saw you hungry and gave you food, or thirsty and gave you something to drink? And when was it that we saw you a stranger and welcomed you, or naked and gave you clothing? And when was it that we saw you sick or in prison and visited you?' And the king will answer them, 'Truly I tell you, just as you did it to one of the least of these who are members of my family, you did it to me.'"

- Where are the hungry, the naked, the homeless who would call on me if they could reach me? Or have I so organized my life that the needy never impinge on me?
- Lord, you have made this the sole criterion of judgment. How will I measure up?

Tuesday 3rd March **Matthew 6:7–13**

"When you are praying, do not heap up empty phrases as the Gentiles do; for they think that they will be heard because of their many words. Do not be like them, for your Father knows what you need before you ask him. "Pray then in this way: Our Father in heaven, hallowed be your name. Your kingdom come. Your will be done, on earth as it is in heaven. Give us this day our daily bread. And forgive us our debts, as we also have forgiven our debtors. And do not bring us to the time of trial, but rescue us from the evil one."

- I need to be an adult, and a disciple of Jesus, before I can pray like this. In the Our Father I glorify God in the first three petitions, and then beg for my own needs, for bread, for forgiveness, and for removal from temptation.
- Let me pray it slowly, plumbing the depths in each phrase.

Wednesday 4th March **Luke 11:29–32**

When the crowds were increasing, he began to say, "This generation is an evil generation; it asks for a sign, but no sign will be given to it except the sign of Jonah. For just as Jonah became a sign to the people of Nineveh, so the Son of Man will be to this generation. The queen of the South will rise at the judgment with the people of this generation and condemn them, because she came from the ends of the earth to listen to the wisdom of Solomon, and see, something greater than Solomon is here! The people of Nineveh will rise up at the judgment with this generation and condemn it, because they repented at the proclamation of Jonah, and see, something greater than Jonah is here!"

- You, Lord Jesus, are the sign of signs. Those who go seeking further wonders have not truly seen you. In you I find all that I need to be fully human and to find my destiny with God.

Thursday 5th March **Matthew 7:7–12**

"Ask, and it will be given you; search, and you will find; knock, and the door will be opened for you. For everyone who asks receives, and everyone who searches finds, and for everyone who knocks, the door will be opened. Is there anyone among you who, if your child asks for bread, will give a stone? Or if the child asks for a fish, will give a snake? If you then, who are evil, know how to give good gifts to your children, how much more will your Father in heaven give good things to those who ask him! In everything do to others as you would have them do to you; for this is the law and the prophets."

- Jesus describes the setting: when we pray, we are not facing a begrudging God, who is easily irked by our requests. We are talking to a father, who wants to give all that is good for his child. The rabbis used to say: God is as near to his creatures as the ear to the mouth.

- Lord, I call on you with confidence, and I know you hear me.

Friday 6th March **Matthew 5:20–24**

Jesus said to his disciples, "For I tell you, unless your righteousness exceeds that of the scribes and Pharisees, you will never enter the kingdom of heaven. You have heard that it was said to those of ancient times, 'You shall not murder'; and 'whoever murders shall be liable to judgment.' But I say to you that if you are angry with a brother or sister, you will be liable to judgment; and if you insult a brother or sister, you will be liable to the council; and if you say, 'You fool,' you will be liable to the hell of fire. So when you are offering your gift at the altar, if you remember that your brother or sister has something against you, leave your gift there before the altar and go; first be reconciled to your brother or sister, and then come and offer your gift."

- Lord, you are pulling me back from the action to the heart that prompts the action: from the good or bad deed to the love or anger that I allow to possess my heart. You want no part of my show of religion if it comes from a heart that is not at peace with those around me.

Saturday 7th March **Matthew 5:43–48**

Jesus said to the disciples, "You have heard that it was said, 'You shall love your neighbor and hate your enemy.' But I say to you, Love your enemies and pray for those who persecute you, so that you may be children of your Father in heaven; for he makes his sun rise on the evil and on the good, and sends rain on the righteous and on the unrighteous. For if you love those who love you, what reward do you have? Do not even the tax collectors do the same? And if you greet only your brothers and sisters, what more are you doing than others? Do not even the Gentiles do the same? Be perfect, therefore, as your heavenly Father is perfect."

- The love to which Jesus calls us is not "passion" or "family feeling," but what the Greeks called *agape*, the habit of benevolence toward all, even those who see us with hostile eyes.
- Jesus admits that this sort of unselfish love is a high ideal, God-like in its perfection. It is the Holy Spirit who pours it out in our hearts.

march 8–14

Something to think and pray about each day this week:

The Taste of Life

When Ignatius Loyola was recovering after breaking his leg in battle, he used to enjoy the romances they gave him to read; but he found that their aftertaste was empty and unsatisfying. When he read the Gospels, the aftertaste was of solid food, something he could live on. He learned to discern the aftertaste of experiences. That is the way the Holy Spirit can shape our lives. It means listening to our hearts to discover the path of God and of the Holy Spirit through us, and to recognize what blocks we place, consciously or unconsciously, to God's work in us.

The Presence of God
For a few moments, I think of God's veiled presence in things:
in the elements, giving them existence;
in plants, giving them life; in animals, giving them sensation;
and finally, in me, giving me all this and more,
making me a temple, a dwelling-place of the Spirit.

Freedom
God is not foreign to my freedom.
Instead the Spirit breathes life into my most intimate desires,
gently nudging me toward all that is good.
I ask for the grace to let myself be enfolded by the Spirit.

Consciousness
Knowing that God loves me unconditionally,
I can afford to be honest about how I am.
How has the last day been, and how do I feel now?
I share my feelings openly with the Lord.

The Word
I take my time to read the Word of God, slowly, a few times, allowing myself to dwell on anything that strikes me. (Please turn to your scripture on the following pages. Inspiration points are there should you need them. When you are ready, return here to continue.)

Conversation
How has God's Word moved me? Has it left me cold?
Has it consoled me or moved me to act in a new way?
I imagine Jesus standing or sitting beside me,
I turn and share my feelings with him.

Conclusion
Glory be to the Father, and to the Son, and to the Holy Spirit,
As it was in the beginning, is now and ever shall be,
World without end. Amen

Sunday 8th March,
Second Sunday of Lent **Mark 9:2–10**

Six days later, Jesus took with him Peter and James and John, and led them up a high mountain apart, by themselves. And he was transfigured before them, and his clothes became dazzling white, such as no one on earth could bleach them. And there appeared to them Elijah with Moses, who were talking with Jesus. Then Peter said to Jesus, "Rabbi, it is good for us to be here; let us make three dwellings, one for you, one for Moses, and one for Elijah." He did not know what to say, for they were terrified. Then a cloud overshadowed them, and from the cloud there came a voice, "This is my Son, the Beloved; listen to him!" Suddenly when they looked around, they saw no one with them any more, but only Jesus. As they were coming down the mountain, he ordered them to tell no one about what they had seen, until after the Son of Man had risen from the dead. So they kept the matter to themselves, questioning what this rising from the dead could mean.

- In our journey to God we have peak moments, when the ground is holy. Like Peter, we want them to last forever.
- But Jesus, "only Jesus," brings us down the mountain and prepares us for the hard times ahead, sustained by the memory of brief transfigurations.
- Can I recall any of my peak moments?

Monday 9th March **Luke 6:36–38**

Be merciful, just as your Father is merciful. "Do not judge, and you will not be judged; do not condemn, and you will not be condemned. Forgive, and you will be forgiven; give, and it will be given to you. A good measure, pressed down, shaken together, running over, will be put into your lap; for the measure you give will be the measure you get back."

- Lord, I do not know enough to form a full judgment on those around me; it is not my business to pass sentence on them.
- But I know enough to forgive them, because I know my own frailty and how often I wish for forgiveness from others.

Tuesday 10th March **Matthew 23:1–3, 6–9**

Then Jesus said to the crowds and to his disciples, "The scribes and the Pharisees sit on Moses' seat; therefore, do whatever they teach you and follow it; but do not do as they do, for they do not practice what they teach. They love to have the place of honor at banquets and the best seats in the synagogues, and to be greeted with respect in the marketplaces, and to have people call them rabbi. But you are not to be called rabbi, for you have one teacher, and you are all students. And call no one your father on earth, for you have one Father—the one in heaven."

- Those are sweet titles, Rabbi or Father. It warms the heart to have the best seats and to be treated with respect.
- You are teaching me something, Lord, when these things change, when the pious are no longer exempt from public mockery. You are bringing me back from the complacency of the Pharisee to the state that you endured.

Wednesday 11th March **Matthew 20:17–22**

While Jesus was going up to Jerusalem, he took the twelve disciples aside by themselves, and said to them on the way, "See, we are going up to Jerusalem, and the Son of Man will be handed over to the chief priests and scribes, and they will condemn him to death; then they will hand him over to the Gentiles to be mocked and flogged and crucified; and on the third day he will be raised." Then the mother of the sons of Zebedee came to him with her sons, and kneeling before him, she asked a favor of him. And he said to her, "What do you want?" She said to him, "Declare that these two sons of mine will sit, one at your right hand and one at your left, in your kingdom." But Jesus answered, "You do not know what you are asking. Are you able to drink the cup that I am about to drink?'"

- This walk to Jerusalem is heavy with foreboding. Jesus tries to tell the Twelve of the fears that fill his soul: He will be betrayed by friends, delivered to his enemies; he will hear the death sentence read over him; he will suffer injustice, mockery, humiliation, insults; he will undergo the torture of scourging and finally face a horrific death on a gibbet.
- That is the cup you drank, Lord. If you ask me to share it, give me the strength.

Thursday 12th March **Luke 16:19–23**

Jesus said to the Pharisees, "There was a rich man who was dressed in purple and fine linen and who feasted sumptuously every day. And at his gate lay a poor man named Lazarus, covered with sores, who longed to satisfy his hunger with what fell from the rich man's table; even the dogs would come and lick his sores. The poor man died and was carried away by the angels to be with Abraham. The rich man also died and was buried. In Hades, where he was being tormented, he looked up and saw Abraham far away with Lazarus by his side."

- There is a moral lesson here: the great danger of attending only to your own pleasures and not noticing those who are suffering.
- In a land where people were lucky to enjoy one good meal in the week, the rich man feasted sumptuously every day and did not notice Lazarus, who would have been glad even to receive crumbs.

- Lord, open my eyes. When I answer to you for my life, you will not ask in what neighborhood I lived, but you will ask how I treated my neighbor.

Friday 13th March **Psalm 103(104):24, 30–33**

O Lord, how manifold are your works! In wisdom you have made them all; the earth is full of your creatures. When you send forth your spirit, they are created; and you renew the face of the ground. May the glory of the Lord endure forever; may the Lord rejoice in his works—who looks on the earth and it trembles, who touches the mountains and they smoke. I will sing to the Lord as long as I live; I will sing praise to my God while I have being.

- Lord, give me this morning the heart of a poet and singer, to sing your praise and see your works—especially this precious planet you entrusted to us—with grateful, astonished eyes.

Saturday 14th March **Luke 15:11–24**

Jesus told this parable: "There was a man who had two sons. The younger of them said to his father, 'Father, give me the share of the property that will belong to me.' So he divided his property between them. A few days later the younger son gathered all he had and traveled to a distant country, and there he squandered his property in dissolute living. When he had spent everything, a severe famine took place throughout that country, and he began to be in need. So he went and hired himself out to one of the citizens of that country, who sent him to his fields to feed the pigs. He would gladly have filled himself with the pods that the pigs were eating; and no one gave him anything. But when he came to himself he said, 'How many of my father's hired hands have bread enough and to spare, but here I am dying of hunger! I will get up and go to my father, and I will say to him, "Father, I have sinned against heaven and before you; I am no longer worthy to be called your son; treat me like one of your hired hands."' So he set off and went to his father. But while he was still far off, his father saw him and was filled with compassion; he ran and put his arms around him and kissed him. Then the son said to him, 'Father, I have sinned against heaven and before you; I am no longer worthy to be called your son.' But the father said to his slaves, 'Quickly, bring out a robe—the best one—and put it on him; put a ring on his finger and sandals on his feet. And get the fatted calf and kill it, and let us eat and celebrate; for this son of mine was dead and is alive again; he was lost and is found!' And they began to celebrate.

- In different cultures over the centuries God has been pictured in all sorts of images and imaginations. In this parable, we have Jesus' astonishing image. God is a fond father who does not stop his wastrel son from bringing shame on himself and the family; then he not only forgives him, but also falls on his neck, interrupts his apology, and throws a big party to express his own joy.
- Dear Lord, whatever happens to me, let me never forget or doubt this picture of you.

march 15–21

Something to think and pray about each day this week:

Really Giving

When we are urged to be generous in these weeks of Lent, two phrases come to mind, the first from II Samuel 24. When King David wanted to buy Araunah's threshing floor in order to build an altar to God, and Araunah offered to give him the land for nothing, David replied: "I will not offer burnt offerings to the Lord my God that cost me nothing." The best giving is like the widow's mite: It twinges our heart and costs us something.

The second phrase is the old pastor's comment in *Babette's Feast*: "The only things we take with us from our life on earth are those which we have given away." It is a more blessed thing to give than to receive, and it brings greater happiness.

The Presence of God

I pause for a moment
and think of the love and the grace that God showers on me,
creating me in his image and likeness, making me his temple.

Freedom

Everything has the potential to draw forth from me a fuller love and life.
Yet my desires are often fixed, caught, on illusions of fulfillment.
I ask that God, through my freedom, may orchestrate
my desires in a vibrant loving melody rich in harmony.

Consciousness

In the presence of my loving Creator,
I look honestly at my feelings over the last day,
the highs, the lows, and the level ground.
Can I see where the Lord has been present?

The Word

God speaks to each one of us individually. I need to listen to what he is saying to me. (Please turn to your scripture on the following pages. Inspiration points are there should you need them. When you are ready, return here to continue.)

Conversation

What feelings are rising in me
as I pray and reflect on God's Word?
I imagine Jesus himself sitting or standing beside me,
and open my heart to him.

Conclusion

Glory be to the Father, and to the Son, and to the Holy Spirit,
As it was in the beginning, is now and ever shall be,
World without end. Amen

Sunday 15th March,
Third Sunday of Lent **John 2:13–17**

The Passover of the Jews was near, and Jesus went up to Jerusalem. In the temple he found people selling cattle, sheep, and doves, and the money changers seated at their tables. Making a whip of cords, he drove all of them out of the temple, both the sheep and the cattle. He also poured out the coins of the money changers and overturned their tables. He told those who were selling the doves, "Take these things out of here! Stop making my Father's house a marketplace!" His disciples remembered that it was written, "Zeal for your house will consume me."

- What was it that roused Jesus' fury? Not just that money changed hands and animals were sold for sacrifice in the Temple; but the fact that the merchants were selling animals at a far higher price in the Temple than would be paid outside and changing money at a rate that brought undue profit to the money changers.
- The hucksters and money changers were profiteering from people's piety, exercising a kind of monopoly that battened on the good will of the worshippers. Trade had taken over from prayer.

Monday 16th March **Luke 4:24–30**

And he said, "Truly I tell you, no prophet is accepted in the prophet's hometown. But the truth is, there were many widows in Israel in the time of Elijah, when the heaven was shut up three years and six months, and there was a severe famine over all the land; yet Elijah was sent to none of them except to a widow at Zarephath in Sidon. There were also many lepers in Israel in the time of the prophet Elisha, and none of them was cleansed except Naaman the Syrian." When they heard this, all in the synagogue were filled with rage. They got up, drove him out of the town, and led him to the brow of the hill on which their town was built, so that they might hurl him off the cliff. But he passed through the midst of them and went on his way.

- Jesus, speaking to his Jewish neighbors in Nazareth, is pointing to instances of God reaching out to the Gentiles, and the listeners are furious.
- How we cherish this illusion that we are the center of the universe, and that outsiders do not count! Unblinker me, Lord.

Tuesday 17th March, St. Patrick **Luke 10:1–2**

After this the Lord appointed seventy others and sent them on ahead of him in pairs to every town and place where he himself intended to go. He said to them, "The harvest is plentiful, but the laborers are few; therefore ask the Lord of the harvest to send out laborers into his harvest."

- Jesus moved from the organized religion of the synagogue to preaching on the shore of the lake and wherever people gathered. St. Patrick did the same, talking to the Irish on hillsides and at river-crossings.
- The Good News cannot be organized into a neat institutional slot with its own buildings and officials. If I carry the sense of God's love with me, I will spread good news wherever I go.

Wednesday 18th March **Matthew 5:17–19**

Jesus said to his disciples, "Do not think that I have come to abolish the law or the prophets; I have come not to abolish but to fulfill. For truly I tell you, until heaven and earth pass away, not one letter, not one stroke of a letter, will pass from the law until all is accomplished. Therefore, whoever breaks one of the least of these commandments, and teaches others to do the same, will be called least in the kingdom of heaven; but whoever does them and teaches them will be called great in the kingdom of heaven.

- Lord, you criticized the petty regulations that had been added to the law of God, and summed up the law and the prophets in the love of God and our neighbor. You were not turning your back on the past, but deepening our sense of where we stand before God: not as scrupulous rule-keepers, but as loving children.

Thursday 19th March, St. Joseph **Psalm 88(89):1–2**

I will sing of your steadfast love, O Lord, forever; with my mouth I will proclaim your faithfulness to all generations. I declare that your steadfast love is established forever; your faithfulness is as firm as the heavens.

- What inspires me in St. Joseph is his faithfulness, firm as the heavens. He was faithful to his fiancée though he could not understand her pregnancy, and he persevered as the faithful father of his family, supporting them through exile and danger.
- He was the quiet father whom many of us remember, there whenever he was needed, and a huge influence on Jesus.

Friday 20th March **Mark 12:28–34**

One of the scribes came near and heard them disputing with one another, and seeing that he answered them well, he asked him, "Which commandment is the first of all?" Jesus answered, "The first is, 'Hear, O Israel: the Lord our God, the Lord is one; you shall love the Lord your God with all your heart, and with all your soul, and with all your mind, and with all your strength.' The second is this, 'You shall love your neighbor as yourself.' There is no other commandment greater than these." Then the scribe said to him, "You are right, Teacher; you have truly said that 'he is one, and besides him there is no other'; and 'to love him with all the heart, and with all the understanding, and with all the strength,' and 'to love one's neighbor as oneself,'—this is much more important than all whole burnt offerings and sacrifices." When Jesus saw that he answered wisely, he said to him, "You are not far from the kingdom of God." After that no one dared to ask him any question.

- From the wordy chapters of the Old Testament, Jesus picks out just two sentences, one from Deuteronomy and one from Leviticus, to give us a guide to life.
- As I listen to his words in prayer, I can share the joy and enthusiasm of the scribe at this lovely simplicity.

Saturday 21st March **Luke 18:9–14**

He also told this parable to some who trusted in themselves that they were righteous and regarded others with contempt: "Two men went up to the temple to pray, one a Pharisee and the other a tax collector. The Pharisee, standing by himself, was praying thus, 'God, I thank you that I am not like other people: thieves, rogues, adulterers, or even like this tax collector. I fast twice a week; I give a tenth of all my income.' But the tax collector, standing far off, would not even look up to heaven, but was beating his breast and saying, 'God, be merciful to me, a sinner!' I tell you, this man went down to his home justified rather than the other; for all who exalt themselves will be humbled, but all who humble themselves will be exalted."

- Today, we might call the Pharisee a snob, a person who has "made it" and attributes all their good fortune to virtue and hard work. Behind this stance is an attitude, stated or unstated, that "I have done this by my own efforts; others can do it too if only they would work hard enough." There is no place for God there.
- Instead, Jesus presents us with the tax collector as the model for a prayerful attitude.
- I imagine myself in the Temple: With whom do I stand?

march 22–28

Something to think and pray about each day this week:

Slow Food

Lent is a good time for thinking about meals: not so much about fish and fasting, as about making the effort—unusual now—to arrange family meals. There was a time when preparing a meal was a slow business, often seen as the main work of the mother of the house. When it was ready, the household gathered and shared the available food. No distractions—this is what we have been waiting for. It embodied the care and skill of the mother or of whoever prepared and cooked it. It was a time you did not miss, because you were hungry and because the action was here. You would feel out of it if you missed the coming together, no matter how rowdy or quarrelsome it might be. You would fight for your corner, and even if you were bested, you stayed at the table. Slow food made for better company.

The Presence of God

I reflect for a moment on God's presence around me and in me.
Creator of the universe, the sun and the moon, the earth,
every molecule, every atom, everything that is:
God is in every beat of my heart. God is with me, now.

Freedom

A thick and shapeless tree-trunk would never believe
that it could become a statue, admired as a miracle of sculpture,
and would never submit itself to the chisel of the sculptor,
who sees by her genius what she can make of it. (St Ignatius)
I ask for the grace to let myself be shaped by my loving Creator.

Consciousness

Knowing that God loves me unconditionally,
I look honestly over the last day, its events and my feelings.
Do I have something to be grateful for? Then I give thanks.
Is there something I am sorry for? Then I ask forgiveness.

The Word

I read the Word of God slowly a few times over, and I listen to what God is saying to me. (Please turn to your scripture on the following pages. Inspiration points are there should you need them. When you are ready, return here to continue.)

Conversation

What is stirring in me as I pray?
Am I consoled, troubled, left cold?
I imagine Jesus himself standing or sitting at my side,
and share my feelings with him.

Conclusion

Glory be to the Father, and to the Son, and to the Holy Spirit,
As it was in the beginning, is now and ever shall be,
World without end. Amen

Sunday 22nd March,
Fourth Sunday of Lent **John 3:14–15**

Jesus said to Nicodemus, "And just as Moses lifted up the serpent in the wilderness, so must the Son of Man be lifted up, that whoever believes in him may have eternal life."

- Jesus is lifted up on the cross, and it is that same lifting that carries him into glory.
- As I look back on the bad times in my life, I can see how they brought me closer to you, Lord. No cross, no crown.

Monday 23rd March **John 4:46b–50**

Now there was a royal official whose son lay ill in Capernaum. When he heard that Jesus had come from Judea to Galilee, he went and begged him to come down and heal his son, for he was at the point of death. Then Jesus said to him, "Unless you see signs and wonders, you will not believe." The official said to him, "Sir, come down before my little boy dies." Jesus said to him, "Go; your son will live." The man believed the word that Jesus spoke to him and started on his way.

- Jesus' first response seems harsh, even cynical: "Unless you see signs and wonders, you will not believe." But the official doesn't seem to notice: "Sir, come down before my little boy dies."
- Jesus tested his faith further, but the man "believed the word that Jesus spoke to him." He went home to his son, without Jesus.
- Lord, teach me to have faith that you are with me always.

Tuesday 24th March **John 5:1–9**

After this there was a festival of the Jews, and Jesus went up to Jerusalem. Now in Jerusalem by the Sheep Gate there is a pool, called in Hebrew Beth-zatha, which has five porticoes. In these lay many invalids—blind, lame, and paralyzed. One man was there who had been ill for thirty-eight years. When Jesus saw him lying there and knew that he had been there a long time, he said to him, "Do you want to be made well?" The sick man answered him, "Sir, I have no one to put me into the pool when the water is stirred up; and while I am making my way, someone else steps down ahead of me." Jesus said to him, "Stand up, take your mat and walk." At once the man was made well, and he took up his mat and began to walk.

- Jesus asks an intriguing question: Do you want to be made well? He knew the strength of habit and inertia: When you have been an invalid for thirty-eight years, a cure will impose responsibilities and make demands that some sick people might shy from.
- Lord, you ask me if I want to change, to go beyond my present state. Give me the strength to make the break.

Wednesday 25th March,
Annunciation of the Lord **Luke 1:26–29**

In the sixth month the angel Gabriel was sent by God to a town in Galilee called Nazareth, to a virgin engaged to a man whose name was Joseph, of the house of David. The virgin's name was Mary. And he came to her and said, "Greetings, favored one! The Lord is with you." But she was much perplexed by his words and pondered what sort of greeting this might be.

- "Hail Mary, full of grace; *Ave Maria, gratia plena.*" As Mary heard that greeting, she grew shy and confused. I can never plumb the meaning of God made man, but that mantra, "Hail full of grace," engages my tongue while my mind tries to follow Mary in her joy and astonishment.
- She ponders the invitation in her heart, as she ponders later events in the life of her son. Then her response is from a full heart.
- Seat of Wisdom, teach me how to use my head and heart in a crisis.

Thursday 26th March **John 5:39–40**

Jesus said to the Jews "You search the scriptures because you think that in them you have eternal life; and it is they that testify on my behalf. Yet you refuse to come to me to have life."

- The Jews worshipped a God who wrote rather than a God who acted, so when Christ came they did not recognize him. The function of the Scriptures is not to give life, but to point to the one who can give life.
- Lord, I cherish your word in the Bible, but it is a signpost, not a destination; it points me on to you, acting in my life.

Friday 27th March **Wisdom 2:12a, 14–15**

The godless say to themselves, "Let us lie in wait for the righteous man, because he is inconvenient to us and opposes our actions . . . He became to us a reproof of our thoughts; the very sight of him is a burden to us, because his manner of life is unlike that of others, and his ways are strange."

- There is something modern about these ancient observations. Opposition to the followers of Christ shows itself not so much in bloody violence as in slander and ribaldry, ridicule and negative publicity.
- Lord Jesus, let me keep my eyes on you and take opposition in my stride as you did.

Saturday 28th March **John 7:43–52**

So there was a division in the crowd because of him. Some of them wanted to arrest him, but no one laid hands on him. Then the temple police went back to the chief priests and Pharisees, who asked them, "Why did you not arrest him?" The police answered, "Never has anyone spoken like this!" Then the Pharisees replied, "Surely you have not been deceived too, have you? Has any one of the authorities or of the Pharisees believed in him? But this crowd, which does not know the law—they are accursed." Nicodemus, who had gone to Jesus before, and who was one of them, asked, "Our law does not judge people without first giving them a hearing to find out what they are doing, does it?" They replied, "Surely you are not also from Galilee, are you? Search and you will see that no prophet is to arise from Galilee."

- Let me watch the movements in the crowd, and ask where I find myself. The chief priests are determined to silence Jesus as a threat to their authority. When Nicodemus quotes a legal principle at them, they ridicule him as soft. Yet as soon as the police hear the voice of the Jesus they have come to arrest, they fall under his spell: "Never has anyone spoken like this!"
- Lord, may I have the courage of Nicodemus and the police and be ready to stand against the crowd.

march 29–april 4

Something to think and pray about each day this week:

Christian Dreamtime

The Aboriginal community of Australia has its Dreamtime, a subconscious world of stories, memories and images that have a powerful effect on our prayer, but are not easily documented in a way that would satisfy historians. The biblical book of Genesis is like the Australian Aboriginals' Dreamtime, full of parables about the creation of the world and its early history, parables that carry a profound truth for our human condition but do not relate to the careful researches of paleontologists. Those who have grown up in the faith find that they warm to certain non-theological images and practices. They light candles. They have their favorite saints. They are deeply moved by devotions such as novenas, the Camino de Santiago, fiestas and processions, which nurture their sense of the transcendent, of another world intersecting our existence. Just because the scholars cannot quote chapter and verse to prove their authenticity, we are not going to write off the Virgin of Guadalupe, or Our Lady of Lourdes, or the images of Padre Pio, or St. Jude's help in hopeless cases, or St. Anthony's help in finding what is lost. These are the treasures of our Dreamtime.

The Presence of God

In the silence of my innermost being,
in the fragments of my yearned-for wholeness,
can I hear the whispers of God's presence?
Can I remember when I felt God's nearness?
When we walked together and I let myself be embraced by God's love.

Freedom

There are very few people
who realize what God would make of them
if they abandoned themselves into his hands,
and let themselves be formed by his grace. (St Ignatius)
I ask for the grace to trust myself totally to God's love.

Consciousness

How do I find myself today?
Where am I with God? With others?
Do I have something to be grateful for? Then I give thanks.
Is there something I am sorry for? Then I ask forgiveness.

The Word

I take my time to read the Word of God, slowly, a few times, allowing myself to dwell on anything that strikes me. (Please turn to your scripture on the following pages. Inspiration points are there should you need them. When you are ready, return here to continue.)

Conversation

Do I notice myself reacting as I pray with the Word of God?
Do I feel challenged, comforted, angry?
Imagining Jesus sitting or standing by me,
I speak out my feelings, as one trusted friend to another.

Conclusion

Glory be to the Father, and to the Son, and to the Holy Spirit,
As it was in the beginning, is now and ever shall be,
World without end. Amen

Sunday 29th March,
Fifth Sunday of Lent **John 12:20–24**

Now among those who went up to worship at the festival were some Greeks. They came to Philip, who was from Bethsaida in Galilee, and said to him, "Sir, we wish to see Jesus." Philip went and told Andrew; then Andrew and Philip went and told Jesus. Jesus answered them, "The hour has come for the Son of Man to be glorified. Very truly, I tell you, unless a grain of wheat falls into the earth and dies, it remains just a single grain; but if it dies, it bears much fruit."

- What the Greeks asked of Philip is what Christians have been seeking in the Gospels and in pilgrimages for two thousand years: We wish to see Jesus. When they found him, they heard those pregnant words: A grain of wheat has to die before it bears fruit.
- Only in Jesus have we a person and a philosophy that makes sense of suffering and death, and that sees the life beyond them.

Monday 30th March **John 11:25–27**

Jesus said to Martha, "I am the resurrection and the life. Those who believe in me, even though they die, will live, and everyone who lives and believes in me will never die. Do you believe this?" She said to him, "Yes, Lord, I believe that you are the Messiah, the Son of God, the one coming into the world."

- I hear you asking me the same question, Lord: Do you believe that I am the resurrection and the life?
- In the long run, nothing is more important than my answer to this. I cannot grasp your words in my imagination, Lord, but I believe. Help my unbelief.

Tuesday 31st March **John 8:28–30**

Jesus said to the Jews, "When you have lifted up the Son of Man, then you will realize that I am he, and that I do nothing on my own, but I speak these things as the Father instructed me. And the one who sent me is with me; he has not left me alone, for I always do what is pleasing to him." As he was saying these things, many believed in him.

- In a society that was used to public cruelty, death on a cross was both violent and a sign of public disgrace. It took centuries before Christians used the cross to represent their faith in the way we do today.
- Christ lifted on the cross says a great deal about God and humankind, about love and hate, and about sin and grace.
- What does the crucifix mean in my life? What is my role at the foot of the cross?

Wednesday 1st April **John 8:31–32**

Then Jesus said to the Jews who had believed in him, "If you continue in my word, you are truly my disciples; and you will know the truth, and the truth will make you free."

- "And the truth will make you free." Your listeners were Jews who faced the choice of following Jesus or remaining disciples of Moses.
- What will it cost me? What will I gain if I continue in the "word"?
- Can I start with the things about myself that I hide from and try to keep hidden from others?

Thursday 2nd April **John 8:51–59**

Jesus said to the Jews, "Very truly, I tell you, whoever keeps my word will never see death." The Jews said to him, "Now we know that you have a demon. Abraham died, and so did the prophets; yet you say, 'Whoever keeps my word will never taste death.' Are you greater than our father Abraham, who died? The prophets also died. Who do you claim to be?" Jesus answered, "If I glorify myself, my glory is nothing. It is my Father who glorifies me, he of whom you say, 'He is our God,' though you do not know him. But I know him; if I were to say that I do not know him, I would be a liar like you. But I do know him, and I keep his word. Your ancestor Abraham rejoiced that he would see my day; he saw it and was glad." Then the Jews said to him, "You are not yet fifty years old, and have you seen Abraham?" Jesus said to them, "Very truly, I tell you, before Abraham was, I am." So they picked up stones to throw at him, but Jesus hid himself and went out of the temple.

- Jesus, in words his audience took as blasphemous, applied the name of God to himself and linked himself squarely to the covenant between God and Abraham, father of the nations.
- Abraham's faithfulness provides us with a model. He searched for God's voice always, he let go of what was precious to him to journey by faith into the unknown.

Friday 3rd April **Jeremiah 20:10–13**

For I hear many whispering: "Terror is all around! Denounce him! Let us denounce him!" All my close friends are watching for me to stumble. "Perhaps he can be enticed, and we can prevail against him, and take our revenge on him." But the Lord is with me like a dread warrior; therefore my persecutors will stumble, and they will not prevail. They will be greatly shamed, for they will not succeed. Their eternal dishonor will never be forgotten. O Lord of hosts, you test the righteous, you see the heart and the mind; let me see your retribution upon them, for to you I have committed my cause. Sing to the Lord; praise the Lord! For he has delivered the life of the needy from the hands of evildoers.

- Jeremiah spoke out on God's behalf. It cost him friends, led to attempts on his life and to prison. He felt alone, betrayed, and angry.
- In the midst of these great trials, he remained faithful. He begins feeling cut off and fearful; he ends in praise of the God who protects him from those who would do him harm.
- Let me take time to reflect on God's love for me and for all his people.

Saturday 4th April **Ezekiel 37:21–23**

Thus says the Lord God: I will take the people of Israel from the nations among which they have gone, and will gather them from every quarter, and bring them to their own land. I will make them one nation in the land, on the mountains of Israel; and one king shall be king over them all. Never again shall they be two nations, and never again shall they be divided into two kingdoms. They shall never again defile themselves with their idols and their detestable things, or with any of their transgressions. I will save them from all the apostasies into which they have fallen, and will cleanse them. Then they shall be my people, and I will be their God.

- "They shall be my people, and I will be their God." This is an age-old promise; it expresses the mutual obligation on God and on his people.
- For Jews or Christians to see themselves as "special" is to miss the point. Along with the call to be faithful is a special responsibility to pass on to others the good news of God's covenant with his people.
- As I approach the time of Jesus' passion and resurrection, let me think about Abraham, Jeremiah, and Ezekiel and their faithful response to God.
- What comfort did Jesus draw from their examples?

april 5–11

Something to think and pray about each day this week:

Carrying the Cross

For those who pray with the Church, this is a painful week, the days in which we remember Jesus' passion and death. At one time, when a murder had been committed in a European village, neighbors were called to lay a hand on the crucifix and say they had no part in the murder. None of us can say that about Jesus' death. We all had a part in it. But we also share in his passion: We experience the cross in our lives, usually in the form of failure. Can I carry that cross as Jesus did, with love, as my share in redeeming the world, and with no bitterness?

The Presence of God

God is with me, but more,
God is within me, giving me existence.
Let me dwell for a moment on God's life-giving presence
in my body, my mind, my heart,
and in the whole of my life.

Freedom

Many countries are at this moment suffering
the agonies of war.
I bow my head in thanksgiving for my freedom.
I pray for all prisoners and captives.

Consciousness

I remind myself that I am in the presence of the Lord.
I will take refuge in His loving heart.
He is my strength in times of weakness.
He is my comforter in times of sorrow.

The Word

I read the Word of God slowly, a few times over, and I listen to what God is saying to me. (Please turn to your scripture on the following pages. Inspiration points are there should you need them. When you are ready, return here to continue.)

Conversation

How has God's Word moved me? Has it left me cold?
Has it consoled me or moved me to act in a new way?
I imagine Jesus standing or sitting beside me,
I turn and share my feelings with him.

Conclusion

Glory be to the Father, and to the Son, and to the Holy Spirit,
As it was in the beginning, is now and ever shall be,
World without end. Amen

Sunday 5th April,
Palm Sunday of the Lord's Passion **Philippians 2:6–11**

Let the same mind be in you that was in Christ Jesus, who, though he was in the form of God, did not regard equality with God as something to be exploited, but emptied himself, taking the form of a slave, being born in human likeness. And being found in human form, he humbled himself and became obedient to the point of death—even death on a cross. Therefore God also highly exalted him and gave him the name that is above every name, so that at the name of Jesus every knee should bend, in heaven and on earth and under the earth, and every tongue should confess that Jesus Christ is Lord, to the glory of God the Father.

- On this Sunday of the passion, we read St. Paul's Christ-hymn, which offers a dense theology of the incarnation. Jesus emptied himself and accepted the loss of everything—family, power, the love and respect of his own people, and finally his own life.
- Lord, you ask me to have the same mind as you had. I can accept the emptying out of my attachments because you have shown me the way.

Monday 6th April **John 12:1–8**

Six days before the Passover Jesus came to Bethany, the home of Lazarus, whom he had raised from the dead. There they gave a dinner for him. Martha served, and Lazarus was one of those at the table with him. Mary took a pound of costly perfume made of pure nard, anointed Jesus' feet, and wiped them with her hair. The house was filled with the fragrance of the perfume. But Judas Iscariot, one of his disciples (the one who was about to betray him), said, "Why was this perfume not sold for three hundred denarii and the money given to the poor?" (He said this not because he cared about the poor, but because he was a thief; he kept the common purse and used to steal what was put into it.) Jesus said, "Leave her alone. She bought it so that she might keep it for the day of my burial. You always have the poor with you, but you do not always have me."

- Let me sit with this love-scene. Overjoyed to have Jesus as her guest, Mary produces her most precious possession, a fragrant perfume, and lavishes it upon Jesus' feet, then wipes them with her hair.
- It is a prodigal, unself-conscious act of love. She does not count the cost, but Judas does. Who am I more like, Mary or Judas?
- Teach me, Lord, to keep my eyes fixed on you.

Tuesday 7th April **Isaiah 49:1–4**

Listen to me, O coastlands, pay attention, you peoples from far away! The Lord called me before I was born, while I was in my mother's womb he named me. He made my mouth like a sharp sword, in the shadow of his hand he hid me; he made me a polished arrow, in his quiver he hid me away. And he said to me, "You are my servant, Israel, in whom I will be glorified." But I said, "I have labored in vain, I have spent my strength for nothing and vanity; yet surely my cause is with the LORD, and my reward with my God.

- Like Israel, I was called by the Lord before I was even born.
- God has a plan for me, despite my sinfulness and weakness, my regular failings. "I will give you as a light to the nations, that my salvation may reach to the end of the earth."
- Can I make this plan my own?

Wednesday 8th April **Matthew 26:19–25**

The disciples did as Jesus had directed them, and they prepared the Passover meal. When it was evening, he took his place with the twelve; and while they were eating, he said, "Truly I tell you, one of you will betray me." And they became greatly distressed and began to say to him one after another, "Surely not I, Lord?" He answered, "The one who has dipped his hand into the bowl with me will betray me. The Son of Man goes as it is written of him, but woe to that one by whom the Son of Man is betrayed! It would have been better for that one not to have been born." Judas, who betrayed him, said, "Surely not I, Rabbi?" He replied, "You have said so."

- We wonder why Judas betrayed Jesus. Avarice? If so, he sold him cheap. More likely he was in some way disillusioned: He had expected Jesus to lead them to a messianic kingdom. Jesus was not the Christ that Judas expected him to be—too gentle and slow-moving. If so, he had tried to second-guess God.
- It is not Jesus who can be changed by us, but we who must be changed by Jesus.

Thursday 9th April, Holy Thursday **John 13:12–16**

After Jesus had washed their feet, had put on his robe, and had returned to the table, he said to them, "Do you know what I have done to you? You call me Teacher and Lord—and you are right, for that is what I am. So if I, your Lord and Teacher, have washed your feet, you also ought to wash one another's feet. For I have set you an example, that you also should do as I have done to you. Very truly, I tell you, servants are not greater than their master, nor are messengers greater than the one who sent them."

- Jesus kneeling with a towel round his waist is pointing to that aspect of Christianity in which there is no hierarchy, and the only rule is to meet the needs of others.
- On this feast of the Last Supper, John does not mention the Eucharist. He speaks only of service, one for another.

Friday 10th April, Good Friday **John 19:1–11**

Then Pilate took Jesus and had him flogged. And the soldiers wove a crown of thorns and put it on his head, and they dressed him in a purple robe. They kept coming up to him, saying, "Hail, King of the Jews!" and striking him on the face. Pilate went out again and said to them, "Look, I am bringing him out to you to let you know that I find no case against him." So Jesus came out, wearing the crown of thorns and the purple robe. Pilate said to them, "Here is the man!" When the chief priests and the police saw him, they shouted, "Crucify him! Crucify him!" Pilate said to them, "Take him yourselves and crucify him; I find no case against him." The Jews answered him, "We have a law, and according to that law he ought to die because he has claimed to be the Son of God." Now when Pilate heard this, he was more afraid than ever. He entered his headquarters again and asked Jesus, "Where are you from?" But Jesus gave him no answer. Pilate therefore said to him, "Do you refuse to speak to me? Do you not know that I have power to release you, and power to crucify you?" Jesus answered him, "You would have no power over me unless it had been given you from above; therefore the one who handed me over to you is guilty of a greater sin."

- St. Peter Claver's life was spent in the holds of slave-ships with African victims who had no hope in this world. Out of that experience he used to say: The only book people should read is the story of the passion.

- A time comes to all of us to stretch out our hands as Jesus did, in passivity, unable to do anything with them: a time when God takes over, and our resistance folds. This is the hardest meditation; it touches a reality that in the long run we cannot escape.
- Love demands that we trust in a goodness and a life beyond our own. Lord, it is hard to contemplate. I pull away from the pain and injustice of this cross. Your love draws me back.

Saturday 11th April, Holy Saturday **John 19:25–30**

Meanwhile, standing near the cross of Jesus were his mother, and his mother's sister, Mary the wife of Clopas, and Mary Magdalene. When Jesus saw his mother and the disciple whom he loved standing beside her, he said to his mother, "Woman, here is your son." Then he said to the disciple, "Here is your mother." And from that hour the disciple took her into his own home. After this, when Jesus knew that all was now finished, he said (in order to fulfill the scripture), "I am thirsty." A jar full of sour wine was standing there. So they put a sponge full of the wine on a branch of hyssop and held it to his mouth. When Jesus had received the wine, he said, "It is finished." Then he bowed his head and gave up his spirit.

- "It is finished." The last words that Jesus speaks from the cross. He completed what he came to do, to show that God is love, and love conquers death.
- As Julian of Norwich wrote: " . . . the love that made him suffer all this—it passes as far beyond all his pains as heaven is above earth. For the passion was a deed done in time by the working of love; but the love is without beginning and is, and ever shall be, without . . . end."

april 12–18

Something to think and pray about each day this week:

The Easter Mystery

On the first Easter morning, the apostles and holy women did not see a ghost of Jesus. They saw him in the flesh, but in a different flesh, as the oak tree is different from the acorn that was its origin. We touch on the mystery of a body, not just Jesus' body but our own; a body which will express us at our best, will not dull our spirit with weariness and rebellion, but will express it with ease and joy. This is a mystery beyond our imagination, but it is the center of our faith. When we wish one another a happy Easter, we should take deep joy in the knowledge that the best part of us will cheat the grave. Our lives sometimes disguise that joy as weary bones and heavy flesh, and addled brains distract us. But our bodies already hold the seeds of resurrection. We are none of us mortal.

The Presence of God

To be present is to arrive as one is and open up to the other.
At this instant, as I arrive here, God is present waiting for me.
God always arrives before me, desiring to connect with me
even more than my most intimate friend.
I take a moment and greet my loving God.

Freedom

"In these days, God taught me
as a schoolteacher teaches a pupil" (St Ignatius).
I remind myself that there are things God has to teach me yet,
and ask for the grace to hear them and let them change me.

Consciousness

How am I really feeling? Light-hearted? Heavy-hearted?
I may be very much at peace, happy to be here.
Equally, I may be frustrated, worried, or angry.
I acknowledge how I really am. It is the real me that the Lord loves.

The Word

I take my time to read the Word of God, slowly, a few times, allowing myself to dwell on anything that strikes me. (Please turn to your scripture on the following pages. Inspiration points are there should you need them. When you are ready, return here to continue.)

Conversation

What feelings are rising in me
as I pray and reflect on God's Word?
I imagine Jesus himself sitting or standing beside me
and open my heart to him.

Conclusion

Glory be to the Father, and to the Son, and to the Holy Spirit,
As it was in the beginning, is now and ever shall be,
World without end. Amen

Sunday 12th April,
Easter Sunday **John 20:1–9**

Early on the first day of the week, while it was still dark, Mary Magdalene came to the tomb and saw that the stone had been removed from the tomb. So she ran and went to Simon Peter and the other disciple, the one whom Jesus loved, and said to them, "They have taken the Lord out of the tomb, and we do not know where they have laid him." Then Peter and the other disciple set out and went toward the tomb. The two were running together, but the other disciple outran Peter and reached the tomb first. He bent down to look in and saw the linen wrappings lying there, but he did not go in. Then Simon Peter came, following him, and went into the tomb. He saw the linen wrappings lying there, and the cloth that had been on Jesus' head, not lying with the linen wrappings but rolled up in a place by itself. Then the other disciple, who reached the tomb first, also went in, and he saw and believed; for as yet they did not understand the scripture, that he must rise from the dead.

- On this strange dawn we are praying in a darkness that is outside time, like that of astronauts circling in space: beyond sunsets and sunrises, seeing the beginning and the end of our days.
- We look back to that breathless morning when the apostles saw the holy women come back from the tomb with a story of angels. A bloodless corpse, transfixed by a spear, had risen again with a mysterious new life. Jesus had kept his promise. Death, our oldest enemy, had been mastered.

Monday 13th April **Matthew 28:8–10**

So the women left the tomb quickly with fear and great joy, and ran to tell his disciples. Suddenly Jesus met them and said, "Greetings!" And they came to him, took hold of his feet, and worshipped him. Then Jesus said to them, "Do not be afraid; go and tell my brothers to go to Galilee; there they will see me."

- "Do not be afraid." This is one of the most common phrases in the scriptures, and it encourages and sustains these women, the messengers of new life.
- Can I embrace my fears and my wariness of what the risen Jesus might achieve if I accept him more fully into my life?

Tuesday 14th April **John 20:11–17**

As Mary wept, she bent over to look into the tomb; and she saw two angels in white, sitting where the body of Jesus had been lying, one at the head and the other at the feet. They said to her, "Woman, why are you weeping?" She said to them, "They have taken away my Lord, and I do not know where they have laid him." When she had said this, she turned around and saw Jesus standing there, but she did not know that it was Jesus. Jesus said to her, "Woman, why are you weeping? Whom are you looking for?" Supposing him to be the gardener, she said to him, "Sir, if you have carried him away, tell me where you have laid him, and I will take him away." Jesus said to her, "Mary!" She turned and said to him in Hebrew, "Rabbouni!" (which means Teacher). Jesus said to her, "Do not hold on to me, because I have not yet ascended to the Father. But go to my brothers and say to them, 'I am ascending to my Father and your Father, to my God and your God.'"

- Jesus said, "Do not hold on to me." He has a mission for Mary, and she must set out to tell the others. There is work to be done.
- You know my name too, Lord, just as you knew Mary's. Do I recognize your voice? Teach me to understand and to respond.

Wednesday 15th April **Acts 3:1–8**

One day Peter and John were going up to the temple at the hour of prayer, at three o'clock in the afternoon. And a man lame from birth was being carried in. People would lay him daily at the gate of the temple called the Beautiful Gate so that he could ask for alms from those entering the temple. When he saw Peter and John about to go into the temple, he asked them for alms. Peter looked intently at him, as did John, and said, "Look at us." And he fixed his attention on them, expecting to receive something from them. But Peter said, "I have no silver or gold, but what I have I give you; in the name of Jesus Christ of Nazareth, stand up and walk." And he took him by the right hand and raised him up; and immediately his feet and ankles were made strong. Jumping up, he stood and began to walk, and he entered the temple with them, walking and leaping and praising God.

- Jesus is alive and active in a new way. He acts through John and Peter, in their response to the man lame from birth. They act with power and complete confidence in Jesus' name.
- What happened at the Beautiful Gate was indeed beautiful to see.
- Can I take some time to think about the new reality for Peter and John? How do I share in that new reality?

Thursday 16th April **Luke 24:36–45**

While they were talking about this, Jesus himself stood among them and said to them, "Peace be with you." They were startled and terrified, and thought that they were seeing a ghost. He said to them, "Why are you frightened, and why do doubts arise in your hearts? Look at my hands and my feet; see that it is I myself. Touch me and see; for a ghost does not have flesh and bones as you see that I have." And when he had said this, he showed them his hands and his feet. While in their joy they were disbelieving and still wondering, he said to them, "Have you anything here to eat?" They gave him a piece of broiled fish, and he took it and ate in their presence. Then he said to them, "These are my words that I spoke to you while I was still with you—that everything written about me in the law of Moses, the prophets, and the psalms must be fulfilled." Then he opened their minds to understand the scriptures.

- Jesus does for the terrified disciples what he did for those he met on the road to Emmaus: As he shared food with them, he opened their minds to understanding the scriptures.
- We do not believe through the eyes of the flesh, but through the faith in his word—that he will be with us always.

Friday 17th April **John 21:4–14**

Just after daybreak, Jesus stood on the beach; but the disciples did not know that it was Jesus. Jesus said to them, "Children, you have no fish, have you?" They answered him, "No." He said to them, "Cast the net to the right side of the boat, and you will find some." So they cast it, and now they were not able to haul it in because there were so many fish. That disciple whom Jesus loved said to Peter, "It is the Lord!" When Simon Peter heard that it was the Lord, he put on some clothes, for he was naked, and jumped into the sea. But the other disciples came in the boat, dragging the net full of fish, for they were not far from the land, only about a hundred yards off. When they had gone ashore, they saw a charcoal fire there, with fish on it, and bread. Jesus said to them, "Bring some of the fish that you have just caught." So Simon Peter went aboard and hauled the net ashore, full of large fish, a hundred and fifty-three of them; and though there were so many, the net was not torn. Jesus said to them, "Come and have breakfast." Now none of the disciples dared to ask him,

"Who are you?" because they knew it was the Lord. Jesus came and took the bread and gave it to them, and did the same with the fish. This was now the third time that Jesus appeared to the disciples after he was raised from the dead.

- "Come and have breakfast." This is such a simple event. Jesus meets and invites his followers to eat together, just as the early communities did—meeting, sharing their food, and breaking bread together.
- The shared meal, the Eucharist, makes us one with the risen Lord and with each other.

Saturday 18th April **Acts 4:18–21**

So they called Peter and John and ordered them not to speak or teach at all in the name of Jesus. But Peter and John answered them, "Whether it is right in God's sight to listen to you rather than to God, you must judge; for we cannot keep from speaking about what we have seen and heard." After threatening them again, they let them go, finding no way to punish them because of the people, for all of them praised God for what had happened.

- Peter and John are gripped by the love of God; they are changed men who cannot keep the good news of the risen Lord to themselves.
- Can I accept the Easter invitation to admire the change that God's love brings about in people? Can I be open to it in my own life?

april 19–25

Something to think and pray about each day this week:

Living in This Body

You know my name and my body, Lord. You see my lived-in face, shaped by my history, showing the lines of love, indulgence, suffering, humor, and gentleness. Teach me to love my face and my body, my temple of the Holy Spirit. My body is sacred, and Easter opens a window for it and me onto a mysterious but endless vista. As we grow older nothing in our faith makes more sense than the passion and the resurrection, the certainty that our body, like Jesus', must suffer and die, and the certainty that we, in our bodies, have a life beyond death.

The Presence of God

What is present to me is what has a hold on my becoming.
I reflect on the presence of God always there in love,
amidst the many things that have a hold on me.
I pause and pray that I may let God
affect my becoming in this precise moment.

Freedom

If God were trying to tell me something, would I know?
If God were reassuring me or challenging me, would I notice?
I ask for the grace to be free of my own preoccupations
and open to what God may be saying to me.

Consciousness

Knowing that God loves me unconditionally,
I can afford to be honest about how I am.
How has the last day been, and how do I feel now?
I share my feelings openly with the Lord.

The Word

God speaks to each one of us individually. I need to listen to what he is saying to me. (Please turn to your scripture on the following pages. Inspiration points are there should you need them. When you are ready, return here to continue.)

Conversation

What is stirring in me as I pray?
Am I consoled, troubled, left cold?
I imagine Jesus himself standing or sitting at my side
and share my feelings with him.

Conclusion

Glory be to the Father, and to the Son, and to the Holy Spirit,
As it was in the beginning, is now and ever shall be,
World without end. Amen

Sunday 19th April,
Second Sunday of Easter **Acts 4:32–35**

Now the whole group of those who believed were of one heart and soul, and no one claimed private ownership of any possessions, but everything they owned was held in common. With great power the apostles gave their testimony to the resurrection of the Lord Jesus, and great grace was upon them all. There was not a needy person among them, for as many as owned lands or houses sold them and brought the proceeds of what was sold. They laid it at the apostles' feet, and it was distributed to each as any had need.

- We see here a community living in the Spirit, as brothers and sisters in Christ, as children of the Father.
- Christian life is meant to be lived in community. It is a sharing of the Spirit with others, in the body of Christ. It is not a private dialogue with Jesus.
- We discover the Lord in relationship with others. Can I work on that today?

Monday 20th April **John 3:1–6**

Now there was a Pharisee named Nicodemus, a leader of the Jews. He came to Jesus by night and said to him, "Rabbi, we know that you are a teacher who has come from God; for no one can do these signs that you do apart from the presence of God." Jesus answered him, "Very truly, I tell you, no one can see the kingdom of God without being born from above." Nicodemus said to him, "How can anyone be born after having grown old? Can one enter a second time into the mother's womb and be born?" Jesus answered, "Very truly, I tell you, no one can enter the kingdom of God without being born of water and Spirit.

What is born of the flesh is flesh, and what is born of the Spirit is spirit."

- Nicodemus was a Pharisee, one of a closely-knit brotherhood who were pledged to keep every detail of the Law. They were good people, but they had created such a maze of obligations that it was a lifetime's work to remember them all.
- In face of that, Jesus was saying something simple: Be born of the Spirit. Love God and love your neighbor.

Tuesday 21st April **John 3:7–8**

Jesus said to Nicodemus, "Do not be astonished that I said to you, 'You must be born from above.' The wind blows where it chooses, and you hear the sound of it, but you do not know where it comes from or where it goes. So it is with everyone who is born of the Spirit."

- The love of God is poured out in our hearts by the Holy Spirit who is given to us and who makes us children of God.
- Lord, may I heed your spirit and live by the spirit.

Wednesday 22nd April **John 3:16–17**

Jesus said to Nicodemus, "For God so loved the world that he gave his only Son, so that everyone who believes in him may not perish but may have eternal life. Indeed, God did not send the Son into the world to condemn the world, but in order that the world might be saved through him."

- To "save" is to take a person away from imminent danger, to liberate from oppression, to heal or to make whole again.
- Jesus instructs Nicodemus, as he instructs us. He came to give us the very life of God, and it flows in us because Jesus was lifted up on the cross and lifted up in his resurrection.

Thursday 23rd April **John 3:31–34a**

John the Baptist said to his disciples, "The one who comes from above is above all; the one who is of the earth belongs to the earth and speaks about earthly things. The one who comes from heaven is above all. He testifies to what he has seen and heard, yet no one accepts his testimony. Whoever has accepted his testimony has certified this, that God is true. He whom God has sent speaks the words of God."

- I am invited to be in the presence of the one who "comes from above." Jesus shares our humanity and is close to us but he is of God.
- Perhaps I too find it hard to accept the full testimony of Jesus and the truth about him.
- Now I can simply ask to know him better.

Friday 24th April **John 6:5–11**

When he looked up and saw a large crowd coming toward him, Jesus said to Philip, "Where are we to buy bread for these people to eat?" He said this to test him, for he himself knew what he was going to do. Philip answered him, "Six months' wages would not buy enough bread for each of them to get a little." One of his disciples, Andrew, Simon Peter's brother, said to him, "There is a boy here who has five barley loaves and two fish. But what are they among so many people?" Jesus said, "Make the people sit down." Now there was a great deal of grass in the place; so they sat down, about five thousand in all. Then Jesus took the loaves, and when he had given thanks, he distributed them to those who were seated; so also the fish, as much as they wanted.

- "Where are we to buy bread for these people?" I imagine myself there. Am I Philip, frustrated at the lack of a solution? Am I the boy, trusting the adults with my meager supplies? Am I Andrew who, like Philip, sees no way of answering Jesus' test?

- Jesus' solution brings together the boy, the few supplies, and an invitation for all to sit on the green grass.
- In this miracle, what is Jesus telling me about God's work?

Saturday 25th April,
St. Mark the Evangelist **Mark 16:15–20**

And Jesus said to the disciples, "Go into all the world and proclaim the good news to the whole creation. The one who believes and is baptized will be saved; but the one who does not believe will be condemned. And these signs will accompany those who believe: by using my name they will cast out demons; they will speak in new tongues; they will pick up snakes in their hands, and if they drink any deadly thing, it will not hurt them; they will lay their hands on the sick, and they will recover." So then the Lord Jesus, after he had spoken to them, was taken up into heaven and sat down at the right hand of God. And they went out and proclaimed the good news everywhere, while the Lord worked with them and confirmed the message by the signs that accompanied it.

- Mark is said to have worked as Peter's secretary, so this may well be Peter's memory of his last meeting with Jesus, when he received his mission—of which I am part: to pass on the good news and to bring healing and health to the whole creation, and all this in the confidence that God is working with us.

april 26–may 2

Something to think and pray about each day this week:

Signs of New Life

At Easter we meditate on the body, my body. This flesh is not distinct from me. It is me. The faces we see around us are lived in, showing the signs of love, suffering, pride, tenderness, arrogance, or indulgence. As the proverb says: The face you have at forty is the face that you deserve. So too our hands are shaped by the skills we give them, our limbs by the exercise we offer them, our lungs, heart, and stomach by the use or abuse we show them. This is a time to converse with this loved but mortal flesh: Do I listen to you? Have I the freedom of you? Do I respect you, my temple of the Holy Spirit? You will indeed grow old and die with me, but that is not the end. You are sacred, and Easter opens a ravishing prospect for both of us.

The Presence of God

At any time of the day or night we can call on Jesus.
He is always waiting, listening for our call.
What a wonderful blessing.
No phone needed, no emails, just a whisper.

Freedom

I need to close out the noise, to rise above the noise;
The noise that interrupts, that separates,
The noise that isolates.
I need to listen to God again.

Consciousness

Help me, Lord, to be more conscious of your presence.
Teach me to recognize your presence in others.
Fill my heart with gratitude for the times your love
has been shown to me through the care of others.

The Word

I read the Word of God slowly, a few times over, and I listen to what God is saying to me. (Please turn to your scripture on the following pages. Inspiration points are there should you need them. When you are ready, return here to continue.)

Conversation

Do I notice myself reacting as I pray with the Word of God?
Do I feel challenged, comforted, angry?
Imagining Jesus sitting or standing by me,
I speak out my feelings, as one trusted friend to another.

Conclusion

Glory be to the Father, and to the Son, and to the Holy Spirit,
As it was in the beginning, is now and ever shall be,
World without end. Amen

Sunday 26th April,
Third Sunday of Easter **Luke 24:36–43**

While they were talking about this, Jesus himself stood among them and said to them, "Peace be with you." They were startled and terrified, and thought that they were seeing a ghost. He said to them, "Why are you frightened, and why do doubts arise in your hearts? Look at my hands and my feet; see that it is I myself. Touch me and see; for a ghost does not have flesh and bones as you see that I have." And when he had said this, he showed them his hands and his feet. While in their joy they were disbelieving and still wondering, he said to them, "Have you anything here to eat?" They gave him a piece of broiled fish, and he took it and ate in their presence.

- In his risen body, Jesus comes as one bringing peace and calming fears.
- I do not understand the biology of it, Lord, eating broiled fish in that glorious body. But I do understand that your resurrection is a promise of my own and that my closeness to you brings a peace that the world cannot give.

Monday 27th April **John 6:26–27**

Jesus answered them, "Very truly, I tell you, you are looking for me, not because you saw signs, but because you ate your fill of the loaves. Do not work for the food that perishes, but for the food that endures for eternal life, which the Son of Man will give you.

- "Do not work for the food which perishes." Lord, I know about what perishes. We are the waste-makers. In the western world we make mountains of garbage, which in the poor countries would supply their daily bread—not just food but clothes, toys, household goods.

- I do not want to set my heart on stuff that will be obsolete tomorrow. You, Lord, are the beauty ever ancient, ever new. You gave us the things of this world to use, but our hearts are made to find joy in you.

Tuesday 28th April **John 6:30–35**

So they said to him, "What sign are you going to give us then, so that we may see it and believe you? What work are you performing? Our ancestors ate the manna in the wilderness; as it is written, 'He gave them bread from heaven to eat.'" Then Jesus said to them, "Very truly, I tell you, it was not Moses who gave you the bread from heaven, but it is my Father who gives you the true bread from heaven. For the bread of God is that which comes down from heaven and gives life to the world." They said to him, "Sir, give us this bread always." Jesus said to them, "I am the bread of life. Whoever comes to me will never be hungry, and whoever believes in me will never be thirsty."

- Lord, I am still trying to satisfy some need of mine, working for food that cannot last.
- It is in prayer that I begin to sense a deeper satisfaction and to know that in this bond with you there is something sacred, and the chance to live at a deeper level than I have ever done.

Wednesday 29th April **John 6:37**

Jesus said to them, "Everything that the Father gives me will come to me, and anyone who comes to me I will never drive away."

- I rely on that, Lord. When I settle into prayer, it is into silence.
- There is nothing in the world that resembles God as much as silence. In that silence I am not going forward nor going back. I am in between past and future, in the gap.

Thursday 30th April **John 6:45**

Jesus said to the people: It is written in the prophets, "And they shall all be taught by God." Everyone who has heard and learned from the Father comes to me.

- "And they shall all be taught by God." When God teaches us, it is usually without words, touching us by the encounters, pleasures, and pains of everyday living.
- Lord, as I pray, show me, in the movements of my heart, what you want me to learn from you.

Friday 1st May **John 6:56–59**

"Those who eat my flesh and drink my blood abide in me, and I in them. Just as the living Father sent me, and I live because of the Father, so whoever eats me will live because of me. This is the bread that came down from heaven, not like that which your ancestors ate, and they died. But the one who eats this bread will live for ever." He said these things while he was teaching in the synagogue at Capernaum.

- We are invited into a most intimate communion with God: As we become more united with Christ, so we grow into a union that flows from the unity of Father and Son.
- Let me contemplate this mystery of Christian life, of how one flows from the other. How do I embrace this life?
- I can talk with God about these things.

Saturday 2nd May **John 6:64–69**

And he said, "But among you there are some who do not believe." For Jesus knew from the first who were the ones that did not believe, and who was the one that would betray him. And he said, "For this reason I have told you that no one can come to me unless it is granted by the Father." Because of his teaching many of his disciples turned back and no longer went about with him. So Jesus asked the twelve, "Do you also wish to go away?" Simon Peter answered him, "Lord, to whom can we go? You have the words of eternal life. We have come to believe and know that you are the Holy One of God."

- Dear Peter, for all his failings, he speaks in memorable phrases: "Lord, to whom can we go?"
- In my faint-hearted moments I hear both Jesus' gentle voice, giving me the freedom to choose, and the strength of Peter's reply: "You have the words of eternal life."

may 3–9

Something to think and pray about each day this week:

Carrying the News

Many of us have experienced the death of somebody close. Grief comes in two parts: facing death as a fact, and facing death as a reality that will last for the rest of your life. When someone is close to us, as spouse, mother, father, or child, we carry them around as an inner loved one. After death people can continue as a powerful force in our lives. You talk to your inner mother, or husband, or child, and even listen to them.

In the weeks after Easter, the apostles were doing more than that. At the very center of our faith is the conviction that Jesus is alive and alive in a glorified body, not just as a ghost. He always comes bringing peace, a deep comfort in the realization of his continuing presence and care for us. The church grew up against all the odds in a hostile world, around the presence of the risen Christ. The apostles knew he was with them through the Holy Spirit. On the strength of that, a handful of uneducated fishermen went on to carry the news of the risen Jesus to the ends of the earth, to over a billion people now.

The Presence of God
As I sit here, the beating of my heart,
the ebb and flow of my breathing, the movements of my mind
are all signs of God's ongoing creation of me.
I pause for a moment, and become aware
of this presence of God within me.

Freedom
I will ask God's help,
to be free from my own preoccupations,
to be open to God in this time of prayer,
to come to love and serve him more.

Consciousness
Knowing that God loves me unconditionally,
I look honestly over the last day, its events, and my feelings.
Do I have something to be grateful for? Then I give thanks.
Is there something I am sorry for? Then I ask forgiveness.

The Word
I take my time to read the Word of God slowly a few times, allowing myself to dwell on anything that strikes me. (Please turn to your scripture on the following pages. Inspiration points are there should you need them. When you are ready, return here to continue.)

Conversation
Remembering that I am still in God's presence,
I imagine Jesus himself standing or sitting beside me
and say whatever is on my mind, whatever is in my heart,
speaking as one friend to another.

Conclusion
Glory be to the Father, and to the Son, and to the Holy Spirit,
As it was in the beginning, is now and ever shall be,
World without end. Amen

Sunday 3rd May,
Fourth Sunday of Easter **John 10:11–13**

"I am the good shepherd. The good shepherd lays down his life for the sheep. The hired hand, who is not the shepherd and does not own the sheep, sees the wolf coming and leaves the sheep and runs away—and the wolf snatches them and scatters them. The hired hand runs away because a hired hand does not care for the sheep."

- We know leaders who want influence or money, who value their own aims above that of their followers, and who can be bought. Such leaders are a sad mistake, and we live to regret them.
- Lord, you are a fearless leader. Death has no terrors for you. You value the life of your followers above your own. You are not in it for the money, but you know me and love me.

Monday 4th May **John 10:14–16**

"I am the good shepherd. I know my own and my own know me, just as the Father knows me and I know the Father. And I lay down my life for the sheep. I have other sheep that do not belong to this fold. I must bring them also, and they will listen to my voice. So there will be one flock, one shepherd."

- Lord, in my love of you I am joined to the millions of fellow-Christians of all churches. May I do everything I can to forge our unity and strengthen the fellow-feeling of all who follow you.

Tuesday 5th May **Acts 11:25–26**

Then Barnabas went to Tarsus to look for Saul, and when he had found him, he brought him to Antioch. So it was that for an entire year they met with the church and taught a great many people, and it was in Antioch that the disciples were first called "Christians."

- In Antioch the disciples were first called "Christians." Nobody is paid royalties for that coinage, yet it was momentous.
- What does it mean to me to carry that title? To know Jesus as the Son of God, to love him and follow his teaching, to hope that others would recognize me as a Christian by my life. Would they?

Wednesday 6th May **John 12:44–46**

Then Jesus cried aloud: "Whoever believes in me believes not in me but in him who sent me. And whoever sees me sees him who sent me. I have come as light into the world, so that everyone who believes in me should not remain in the darkness."

- Many of the ancients paid homage to the unknown God. Peoples sought God in the shape of animals like the Egyptian Anubis, or of wayward humans like Dionysus.
- Now Jesus says: The one who sees me sees the one who sent me. That is why your words, Lord, have a depth I can never fathom. I love to seek God in the person of Christ.

Thursday 7th May **John 13:16–17**

After he had washed their feet, had put on his robe, and had returned to the table, he said to them, "Very truly, I tell you, servants are not greater than their master, nor are messengers greater than the one who sent them. If you know these things, you are blessed if you do them."

- Can I imagine the tenderness with which Jesus touches the feet of each disciple? What he says to them?
- At the meal he speaks to them all; he reveals his love, which is both comforting and challenging.
- Lord, encourage me to accept the challenge, to stand up and do the work of God, to serve as you serve.

Friday 8th May **John 14:1–3**

Jesus said to his disciples, "Do not let your hearts be troubled. Believe in God, believe also in me. In my Father's house there are many dwelling places. If it were not so, would I have told you that I go to prepare a place for you? And if I go and prepare a place for you, I will come again and will take you to myself, so that where I am, there you may be also."

- Paradise can seem too lofty and shining a place for me to feel at home. I find comfort in Jesus' words: "In my father's house there are many dwelling-places . . . I go to prepare a place for you."
- Where you are, Lord, I will know I am at home.

Saturday 9th May **John 14:12–14**

Jesus said to his disciples, "Very truly, I tell you, the one who believes in me will also do the works that I do and, in fact, will do greater works than these, because I am going to the Father. I will do whatever you ask in my name, so that the Father may be glorified in the Son. If in my name you ask me for anything, I will do it."

- How can we do greater works than Jesus did? Over the centuries, filled with the desire to heal and to make the world a better place, we have mastered diseases, combated famine, tamed the flooding of rivers, and built alliances like the United Nations to make peace more possible.
- Lord, let me continue your work, filled with your spirit.

may 10–16

Something to think and pray about each day this week:

Embracing Our Weakness

The experience of weakness deepens both our sensitivity to human need and our experience of prayer. There is an important consequence for all of us: We must make such a life possible for one another. We must support one another in weakness, forgiving one another our daily faults and carrying one another's burdens. It would be absurd to see weakness as an essential part of our calling, and then to belittle those who are deficient, to resent those who are insensitive, unsophisticated, or clumsy, to allow disagreements to become hostilities, or to continue battles and angers because of personal histories.

The Presence of God
I pause for a moment
and reflect on God's life-giving presence
in every part of my body, in everything around me,
in the whole of my life.

Freedom
God is not foreign to my freedom.
Instead the Spirit breathes life into my most intimate desires,
gently nudging me towards all that is good.
I ask for the grace to let myself be enfolded by the Spirit.

Consciousness
How do I find myself today?
Where am I with God? With others?
Do I have something to be grateful for? Then I give thanks.
Is there something I am sorry for? Then I ask forgiveness.

The Word
God speaks to each one of us individually. I need to listen to what he is saying to me. (Please turn to your scripture on the following pages. Inspiration points are there should you need them. When you are ready, return here to continue.)

Conversation
How has God's Word moved me? Has it left me cold?
Has it consoled me or moved me to act in a new way?
I imagine Jesus standing or sitting beside me,
I turn and share my feelings with him.

Conclusion
Glory be to the Father, and to the Son, and to the Holy Spirit,
As it was in the beginning, is now and ever shall be,
World without end. Amen

Sunday 10th May,
Fifth Sunday of Easter **John 15:1–2, 5**

Jesus said, "I am the true vine, and my Father is the vine-grower. He removes every branch in me that bears no fruit. Every branch that bears fruit he prunes to make it bear more fruit. I am the vine, you are the branches. Those who abide in me and I in them bear much fruit, because apart from me you can do nothing."

- Here is a new image of God. The vine-grower has a sharp knife and a keen eye to the vine's health. If he cuts it, it is to make the plant more vigorous and fruitful.
- Lord, when I feel your sharp touch, I may resent it, but I trust your love for me.

Monday 11th May **John 14:25–26**

Jesus said to his disciples: "I have said these things to you while I am still with you. The Advocate, the Holy Spirit, whom the Father will send in my name, will teach you everything, and remind you of all that I have said to you."

- The Holy Spirit, the ally and spirit of Jesus, remains with me through my life, keeping the words of Jesus in my mind, helping me to deepen my understanding of them, as I apply them to the constantly changing situations that I face.

Tuesday 12th May **John 14:27, 31b**

Jesus said to his disciples, "Peace I leave with you; my peace I give to you. I do not give to you as the world gives. Do not let your hearts be troubled, and do not let them be afraid. Rise, let us be on our way."

- The peace that Jesus promises is not an escape from trouble—the peace that the world gives—but rather the courage to face it calmly. As he spoke these words of peace, he was walking out to Gethsemane and his passion.

- Lord, that is the peace I seek: to be able to face sorrow and pain without the overwhelming fear that all is lost.

Wednesday 13th May **John 15:1–8**

Jesus said to his disciples, "I am the true vine, and my Father is the vine-grower. He removes every branch in me that bears no fruit. Every branch that bears fruit he prunes to make it bear more fruit. You have already been cleansed by the word that I have spoken to you. Abide in me as I abide in you. Just as the branch cannot bear fruit by itself unless it abides in the vine, neither can you unless you abide in me. I am the vine, you are the branches. Those who abide in me and I in them bear much fruit because apart from me you can do nothing. Whoever does not abide in me is thrown away like a branch and withers; such branches are gathered, thrown into the fire, and burned. If you abide in me, and my words abide in you, ask for whatever you wish, and it will be done for you. My Father is glorified by this, that you bear much fruit and become my disciples."

- A vine can easily run wild. It needs careful tending of the soil and constant pruning. Otherwise it shows barren branches. Jesus' image suggests the intimate bond between vine and branches, the sap flowing, the buds fruiting.
- Lord, I have learned this well: It is only if I bring you to others that I can be of any help to them. If I bring myself, my contact is barren and sterile. Let me abide in you.

Thursday 14th May **Acts 15:7–21**

The apostles and the elders met together to consider this matter. After there had been much debate, Peter stood up and said to them, "My brothers, you know that in the early days God made a choice among you, that I should be the one through whom the Gentiles would hear the message of the good news and become believers. And God, who knows the human heart, testified to them by giving them the Holy Spirit, just as he did to us; and in cleansing their hearts by faith he has made no distinction between them and us. Now therefore why are you putting God to the test by placing on the neck of the disciples a yoke that neither our ancestors nor we have been able to bear? On the contrary, we believe that we will be saved through the grace of the Lord Jesus, just as they will." The whole assembly kept silence, and listened to Barnabas and Paul as they told of all the signs and wonders that God had done through them among the Gentiles.

- There is drama in this scene. The disciples did not know how the meeting would deal with the conflicting views of the strongly Jewish group from Jerusalem and the enthusiastic apostles of the Gentiles. How much of the Jewish law—circumcision, diet, contact with Gentiles—should survive in the Church?
- The Holy Spirit shines not merely in the results, but in the way the Spirit was reached—by listening to one another, searching for the signs, and by leaving a model for how Christians should come to decisions.

Friday 15th May **John 15:12–17**

This is my commandment, that you love one another as I have loved you. No one has greater love than this, to lay down one's life for one's friends. You are my friends if you do what I command you. I do not call you servants any longer, because the servant does not know what the master is doing; but I have called you friends, because I have made known to you everything that I have heard from my Father. You did not choose me but I chose you. And I appointed you to go and bear fruit,

fruit that will last, so that the Father will give you whatever you ask him in my name. I am giving you these commands so that you may love one another.

- In the Roman Empire and the Middle Eastern kingdoms of Jesus' time, the "friends of the king" were a privileged group of insiders who had access to his bedchamber and with whom he would discuss his plans and concerns.
- Lord, you are inviting me, choosing me, to be your intimate friend, to go out in your name, to make an impact on this precious world, and to bear lasting fruit.

Saturday 16th May **John 15:18–21**

Jesus said to his disciples: "If the world hates you, be aware that it hated me before it hated you. If you belonged to the world, the world would love you as its own. Because you do not belong to the world, but I have chosen you out of the world—therefore the world hates you. Remember the word that I said to you, 'Servants are not greater than their master.' If they persecuted me, they will persecute you; if they kept my word, they will keep yours also. But they will do all these things to you on account of my name, because they do not know him who sent me."

- Lord, you speak of being hated. Am I hated? It is hard to live with the awareness of being hated, or even disliked, so I hide it from myself.
- But I wonder: Those who dislike or hate me—is it because I do not belong to the world and threaten it with my spiritual values? Or is it because I am vain, or mean, or malicious?

may 17–23

Something to think and pray about each day this week:

Here I Am, Lord

In the *Spiritual Exercises*, St. Ignatius writes: "I will stand for the space of an *Our Father*, a step or two before the place where I am to meditate or contemplate, and with my mind raised on high, consider that God our Lord beholds me. Then I will make an act of reverence or humility." This is a beautiful and simple way of entering sacred space. I am not alone with my thoughts and feelings. God is here with me. So I can say to him, "Here I am, Lord." Let me repeat this inwardly several times. Here I am, Lord. Here I am, in this place, for this day. Here I am, Lord, as I am, just as I am, not as I feel I ought to be. No, here I am, just as I am, with all my *real* thoughts, *real* feelings, *real* worries and concerns, and also my deeper wishes and desires. I come before you Lord just as I am.

The Presence of God

The world is charged with the grandeur of God
(Gerard Manley Hopkins).
I dwell for a moment on the presence of God
around me, in every part of my body,
and deep within my being.

Freedom

Everything has the potential to draw forth from me a fuller love and life.
Yet my desires are often fixed, caught, on illusions of fulfillment.
I ask that God, through my freedom, may orchestrate
my desires in a vibrant loving melody rich in harmony.

Consciousness

In God's loving presence I unwind the past day,
starting from now and looking back, moment by moment.
I gather in all the goodness and light, in gratitude.
I attend to the shadows and what they say to me,
seeking healing, courage, forgiveness.

The Word

I read the Word of God slowly a few times over, and I listen to what God is saying to me. (Please turn to your scripture on the following pages. Inspiration points are there should you need them. When you are ready, return here to continue.)

Conversation

What feelings are rising in me
as I pray and reflect on God's Word?
I imagine Jesus himself sitting or standing beside me
and open my heart to him.

Conclusion

Glory be to the Father, and to the Son, and to the Holy Spirit,
As it was in the beginning, is now and ever shall be,
World without end. Amen

Sunday 17th May,
Sixth Sunday of Easter **John 15:9–17**

Jesus said to his disciples, "As the Father has loved me, so I have loved you; abide in my love. If you keep my commandments, you will abide in my love, just as I have kept my Father's commandments and abide in his love. I have said these things to you so that my joy may be in you, and that your joy may be complete. This is my commandment, that you love one another as I have loved you. No one has greater love than this, to lay down one's life for one's friends. You are my friends if you do what I command you. I do not call you servants any longer because the servant does not know what the master is doing; but I have called you friends, because I have made known to you everything that I have heard from my Father. You did not choose me but I chose you. And I appointed you to go and bear fruit, fruit that will last, so that the Father will give you whatever you ask him in my name. I am giving you these commands so that you may love one another."

- A person blind from birth cannot understand color. A person who has never been loved can find love a baffling word. I feel I have an inkling of love's meaning, but how? Whose love was it that taught me the meaning of the word?
- What do I know about the sort of self-giving that is unearned, unquestioning, looking for no return?
- Lord, I have so much to learn from you about love.

Monday 18th May **Acts 16:11–14**

We set sail from Troas and took a straight course to Samothrace, the following day to Neapolis, and from there to Philippi, which is a leading city of the district of Macedonia and a Roman colony. We remained in this city for some days. On the sabbath day we went outside the gate by the river, where we supposed there was a place of prayer; and we sat down and spoke to the women who had gathered there. A certain woman named Lydia, a worshipper of God, was listening to us; she was from the city of Thyatira and a dealer in purple cloth. The Lord opened her heart to listen eagerly to what was said by Paul.

- The scripture presents us with a wonderful eyewitness account of Paul bringing the good news to a small Jewish community in Roman Philippi. He joins the local people at their place of worship, converting a businesswoman, Lydia, and her household.
- Lord, teach me the simple ways I can spread your good news, in my travels and my conversations. Let me share your journey.

Tuesday 19th May **John 16:5–7**

Jesus said to his disciples, "But now I am going to him who sent me; yet none of you asks me, 'Where are you going?' But because I have said these things to you, sorrow has filled your hearts. Nevertheless I tell you the truth: it is to your advantage that I go away, for if I do not go away, the Advocate will not come to you; but if I go, I will send him to you."

- I did not know you in the flesh, Lord, but you promised not to leave me an orphan. You sent me the Holy Spirit, the Advocate and Paraclete, the comforter who linked you, and now links me, to the Father.
- Through the Holy Spirit, I am caught into the life of the Blessed Trinity.

Wednesday 20th May **Acts 17:22–28**

Then Paul stood in front of the Areopagus and said, "Athenians, I see how extremely religious you are in every way. For as I went through the city and looked carefully at the objects of your worship, I found among them an altar with the inscription, 'To an unknown god.' What therefore you worship as unknown, this I proclaim to you. The God who made the world and everything in it, he who is Lord of heaven and earth, does not live in shrines made by human hands, nor is he served by human hands, as though he needed anything, since he himself gives to all mortals life and breath and all things. From one ancestor he made all nations to inhabit the whole earth, and he allotted the times of their existence and the boundaries of the places where they would live, so that they would search for God and perhaps grope for him and find him—though indeed he is not far from each one of us. For 'In him we live and move and have our being'; as even some of your own poets have said, 'For we too are his offspring.'"

- Paul is facing the most exclusive Athenian court, the Areopagus, in the most learned city in the world. Where can he find the words for his message?
- He starts with what he knows of their searching—for an unknown God. How can I find points of contact with those who disagree with how I see things?
- Loving God, you are no longer unknown. I know you, through Jesus. Give me the words to make you known to others.

Thursday 21st May **Acts 18:1–3**

After this Paul left Athens and went to Corinth. There he found a Jew named Aquila, a native of Pontus, who had recently come from Italy with his wife Priscilla, because Claudius had ordered all Jews to leave Rome. Paul went to see them, and, because he was of the same trade, he stayed with them, and they worked together—by trade they were tentmakers.

- Here is a welcome reminder of Paul's style of life. As a Jewish rabbi he had to have a trade so that he need take no money for preaching and teaching, but earn his own living.
- This speaks to me, Lord. There are echoes here of Freud's neat definition of mental health: the ability to work and the ability to love. In you—the carpenter and the lover—I see them both.

Friday 22nd May **John 16:20–23**

Jesus said to his disciples, "Very truly, I tell you, you will weep and mourn, but the world will rejoice; you will have pain, but your pain will turn into joy. When a woman is in labor, she has pain, because her hour has come. But when her child is born, she no longer remembers the anguish because of the joy of having brought a human being into the world. So you have pain now; but I will see you again, and your hearts will rejoice, and no one will take your joy from you. On that day you will ask nothing of me. Very truly, I tell you, if you ask anything of the Father in my name, he will give it to you."

- You bring me back to the basics, Lord: pain and joy. The labor does not last forever, and I can bear it with your support, with the prospect of being with you.

Saturday 23rd May **Acts 18:24–26**

Now there came to Ephesus a Jew named Apollos, a native of Alexandria. He was an eloquent man, well-versed in the scriptures. He had been instructed in the Way of the Lord; and he spoke with burning enthusiasm and taught accurately the things concerning Jesus, though he knew only the baptism of John. He began to speak boldly in the synagogue; but when Priscilla and Aquila heard him, they took him aside and explained the Way of God to him more accurately.

- Priscilla and Aquila from the circle of Paul notice that this scholarly Egyptian Apollos, full of a convert's enthusiasm, is still unaware of the work of the Holy Spirit. The two Christian women take him aside quietly and fill in the gaps in his knowledge of Jesus and of Jesus' message.
- I give thanks for those who have taken me aside and bring to mind the people I influence.
- Thank you, Lord, for the gentle wisdom of these women theologians and for all that their successors have given to the Church.

may 24–30

Something to think and pray about each day this week:

God of Consolation

We sense God's effect on us in consoling times. When we feel a happiness that carries us beyond ourselves and there is no obvious cause such as good news, or physical pleasures, we may see the hand of God in it. It may be in the experience of trust and security: Psalm 131—Lord my heart has no lofty ambitions; my eyes do not look too high. I am not concerned with great affairs, or marvels beyond my scope. Enough for me to keep my soul tranquil and quiet, like a child in its mother's arms, as content as a child that has been weaned.

Consolation may also come in the realization that God is central to our existence, deeper in us than we can imagine: Psalm 139—Lord you examine me and you know me. You know if I am standing or sitting. You read my thoughts from far away. Whether I walk or lie down you are watching. You know every detail of my conduct. The word is not even on my tongue, Lord, before you know all about it. Close behind and in front you fence me round, shielding me with your hand. Such knowledge is beyond my understanding. If I asked darkness to cover me, and light to become night around me, that darkness would not be dark to you, night would be as light as day. It was you who created my inmost self, and put me together in my mother's womb. For all these mysteries I thank you, for the wonder of myself, for the wonder of your works.

The Presence of God
I pause for a moment
and think of the love and the grace that God showers on me,
creating me in his image and likeness, making me his temple.

Freedom
Lord, grant me the grace to be free from the excesses of this life.
Let me not get caught up with the desire for wealth.
Keep my heart and mind free to love and serve you.

Consciousness
In the presence of my loving Creator,
I look honestly at my feelings over the last day,
the highs, the lows, and the level ground.
Can I see where the Lord has been present?

The Word
God speaks to each one of us individually. I need to listen to what he is saying to me. (Please turn to your scripture on the following pages. Inspiration points are there should you need them. When you are ready, return here to continue.)

Conversation
Sometimes I wonder what I might say
if I were to meet You in person, Lord.
I might say "Thank You, Lord" for always being there for me.
I know with certainty there were times when you carried me,
when through your strength I got through the dark times in my life.

Conclusion
Glory be to the Father, and to the Son, and to the Holy Spirit,
As it was in the beginning, is now and ever shall be,
World without end. Amen

Sunday 24th May, Ascension of the Lord **Acts 1:6–11**

So when they had come together, the disciples asked him, "Lord, is this the time when you will restore the kingdom to Israel?" He replied, "It is not for you to know the times or periods that the Father has set by his own authority. But you will receive power when the Holy Spirit has come upon you; and you will be my witnesses in Jerusalem, in all Judea and Samaria, and to the ends of the earth." When he had said this, as they were watching, he was lifted up, and a cloud took him out of their sight. While he was going and they were gazing up toward heaven, suddenly two men in white robes stood by them. They said, "Men of Galilee, why do you stand looking up toward heaven? This Jesus, who has been taken up from you into heaven, will come in the same way as you saw him go into heaven."

- Because of Jesus' Ascension to the Father, humankind now has a place in heaven. We will no longer be out of place there. "One of our own" sits at God's right hand.
- If I have difficulty appreciating this, I can look at the disciples in the scene. Even at the end they seem not to understand.

Monday 25th May **John 16:29–33**

The disciples said to Jesus, "Yes, now you are speaking plainly, not in any figure of speech! Now we know that you know all things and do not need to have anyone question you; by this we believe that you came from God. Jesus answered them, "Do you now believe? The hour is coming, indeed it has come, when you will be scattered, each one to his home, and you will leave me alone. Yet I am not alone because the Father is with me. I have said this to you, so that in me you may have peace. In the world you face persecution. But take courage; I have conquered the world!"

- There is a slightly manic tinge about the disciples' speech. Jesus looks into their hearts and brings them back to the grim realities that he and they face. He knows how they will fail—"you will leave me alone"—and he loves them as they are, promises them peace, and urges them to courage.
- Lord, you have no illusions about my fallible heart, but you promise peace to me too.

Tuesday 26th May **John 17:1–3**

After Jesus had spoken these words, he looked up to heaven and said, "Father, the hour has come; glorify your Son so that the Son may glorify you, since you have given him authority over all people, to give eternal life to all whom you have given him. And this is eternal life, that they may know you, the only true God, and Jesus Christ whom you have sent."

- I have to work at this, Lord. The description of eternal life is stark. To know the only true God is beyond my imagination.
- Do we, in our glorified bodies, leave behind our senses of smell, taste, touch, hearing, and vision that delight us now and seem to be harbingers of better things to come? Somehow the knowledge of the one true God must bring all these joys to a new level.

Wednesday 27th May **John 17:15–18**

I am not asking you to take them out of the world, but I ask you to protect them from the evil one. They do not belong to the world, just as I do not belong to the world. Sanctify them in the truth; your word is truth. As you have sent me into the world, so I have sent them into the world.

- No, Lord, do not take me out of the world. I belong here, with all its messiness, just as you belonged here and took all the risks it involved.

- I do not seek a lily-pure existence untouched by the struggle for survival. But I do beg you to protect me from the evil one, from the malice in my own heart.

Thursday 28th May **John 17:20–23**

Jesus looked up to heaven and said, "Father, I ask not only on behalf of these, but also on behalf of those who will believe in me through their word, that they may all be one. As you, Father, are in me and I am in you, may they also be in us, so that the world may believe that you have sent me. The glory that you have given me I have given them, so that they may be one, as we are one, I in them and you in me, that they may become completely one, so that the world may know that you have sent me and have loved them even as you have loved me."

- "That they may become one so that the world may know that you have sent me"... That is the scandal of division, the hardest question we Christians have to face.
- What is it in me, what sort of egotism, that makes me inclined to split rather than join?

Friday 29th May **John 21:15–17**

When they had finished breakfast, Jesus said to Simon Peter, "Simon son of John, do you love me more than these?" He said to him, "Yes, Lord; you know that I love you." Jesus said to him, "Feed my lambs." A second time he said to him, "Simon son of John, do you love me?" He said to him, "Yes, Lord; you know that I love you." Jesus said to him, "Tend my sheep." He said to him the third time, "Simon son of John, do you love me?" Peter felt hurt because he said to him the third time, "Do you love me?" And he said to him, "Lord, you know everything; you know that I love you." Jesus said to him, "Feed my sheep."

- Lord, I feel this is a telegraphic version of your dealings with Simon Peter. You probably took him for a long, tearful walk, talking through the horror of the disciples' betrayal and abandonment of Jesus.
- What the gospel describes here is a summary, but it tells me how you understand love. It means fidelity that can grow from betrayal, courage that can grow from cowardice. The one quality that is demanded of the future shepherd of the church is that he love you with all his fallible heart.
- This is what you ask of me too.

Saturday 30th May **John 21:20–23**

Peter turned and saw the disciple whom Jesus loved following them; he was the one who had reclined next to Jesus at the supper and had said, "Lord, who is it that is going to betray you?" When Peter saw him, he said to Jesus, "Lord, what about him?" Jesus said to him, "If it is my will that he remain until I come, what is that to you? Follow me!" So the rumor spread in the community that this disciple would not die. Yet Jesus did not say to him that he would not die, but, "If it is my will that he remain until I come, what is that to you?"

- "What about him?" asked Peter. Is there a hint here of sibling rivalry, jealous curiosity? There is a reproach in Jesus' comment: "What is that to you?"
- Lord, will I ever outgrow this sense of rivalry, wanting to be the center of attention? Let your love flow through me in an unselfish way.

may 31–june 6

Something to think and pray about each day this week:

Growing in the Spirit

Pentecost is about the Now. The Holy Spirit gives us the confidence to be where we are, possibly depressed, old, with sicknesses. We do not look at trees and say they have to be saplings. Ancient trees may have rotten branches, but they have a beauty that comes from all the years they have lived. In the Holy Spirit nothing goes out of fashion; it grows and never dies. The body may die, but you and I will not. When you are fifteen, you do not necessarily want to draw from knowledge about life gained when you were ten. Instead, you are looking ahead, hoping to be something else. But that does not give peace. Peace comes from knowing: *I am fifteen, which means that each of those fifteen years has added something to me. My successes come from what I did with my failures. I have survived some sufferings and have learned from them.* The Holy Spirit would have taught St. Peter to think about the denial of Christ and the crowing of the cock. He would rather have forgotten about it, undone it. Instead he learned to make it part of the Lord's dealing with him, as much a part as Jesus' tender words to him after the resurrection: "Feed my sheep."

The Presence of God

As I sit here with my book, God is here,
around me, in my sensations, in my thoughts and deep within me.
I pause for a moment, and become aware
of God's life-giving presence.

Freedom

A thick and shapeless tree-trunk would never believe
that it could become a statue, admired as a miracle of sculpture,
and would never submit itself to the chisel of the sculptor,
who sees by her genius what she can make of it. (St Ignatius)
I ask for the grace to let myself be shaped by my loving Creator.

Consciousness

How am I really feeling? Light-hearted? Heavy-hearted?
I may be very much at peace, happy to be here.
Equally, I may be frustrated, worried, or angry.
I acknowledge how I really am. It is the real me that the Lord loves.

The Word

The Word of God comes down to us through the scriptures. May the Holy Spirit enlighten my mind and my heart to respond to the gospel teachings. (Please turn to your scripture on the following pages. Inspiration points are there should you need them. When you are ready, return here to continue.)

Conversation

Do I notice myself reacting as I pray with the Word of God?
Do I feel challenged, comforted, angry?
Imagining Jesus sitting or standing by me,
I speak out my feelings, as one trusted friend to another.

Conclusion

Glory be to the Father, and to the Son, and to the Holy Spirit,
As it was in the beginning, is now and ever shall be,
World without end. Amen

Sunday 31st May, Pentecost **Acts 2:1–4**

When the day of Pentecost had come, they were all together in one place. And suddenly from heaven there came a sound like the rush of a violent wind, and it filled the entire house where they were sitting. Divided tongues, as of fire, appeared among them, and a tongue rested on each of them. All of them were filled with the Holy Spirit and began to speak in other languages, as the Spirit gave them ability.

- "Speaking in other languages": the words you might read in *Sacred Space* online are translated into nineteen languages, and they reach the ends of the earth, thanks to the marvelous creators of the Internet, the World Wide Web.
- Lord, send tongues of fire on all in *Sacred Space*. Bond them with you through your Holy Spirit.

Monday 1st June **Tobit 2:3–8**

Tobias my son went to look for some poor person of our people. When he had returned he said, "Father!" And I replied, "Here I am, my child." Then he went on to say, "Look, father, one of our own people has been murdered and thrown into the market place, and now he lies there strangled." Then I sprang up, left the dinner before even tasting it, and removed the body from the square and laid it in one of the rooms until sunset when I might bury it. When I returned, I washed myself and ate my food in sorrow. Then I remembered the prophecy of Amos, how he said against Bethel,

> Your festivals shall be turned into mourning,
> and all your songs into lamentation.

And I wept. When the sun had set, I went and dug a grave and buried him. And my neighbors laughed and said, "Is he still not afraid? He has already been hunted down to be put to death for doing this, and he ran away; yet here he is again burying the dead!"

- The story of Tobit is that of a just man living under an unjust civil law, and facing death for following his conscience: He risks his life by burying a fellow Jew.
- Am I ever placed in such a dilemma? Is my conscience up to the challenge if it comes?

Tuesday 2nd June **Mark 12:13–17**

Then they sent to Jesus some Pharisees and some Herodians to trap him in what he said. And they came and said to him, "Teacher, we know that you are sincere, and show deference to no one; for you do not regard people with partiality, but teach the way of God in accordance with truth. Is it lawful to pay taxes to the emperor, or not? Should we pay them, or should we not?" But knowing their hypocrisy, he said to them, "Why are you putting me to the test? Bring me a denarius and let me see it." And they brought one. Then he said to them, "Whose head is this, and whose title?" They answered, "The emperor's." Jesus said to them, "Give to the emperor the things that are the emperor's, and to God the things that are God's." And they were utterly amazed at him.

- Jesus, faced with the trickiest of dilemmas, gives a momentous answer. If I accept the benefits of the state and the rule of law, then I have responsibilities toward it; but there is a sphere of life that belongs to God and not to Caesar. If their claims conflict, loyalty to God comes first.
- Does my following of Jesus make me a better citizen?

Wednesday 3rd June **Mark 12:18–27**

Some Sadducees, who say there is no resurrection, came to Jesus and asked him a question, saying, "Teacher, Moses wrote for us that 'if a man's brother dies, leaving a wife but no child, the man shall marry the widow and raise up children for his brother.' There were seven brothers; the first married and, when he died, left no children; and the second married her and died, leaving no children; and the third likewise; none of the seven left children. Last of all the woman herself died. In the resurrection whose wife will she be? For the seven had married her." Jesus said to them, "Is not this the reason you are wrong, that you know neither the scriptures nor the power of God? For when they rise from the dead, they neither marry nor are given in marriage, but are like angels in heaven. And as for the dead being raised, have you not read in the book of Moses, in the story about the bush, how God said to him, 'I am the God of Abraham, the God of Isaac, and the God of Jacob'? He is God not of the dead, but of the living; you are quite wrong."

- In the resurrection we touch on the mystery of a body, not just Jesus' body, but our own, which will express us at our best, will not dull our spirit with weariness and rebellion, but express it with ease and joy.
- This is a mystery beyond our imagination, but it is the center of our faith. As we grow older, nothing in our faith makes more sense than the passion and the resurrection, the certainty that our bodies, like Jesus', must suffer and die, and the certainty that we, in our bodies, have a life beyond death.

Thursday 4th June **Mark 12:28–34**

One of the scribes came near and heard them disputing with one another, and seeing that Jesus answered them well, he asked him, "Which commandment is the first of all?" Jesus answered, "The first is, 'Hear, O Israel: the Lord our God, the Lord is one; you shall love the Lord your God with all your heart, and with all your soul, and with all your mind, and with all your strength.' The second is this, 'You shall love your neighbor as yourself.' There is no other commandment greater than these." Then the scribe said to him, "You are right, Teacher; you have truly said that 'he is one, and besides him there is no other'; and 'to love him with all the heart, and with all the understanding, and with all the strength,' and 'to love one's neighbor as oneself,'—this is much more important than all whole burnt offerings and sacrifices." When Jesus saw that he answered wisely, he said to him, "You are not far from the kingdom of God." After that no one dared to ask him any question.

- "Love your neighbor as yourself." Just how do I love myself? I am not just aware of present pleasure or pain. I think ahead, protect my routines, and give energy to ensuring my comfort.
- Lord, if you are asking me to do all that for my neighbor, I will need to try much harder than I am trying.

Friday 5th June **Mark 12:35–37**

While Jesus was teaching in the temple, he said, "How can the scribes say that the Messiah is the son of David? David himself, by the Holy Spirit, declared, 'The Lord said to my Lord, "Sit at my right hand, until I put your enemies under your feet."' David himself calls him Lord; so how can he be his son?" And the large crowd was listening to him with delight.

- "They listened with delight." Lord, may I listen to you in this way, relish your goodness and insight, and nourish myself daily on your words.

Saturday 6th June, St. Colmcille **Mark 10:23-30**

Then Jesus looked around and said to his disciples, "How hard it will be for those who have wealth to enter the kingdom of God!" And the disciples were perplexed at these words. But Jesus said to them again, "Children, how hard it is to enter the kingdom of God! It is easier for a camel to go through the eye of a needle than for someone who is rich to enter the kingdom of God." They were greatly astounded and said to one another, "Then who can be saved?" Jesus looked at them and said, "For mortals it is impossible, but not for God; for God all things are possible." Peter began to say to him, "Look, we have left everything and followed you." Jesus said, "Truly I tell you, there is no one who has left house or brothers or sisters or mother or father or children or fields, for my sake and for the sake of the good news, who will not receive a hundredfold now in this age—houses, brothers and sisters, mothers and children, and fields, with persecutions—and in the age to come eternal life.

- You ask us to leave everything and follow you. Sometimes, Lord, you send us a special blessing, under the form of a fire, a theft, or some other disaster, to help us to leave everything and discover whether we miss what has gone.
- Our riches are not bad unless they wean our hearts from you. It comforts me that you are working to purify my heart.

june 7–13

Something to think and pray about each day this week:

The Truth in Jesus

Jesus urged us not to swear at all: "All you need say is 'Yes' if you mean yes, 'No' if you mean no." Only constant honesty with ourselves can make us really sincere. The world knows an honest person. Many would not tell a downright lie, but few, even of the pious, always tell the truth. It was the truth in Jesus that devastated his enemies. In proportion as we live a recollected life, with Jesus as model, we attain a simplicity and lucidity of character that has less and less need for untruth.

The Presence of God

For a few moments, I think of God's veiled presence in things:
in the elements, giving them existence;
in plants, giving them life; in animals, giving them sensation;
and finally, in me, giving me all this and more,
making me a temple, a dwelling-place of the Spirit.

Freedom

I ask for the grace to believe
in what I could be and do
if I only allowed God, my loving Creator,
to continue to create me, guide me, and shape me.

Consciousness

In the presence of my loving Creator,
I look honestly at my feelings over the last day,
the highs, the lows, and the level ground.
Can I see where the Lord has been present?

The Word

I take my time to read the Word of God slowly a few times, allowing myself to dwell on anything that strikes me. (Please turn to your scripture on the following pages. Inspiration points are there should you need them. When you are ready, return here to continue.)

Conversation

How has God's Word moved me? Has it left me cold?
Has it consoled me or moved me to act in a new way?
I imagine Jesus standing or sitting beside me,
I turn and share my feelings with him.

Conclusion

Glory be to the Father, and to the Son, and to the Holy Spirit,
As it was in the beginning, is now and ever shall be,
World without end. Amen

Sunday 7th June,
Feast of the Holy Trinity **Matthew 28:16–20**

Now the eleven disciples went to Galilee, to the mountain to which Jesus had directed them. When they saw him, they worshiped him; but some doubted. And Jesus came and said to them, "All authority in heaven and on earth has been given to me. Go, therefore, and make disciples of all nations, baptizing them in the name of the Father and of the Son and of the Holy Spirit, and teaching them to obey everything that I have commanded you. And remember, I am with you always, to the end of the age."

- I put myself in the skin of one of the eleven disciples, still fearful of those who had arrested and crucified my master, sensing how forlorn I will be without his presence, and, as the text says, doubtful.
- I hear Jesus' commission: "Go, and teach all nations." My heart sinks. Where do I start? Then I hear his promise: "I am with you always." Thanks be to God.

Monday 8th June **Matthew 5:1–3**

When Jesus saw the crowds, he went up the mountain; and after he sat down, his disciples came to him. Then he began to speak, and taught them, saying: "Blessed are the poor in spirit, for theirs is the kingdom of heaven."

- In the Bible, poverty is an evil to be corrected; wealth is not an evil, but a necessity for the well-being of the kingdom. The love of riches, however, can lead to the neglect of God and of the poor.
- The Christian community has always tried to make the care of the poor its priority, as it is God's priority. Is it mine?

Tuesday 9th June **Matthew 5:13–16**

Jesus said to the disciples, "You are the salt of the earth; but if salt has lost its taste, how can its saltiness be restored? It is no longer good for anything, but is thrown out and trampled under foot. "You are the light of the world. A city built on a hill cannot be hidden. No one after lighting a lamp puts it under the bushel basket, but on the lampstand, and it gives light to all in the house. In the same way, let your light shine before others so that they may see your good works and give glory to your Father in heaven."

- Lord, you are telling me something urgent here: In the moral blandness of Western culture, you tell me to be counter-cultural, a strong taste, a light on a lampstand, proud not of myself, but of the gospel.

Wednesday 10th June **2 Corinthians 3:4–6**

Such is the confidence that we have through Christ toward God. Not that we are competent of ourselves to claim anything as coming from us; our competence is from God, who has made us competent to be ministers of a new covenant, not of letter but of spirit; for the letter kills, but the Spirit gives life.

- Lest he seem to be praising himself, Paul protests that any good he does is through God's grace.
- Am I ever tempted by the world of testimonials, public tributes, and personal publicity? Ego-massage is the path of illusion. Lord, my competence is from you.

Thursday 11th June,
St. Barnabas, Apostle **Matthew 10:7–10**

Jesus said to the disciples, "As you go, proclaim the good news, 'The kingdom of heaven has come near.' Cure the sick, raise the dead, cleanse the lepers, cast out demons. You received without payment; give without payment. Take no gold, or silver, or copper in your belts, no bag for your journey, or two tunics, or sandals, or a staff; for laborers deserve their food."

- Lord, I have received freely so I should give without payment. That should be a simple matter, but in a society where everything has its price, it is horribly complicated.
- As I listen to you, let me pray for light on how to follow your bidding with a free heart.

Friday 12th June **2 Corinthians 4:7–10**

But we have this treasure in clay jars, so that it may be made clear that this extraordinary power belongs to God and does not come from us. We are afflicted in every way, but not crushed; perplexed, but not driven to despair; persecuted, but not forsaken; struck down, but not destroyed; always carrying in the body the death of Jesus, so that the life of Jesus may also be made visible in our bodies.

- Christians look the same as other people. They live across the whole world, speak in many languages, and follow many different customs. So, what distinguishes them?
- In Paul's elegant language, we are earthenware; we suffer "in every way," but are "not crushed," we doubt, but do not despair. We live our days on earth, but as a people with eyes fixed beyond this earth.
- In our human frailty and failures, we can make Christ visible.

Saturday 13th June, St. Anthony of Padua **Luke 10:1–7a**

After this the Lord appointed seventy others and sent them on ahead of him in pairs to every town and place where he himself intended to go. He said to them, "The harvest is plentiful, but the laborers are few; therefore ask the Lord of the harvest to send out laborers into his harvest. Go on your way. See, I am sending you out like lambs into the midst of wolves. Carry no purse, no bag, no sandals; and greet no one on the road. Whatever house you enter, first say, 'Peace to this house!' And if anyone is there who shares in peace, your peace will rest on that person; but if not, it will return to you. Remain in the same house, eating and drinking whatever they provide, for the laborer deserves to be paid."

- Anthony was a young Franciscan from Portugal who set out for Africa as a missionary, but ended up in Italy after illness and shipwreck. He preached across Italy and France until his early death.
- Like Anthony, we are also called to bring the good news of Jesus. We are called to do it every day.

june 14–20

Something to think and pray about each day this week:

Family Dreams

We all know about families. There are a variety of kinds of family, and each of us has had a mix of good and bad experiences. The clearest family portrait in the gospel is of a father (and Jesus is talking about God) who was made a fool of, a young son who went prodigal and squandered the family fortune and reputation, and an older son who was so jealous of his young brother that he would not attend the homecoming party. God knows about troubled families. They are nothing out of the ordinary. We may have a dream of an ideal family with lively, intelligent, obedient children who line up with their parents for church on Sunday, pass their exams, compete in community sports, and visit their grandparents. Perhaps we need to move away from such rosy pictures. There is no such thing as perfect parents or perfect children. God is not the presenter of prizes at a high-powered graduation, but the one who helps us to recognize our need of help and to accept our blessings.

The Presence of God
I remind myself that, as I sit here now,
God is gazing on me with love and holding me in being.
I pause for a moment and think of this.

Freedom
I need to close out the noise, to rise above the noise;
The noise that interrupts, that separates,
The noise that isolates.
I need to listen to God again.

Consciousness
In God's loving presence, I unwind the past day,
starting from now and looking back, moment by moment.
I gather in all the goodness and light, in gratitude.
I attend to the shadows and what they say to me,
seeking healing, courage, forgiveness.

The Word
I take my time to read the Word of God, slowly, a few times, allowing myself to dwell on anything that strikes me. (Please turn to your scripture on the following pages. Inspiration points are there should you need them. When you are ready, return here to continue.)

Conversation
Do I notice myself reacting as I pray with the Word of God?
Do I feel challenged, comforted, angry?
Imagining Jesus sitting or standing by me,
I speak out my feelings, as one trusted friend to another.

Conclusion
Glory be to the Father, and to the Son, and to the Holy Spirit,
As it was in the beginning, is now and ever shall be,
World without end. Amen

Sunday 14th June,
The Body and Blood of Christ **Mark 14:22–26a**

While they were eating, Jesus took a loaf of bread, and after blessing it he broke it, gave it to them, and said, "Take; this is my body." Then he took a cup, and after giving thanks he gave it to them, and all of them drank from it. He said to them, "This is my blood of the covenant, which is poured out for many. Truly I tell you, I will never again drink of the fruit of the vine until that day when I drink it new in the kingdom of God."

- In this extraordinary mystery of the Eucharist, Lord, you become part of me and I of you. I celebrate this Eucharist in memory of you: slake my hunger and thirst on the bread and wine. Through this Eucharist, I come closest to meeting my deepest desire—union with God.

Monday 15th June **Matthew 5:38–42**

Jesus said to the crowds, "You have heard that it was said, 'An eye for an eye and a tooth for a tooth.' But I say to you, do not resist an evildoer. But if anyone strikes you on the right cheek, turn the other also; and if anyone wants to sue you and take your coat, give your cloak as well; and if anyone forces you to go one mile, go also the second mile. Give to everyone who begs from you, and do not refuse anyone who wants to borrow from you."

- To this day, the tit-for-tat law, *lex talionis,* is seen as a sensible custom across many cultures, but Jesus raises us beyond it.
- Nowhere is he more radical than here: challenging us to accept attacks and insults without resentment and to respond with love. Can I rise to the challenge?

Tuesday 16th June **Matthew 5:43–48**

Jesus said to the crowds, "You have heard that it was said, 'You shall love your neighbor and hate your enemy.' But I say to you, Love your enemies, and pray for those who persecute you so that you may be children of your Father in heaven; for he makes his sun rise on the evil and on the good and sends rain on the righteous and on the unrighteous. For if you love those who love you, what reward do you have? Do not even the tax collectors do the same? And if you greet only your brothers and sisters, what more are you doing than others? Do not even the Gentiles do the same? Be perfect, therefore, as your heavenly Father is perfect."

- Jesus is laying down a marker for personal relationships.
- Here is the apex of Christianity: to strive to be godlike in our dealings even with those we dislike; wishing them well, praying for them, refusing to indulge feelings of hatred or resentment.

Wednesday 17th June **Matthew 6:5–6**

Jesus said to the disciples, "Whenever you pray, do not be like the hypocrites; for they love to stand and pray in the synagogues and at the street corners, so that they may be seen by others. Truly I tell you, they have received their reward. But whenever you pray, go into your room and shut the door and pray to your Father who is in secret; and your Father who sees in secret will reward you."

- Lord, when you teach how to pray, I listen hard.
- This is the first lesson: to pray privately, with no ostentation. God is closer than the ear to the lips: no need to shout or advertise. You read my heart, Lord, and when I pray I get a glimpse of it too.

Thursday 18th June **Matthew 6:7–13**

Jesus said to the crowds, "When you are praying, do not heap up empty phrases as the Gentiles do; for they think that they will be heard because of their many words. Do not be like them, for your Father knows what you need before you ask him. "Pray then in this way: Our Father in heaven, hallowed be your name. Your kingdom come. Your will be done, on earth as it is in heaven. Give us this day our daily bread. And forgive us our debts, as we also have forgiven our debtors. And do not bring us to the time of trial, but rescue us from the evil one."

- I hear you, Lord. Forms of prayer do not matter. I do not need many words—you know what I need.
- But if I am to speak to you, I need peace in my heart, or at least a desire to be at peace with all I know and to forgive.

Friday 19th June,
Feast of the Sacred Heart **Ephesians 3:14–19**

For this reason I bow my knees before the Father, from whom every family in heaven and on earth takes its name. I pray that, according to the riches of his glory, he may grant that you may be strengthened in your inner being with power through his Spirit, and that Christ may dwell in your hearts through faith, as you are being rooted and grounded in love. I pray that you may have the power to comprehend, with all the saints, what is the breadth and length and height and depth, and to know the love of Christ that surpasses knowledge, so that you may be filled with all the fullness of God.

- "I pray . . . that Christ may dwell in your hearts through faith." The invitation we receive is to be "rooted and grounded in love" so that we grow into "fullness of God."

- Let me take my time to pray this prayer, to begin to immerse myself in the love of Christ "that surpasses all knowledge."
- God is with me.

Saturday 20th June,
Immaculate Heart of Mary **Luke 2:48–51**

When his parents saw him they were astonished; and his mother said to him, "Child, why have you treated us like this? Look, your father and I have been searching for you in great anxiety." He said to them, "Why were you searching for me? Did you not know that I must be in my Father's house?" But they did not understand what he said to them. Then he went down with them and came to Nazareth and was obedient to them. His mother treasured all these things in her heart.

- This is a tense encounter. Mary, the protective mother, is reproachful. Jesus, on the cusp of adolescence, protests, "Stop worrying. I'm old enough to look after myself."
- Lord, as I watch, I pray for parents who are trying to temper protectiveness with trust and for adolescents who are impatient to grow.

june 21–27

Something to think and pray about each day this week:

A Change in Direction

In the northern hemisphere, this week begins with the longest day of the year, a time to look backwards and forwards too; a central date, a pivotal point. On such a day, "halfway through life's journey," Dante started his *Divina Commedia* with the words, *Nel mezzo del camin di nostra vita*. ("How do I see my life, moving steadily upwards?") The Church placed the birth of John the Baptist at the northern mid-summer, when the days start to shorten, remembering his prayer: "Jesus must increase, and I must decrease." We see women and men who, while their senses grow blunter and their bodies slower, are steadily shedding their egos, growing in an openness to God, becoming more and more transparently a vessel of love.

The Presence of God

At any time of the day or night we can call on Jesus.
He is always waiting, listening for our call.
What a wonderful blessing.
No phone needed, no emails, just a whisper.

Freedom

Lord, grant me the grace to be free from the excesses of this life.
Let me not get caught up with the desire for wealth.
Keep my heart and mind free to love and serve you.

Consciousness

I exist in a web of relationships—links to nature, people, God.
I trace out these links, giving thanks for the life that flows through them.
Some links are twisted or broken: I may feel regret, anger, disappointment.
I pray for the gift of acceptance and forgiveness.

The Word

God speaks to each one of us individually. I need to listen to what he is saying to me. (Please turn to your scripture on the following pages. Inspiration points are there should you need them. When you are ready, return here to continue.)

Conversation

Remembering that I am still in God's presence,
I imagine Jesus himself standing or sitting beside me
and say whatever is on my mind, whatever is in my heart,
speaking as one friend to another.

Conclusion

Glory be to the Father, and to the Son, and to the Holy Spirit,
As it was in the beginning, is now and ever shall be,
World without end. Amen

Sunday 21st June,
Twelfth Sunday in Ordinary Time **Mark 4:35–41**

On that day, when evening had come, Jesus said to the disciples, "Let us go across to the other side." And leaving the crowd behind, they took him with them in the boat, just as he was. Other boats were with him. A great windstorm arose, and the waves beat into the boat, so that the boat was already being swamped. But he was in the stern, asleep on the cushion; and they woke him up and said to him, "Teacher, do you not care that we are perishing?" He woke up and rebuked the wind, and said to the sea, "Peace! Be still!" Then the wind ceased, and there was a dead calm. He said to them, "Why are you afraid? Have you still no faith?" And they were filled with great awe and said to one another, "Who then is this, that even the wind and the sea obey him?"

- Lord, I know no better proof of your health and strength than this scene. You had the gift of sleeping in any situation. You slept on the cushion in the stern while the waves were beating and almost swamping the boat.
- And when you awoke, you brought calm. To voyage with you is to voyage in peace even in a storm.

Monday 22nd June **Matthew 7:1–5**

Jesus said to the crowds, "Do not judge, so that you may not be judged. For with the judgment you make you will be judged, and the measure you give will be the measure you get. Why do you see the speck in your neighbor's eye, but do not notice the log in your own eye? Or how can you say to your neighbor, 'Let me take the speck out of your eye,' while the log is in your own eye? You hypocrite, first take the log out of your own eye, and then you will see clearly to take the speck out of your neighbor's eye."

- The thought of judgment makes me nervous, Lord: As I give, so will I receive.
- May I learn in time to see the log in my own eye, to temper my judgments with compassion for the other's situation, and to be generous as I would wish to receive your bounty.

Tuesday 23rd June **Matthew 7:6**

"Do not give what is holy to dogs; and do not throw your pearls before swine, or they will trample them under foot and turn and maul you."

- Most people can only understand what they are prepared to understand. They may respond to gospel talk with anger or contempt.
- Perhaps the only Christian message they can take in is that of a good life. As Helder Camara urged his catechists, "Watch how you live. Your lives may be the only gospel that others can understand."

Wednesday 24th June,
Birth of St. John the Baptist **Luke 1:57–66**

Now the time came for Elizabeth to give birth, and she bore a son. Her neighbors and relatives heard that the Lord had shown his great mercy to her, and they rejoiced with her. On the eighth day they came to circumcise the child, and they were going to name him Zechariah after his father. But his mother said, "No; he is to be called John." They said to her, "None of your relatives has this name." Then they began motioning to his father to find out what name he wanted to give him. He asked for a writing tablet and wrote, "His name is John." And all of them were amazed. Immediately his mouth was opened, and his tongue freed, and he began to speak, praising God. Fear came over all their neighbors, and all these things were talked about throughout the entire hill country of Judea. All who heard them pondered them and said, "What then will this child become?" For, indeed, the hand of the Lord was with him.

- Lord, that sense of promise must have attended my birth, too, as my family wondered what would I become. The hand of the Lord was with me, too.
- Thank you for keeping your hand upon me, even when I did not recognize it. Stay with me, even when I look away.

Thursday 25th June **Matthew 7:21–27**

Jesus said to his disciples, "Not everyone who says to me, 'Lord, Lord,' will enter the kingdom of heaven, but only the one who does the will of my Father in heaven. On that day many will say to me, 'Lord, Lord, did we not prophesy in your name, and cast out demons in your name, and do many deeds of power in your name?' Then I will declare to them, 'I never knew you; go away from me, you evildoers.' Everyone then who hears these words of mine and acts on them will be like a wise man who built his house on rock. The rain fell, the floods came, and the winds blew and beat on that house, but it did not fall because it had been founded on rock. And everyone who hears these words of mine and does not act on them will be like a foolish man who built his house on sand. The rain fell, and the floods came, and the winds blew and beat against that house, and it fell—and great was its fall!"

- Signs and wonders, and words about them, are not what God seeks from us. As we possess this planet and make it our own, our technology can do things that would once have seemed miraculous.
- What you, Lord, ask of me is a good life, hearing your words and acting on them: That is the solid foundation.

Friday 26th June **Matthew 8:1–3**

When Jesus had come down from the mountain, great crowds followed him; and there was a leper who came to him and knelt before him, saying, "Lord, if you choose, you can make me clean." He stretched out his hand and touched him, saying, "I do choose. Be made clean!" Immediately his leprosy was cleansed.

- The onlookers saw this leper as a man punished by God, an outsider without the right to speak, a person full of sin. Jesus "stretched out his hand and touched him" and spoke to him.
- St Francis of Assisi embraced a leper at the turning point of his conversion. "What before seemed bitter was changed into sweetness of body and soul," he said.
- What "leprosy" am I called to heal in my life? Lord, help me.

Saturday 27th June **Matthew 8:5–13**

When he entered Capernaum, a centurion came to him, appealing to him and saying, "Lord, my servant is lying at home paralyzed, in terrible distress." And he said to him, "I will come and cure him." The centurion answered, "Lord, I am not worthy to have you come under my roof; but only speak the word, and my servant will be healed. For I also am a man under authority, with soldiers under me; and I say to one, 'Go,' and he goes, and to another, 'Come,' and he comes, and to my slave, 'Do this,' and the slave does it." When Jesus heard him, he was amazed and said to those who followed him, "Truly I tell you, in no one in Israel have I found such faith. I tell you, many will come from east and west and will eat with Abraham and Isaac and Jacob in the kingdom of heaven, while the heirs of the kingdom will be thrown into the outer darkness, where there will be weeping and gnashing of teeth." And to the centurion Jesus said,

"Go; let it be done for you according to your faith." And the servant was healed in that hour.

- This centurion is saintly. He recognizes Jesus' authority and power over sickness such that he can cure at a distance. Though an officer of the occupying power, he respects the Jewish reluctance to enter a Gentile's house.
- Most astonishing of all, though a slave was simply a piece of property with no legal rights, the centurion loves his slave and begs a favor for him. It was enough to amaze Jesus.

june 28–july 4

Something to think and pray about each day this week:

God's Children

The Old Testament tradition was not exactly child-centered: "The stick and the reprimand bestow wisdom . . . Correct your son and he will delight your soul." (Prv 29). The Gospels (Mt 18: 1-10; Mk 9: 35-37) give us a precious glimpse of how Jesus related to children. He gave them time and touch and urged the disciples: "Change, and become like little children." Why is theirs the kingdom of heaven? Perhaps because of their sense of wonder, their readiness to be unnoticed, their acceptance of dependence on those who love them. They know what it is to be told off, corrected, punished—and mostly take it in their stride. They are constantly challenged in learning, ready to tackle more new things; they know they have a future and look forward to it. Thank God for children.

The Presence of God
God is with me, but more,
God is within me, giving me existence.
Let me dwell for a moment on God's life-giving presence
in my body, my mind, my heart,
and in the whole of my life.

Freedom
God is not foreign to my freedom.
Instead the Spirit breathes life into my most intimate desires,
gently nudging me toward all that is good.
I ask for the grace to let myself be enfolded by the Spirit.

Consciousness
How am I really feeling? Light-hearted? Heavy-hearted?
I may be very much at peace, happy to be here.
Equally, I may be frustrated, worried or angry.
I acknowledge how I really am. It is the real me that the Lord loves.

The Word
I read the Word of God slowly, a few times over, and I listen to what God is saying to me. (Please turn to your scripture on the following pages. Inspiration points are there should you need them. When you are ready, return here to continue.)

Conversation
How has God's Word moved me? Has it left me cold?
Has it consoled me or moved me to act in a new way?
I imagine Jesus standing or sitting beside me,
I turn and share my feelings with him.

Conclusion
Glory be to the Father, and to the Son, and to the Holy Spirit,
As it was in the beginning, is now and ever shall be,
World without end. Amen

Sunday 28th June, Thirteenth Sunday in Ordinary Time **Mark 5:25–30, 33, 34**

Now there was a woman who had been suffering from hemorrhages for twelve years. She had endured much under many physicians, and had spent all that she had; and she was no better, but rather grew worse. She had heard about Jesus, and came up behind him in the crowd and touched his cloak, for she said, "If I but touch his clothes, I will be made well." Immediately her hemorrhage stopped; and she felt in her body that she was healed of her disease. Immediately aware that power had gone forth from him, Jesus turned about in the crowd and said, "Who touched my clothes?" But the woman, knowing what had happened to her, came in fear and trembling, fell down before him, and told him the whole truth. He said to her, "Daughter, your faith has made you well; go in peace, and be healed of your disease."

- Jesus was being pushed from all sides, but he could distinguish between the anonymous jostling of bodies in a crowd, and the visceral desire for healing in the touch of the ailing woman.
- His healing action was never magical or impersonal. It cost him, for it was empowered by prayer, fasting, and a personal affection for those he cured.

Monday 29th June, Sts. Peter & Paul **Matthew 16:13-19**

Now when Jesus came into the district of Caesarea Philippi, he asked his disciples, "Who do people say that the Son of Man is?" And they said, "Some say John the Baptist, but others Elijah, and still others Jeremiah or one of the prophets." He said to them, "But who do you say that I am?" Simon Peter answered, "You are the Messiah, the Son of the living God." And Jesus answered him, "Blessed are you, Simon son of Jonah! For flesh and blood has not revealed this to you, but my Father in heaven. And I tell you, you are Peter, and on this rock I will build my church, and the gates of Hades will not prevail against it. I will give you the keys of the kingdom of heaven, and whatever you bind on earth will be bound in heaven, and whatever you loose on earth will be loosed in heaven."

- As I read these seminal verses, I pray to have the faith of Peter, who, despite his failings, was the rock on whom the early Christians leaned.
- I look at Jesus and seek words to express what he means to me, and I open my heart to God's revelation.

Tuesday 30th June **Matthew 8:23–27**

And when Jesus got into the boat, his disciples followed him. A windstorm arose on the sea, so great that the boat was being swamped by the waves; but he was asleep. And they went and woke him up, saying, "Lord, save us! We are perishing!" And he said to them, "Why are you afraid, you of little faith?" Then he got up and rebuked the winds and the sea; and there was a dead calm. They were amazed, saying, "What sort of man is this, that even the winds and the sea obey him?"

- "He was asleep." As the mystic Meister Eckhart wrote, "There is nothing so much like God as silence." Silence is the source of creation; the Word proceeds from the silence of the Father.
- Do I feel that God is silent in my life when I feel buffeted by life's struggles? Does this silence frighten me?
- Lord, teach me to embrace your silence.

Wednesday 1st July **Matthew 8:28–34**

When he came to the other side, to the country of the Gadarenes, two demoniacs coming out of the tombs met him.

They were so fierce that no one could pass that way. Suddenly they shouted, "What have you to do with us, Son of God? Have you come here to torment us before the time?" Now a large herd of swine was feeding at some distance from them. The demons begged him, "If you cast us out, send us into the herd of swine." And he said to them, "Go!" So they came out and entered the swine; and suddenly, the whole herd rushed down the steep bank into the sea and perished in the water. The swineherds ran off, and on going into the town, they told the whole story about what had happened to the demoniacs. Then the whole town came out to meet Jesus; and when they saw him, they begged him to leave their neighborhood.

- Lord, at times I have been afraid of mad or paranoid people who behave strangely and unpredictably. You did not fear these naked demoniacs. They feared you.
- In you I feel a strength that can withstand and master whatever evil is in the world. The sad note at the end is that the locals also feared a man who had such courage; they did not want him around.
- I wonder about my own worth when I meet exceptional people. Do I shy away from their company?

Thursday 2nd July **Matthew 9:1–8**

And after getting into a boat he crossed the water and came to his own town. And just then some people were carrying a paralyzed man lying on a bed. When Jesus saw their faith, he said to the paralytic, "Take heart, son; your sins are forgiven." Then some of the scribes said to themselves, "This man is blaspheming." But Jesus, perceiving their thoughts, said, "Why do you think evil in your hearts? For which is easier, to say, 'Your sins are forgiven,' or to say, 'Stand up and walk'? But so that you may know that the Son of Man has authority on earth to forgive sins"—he then said to the paralytic—"Stand up, take your bed and go to your home." And he stood up and went to his home. When the crowds saw it, they were filled with awe, and they glorified God, who had given such authority to human beings.

- Jesus' act of forgiveness was part of the healing. For the Jews, sickness was closely linked with sin and could not be cured until sins were forgiven.
- Jesus sensed some unresolved wrongness in the paralytic's heart; because he felt God was his enemy, he was paralyzed. Jesus' words enabled him to say "yes" to life.
- Lord, I know that you delight in me and count me as your friend. Grant me joy in this body and in the life that I live.

Friday 3rd July, St. Thomas, Apostle **John 20:24–29**

But Thomas (who was called the Twin), one of the twelve, was not with them when Jesus came. So the other disciples told him, "We have seen the Lord." But he said to them, "Unless I see the mark of the nails in his hands and put my finger in the mark of the nails and my hand in his side, I will not believe." A week later his disciples were again in the house, and Thomas was with them. Although the doors were shut, Jesus came and stood among them and said, "Peace be with you." Then he said to Thomas, "Put your finger here and see my hands. Reach out your hand and put it in my side. Do not doubt, but believe." Thomas answered him, "My Lord and my God!" Jesus said to him, "Have you believed because you have seen me? Blessed are those who have not seen and yet have come to believe."

- We can imagine the tension in the group as Thomas implied that the disciples were imagining things.
- A week later Jesus appears to them and wishes "Peace" on the whole company. Suddenly the tensions and irritations in the group

appear silly and irrelevant. In the light of Jesus' love, quarrels make no sense. Jesus picks out Thomas and answers his question by guiding his hand into the wounds in his body.

- Thank you, Lord, for the skepticism of Thomas, which led to your blessing on all of us who seek you, who have not seen and yet believe.

Saturday 4th July **Matthew 9:14–15**

Then the disciples of John came to him, saying, "Why do we and the Pharisees fast often, but your disciples do not fast?" And Jesus said to them, "The wedding guests cannot mourn as long as the bridegroom is with them, can they? The days will come when the bridegroom is taken away from them, and then they will fast."

- Lord, when I sense how John's disciples viewed you, I feel relieved. John the Baptist was admirable, but you are my model, and you were seen as a man given to joy and celebration.
- People were high-spirited in your company, as at a wedding feast. The feast would not last forever—you had no illusions and would not encourage illusions. But long faces do not suit your companions.

july 5–11

Something to think and pray about each day this week:

Growing in Faith

The mark of childhood on our faith is deep and pervasive. The prayers we say—even Jesus' prayer on the cross as he died—are largely those we learned as children, when we may have been introduced to Christ and his mother and the saints in a way that has endured. We can learn, as Jesus urged us to learn, from children's innocence and sense of wonder. But the Gospels are essentially for adults, not children; and even adults do not easily find language apt to convey a religion or spirit of truth. As our faith matures, we learn to live with the mystery of suffering and evil; and we learn the limits of our knowledge of God. Augustine put it starkly: "God is not what you imagine or think you understand. If you understand him, you have failed." Has my faith grown with my years of experience and prayer?

The Presence of God
To be present is to arrive as one is and open up to the other.
At this instant, as I arrive here, God is present waiting for me.
God always arrives before me, desiring to connect with me
even more than my most intimate friend.
I take a moment and greet my loving God.

Freedom
Everything has the potential to draw forth from me a fuller love and life.
Yet my desires are often fixed, caught, on illusions of fulfillment.
I ask that God, through my freedom, may orchestrate
my desires in a vibrant loving melody rich in harmony.

Consciousness
Knowing that God loves me unconditionally,
I can afford to be honest about how I am.
How has the last day been, and how do I feel now?
I share my feelings openly with the Lord.

The Word
I take my time to read the Word of God slowly a few times, allowing myself to dwell on anything that strikes me. (Please turn to your scripture on the following pages. Inspiration points are there should you need them. When you are ready, return here to continue.)

Conversation
What feelings are rising in me
as I pray and reflect on God's Word?
I imagine Jesus himself sitting or standing beside me
and open my heart to him.

Conclusion
Glory be to the Father, and to the Son, and to the Holy Spirit,
As it was in the beginning, is now and ever shall be,
World without end. Amen

Sunday 5th July,
Fourteenth Sunday in Ordinary Time **Mark 6:1–6**

Jesus left that place and came to his hometown, and his disciples followed him. On the sabbath he began to teach in the synagogue, and many who heard him were astounded. They said, "Where did this man get all this? What is this wisdom that has been given to him? What deeds of power are being done by his hands! Is not this the carpenter, the son of Mary and brother of James and Joses and Judas and Simon, and are not his sisters here with us?" And they took offense at him. Then Jesus said to them, "Prophets are not without honor, except in their hometown, and among their own kin, and in their own house." And he could do no deed of power there, except that he laid his hands on a few sick people and cured them. And he was amazed at their unbelief. Then he went about among the villages teaching.

- Jesus is a prophet in his own country, undervalued, talked down. Am I guilty of this sort of undervaluing? You go to a party to honor a person in your family or someone you work with. Suddenly the tributes show how strangers love and admire her (or him) in a way you would never have suspected. You see that person with fresh eyes.
- The fact that I know someone's family and history can blind me to the depths and dreams that make that person precious to others.

Monday 6th July **Genesis 28:10–17**

Jacob left Beer-sheba and went towards Haran. He came to a certain place and stayed there for the night because the sun had set. Taking one of the stones of the place, he put it under his head and lay down in that place. And he dreamed that there was a ladder set up on the earth, the top of it reaching to heaven; and the angels of God were ascending and descending on it. And the LORD stood beside him and said, "I am the LORD, the God of Abraham your father and the God of Isaac; the land on which you lie I will give to you and to your offspring; and your offspring shall be like the dust of the earth, and you shall spread abroad to the west and to the east and to the north and to the south; and all the families of the earth shall be blessed in you and in your offspring. Know that I am with you and will keep you wherever you go and will bring you back to this land; for I will not leave you until I have done what I have promised you." Then Jacob woke from his sleep and said, "Surely the LORD is in this place—and I did not know it!" And he was afraid, and said, "How awesome is this place! This is none other than the house of God, and this is the gate of heaven."

- That vision of a ladder touches me, Lord, especially when I am low. I look for a short-cut to a happier place and friendly angels to escort me. But Jacob wakes up and realizes: "This is the holy place. The Lord is here—and I did not know it."
- Help me to recognize you in the here and now.

Tuesday 7th July **Matthew 9:36–38**

When Jesus saw the crowds, he had compassion for them, because they were harassed and helpless, like sheep without a shepherd. Then he said to his disciples, "The harvest is plentiful, but the laborers are few; therefore ask the Lord of the harvest to send out laborers into his harvest."

- How do I see the crowds? Do I focus on their violence or mindless greed? But so many are like sheep without a shepherd, without direction.
- I am often like that myself. They call for compassion, as I do.

Wednesday 8th July **Matthew 10:1–7**

Then Jesus summoned his twelve disciples and gave them authority over unclean spirits, to cast them out, and to cure every disease and every sickness. These are the names of the twelve apostles: first, Simon, also known as Peter, and his brother Andrew; James son of Zebedee, and his brother John; Philip and Bartholomew; Thomas and Matthew the tax collector; James son of Alphaeus, and Thaddaeus; Simon the Cananaean, and Judas Iscariot, the one who betrayed him. These twelve Jesus sent out with the following instructions: "Go nowhere among the Gentiles, and enter no town of the Samaritans, but go rather to the lost sheep of the house of Israel. As you go, proclaim the good news, 'The kingdom of heaven has come near.'"

- You called the apostles by name, Lord, and you call me too: Julie or Helen, Tim or John. You have a mission for me, too. To be your follower is to bring good news, to lift the spirits of those I meet.
- Help me, Lord, to be a source of blessings, to leave others more contented and hopeful than I found them.

Thursday 9th July **Matthew 10:7–10**

As you go, proclaim the good news, "The kingdom of heaven has come near." Cure the sick, raise the dead, cleanse the lepers, cast out demons. You received without payment; give without payment. Take no gold, or silver, or copper in your belts, no bag for your journey, or two tunics, or sandals, or a staff; for laborers deserve their food.

- "Cure the sick," you say, Lord. The Greek word for sick, *astheneis*, means "without strength." You ask us to give one another energy and purpose, to make life worth living.
- The kingdom of God is here among us, in the person of Jesus, and in the life of those whom he touches. They move away from the

false gods of silver and gold, bags for the journey and unnecessary clothes, and find the freedom and strength to live their lives by love.

Friday 10th July **Matthew 10:16–23**

"See, I am sending you out like sheep into the midst of wolves; so be wise as serpents and innocent as doves. Beware of them, for they will hand you over to councils and flog you in their synagogues; and you will be dragged before governors and kings because of me, as a testimony to them and the Gentiles. When they hand you over, do not worry about how you are to speak or what you are to say; for what you are to say will be given to you at that time; for it is not you who speak, but the Spirit of your Father speaking through you. Brother will betray brother to death, and a father his child, and children will rise against parents and have them put to death; and you will be hated by all because of my name. But the one who endures to the end will be saved. When they persecute you in one town, flee to the next; for truly I tell you, you will not have gone through all the towns of Israel before the Son of Man comes."

- You are not trying to lure me with sweet promises, Lord. You guarantee persecution and hatred to those who follow you. You do not try to seduce us, as advertisers do, with promises of pleasure and success.
- If we are true to you, we will meet opposition and worse. Freedom from criticism belongs only to the bland and spineless who say and do nothing and keep their heads below the parapet.

Saturday 11th July, St. Benedict **Matthew 19:27–29**

Then Peter said in reply, "Look, we have left everything and followed you. What then will we have?" Jesus said to them, "Truly I tell you, at the renewal of all things, when the Son of

Man is seated on the throne of his glory, you who have followed me will also sit on twelve thrones, judging the twelve tribes of Israel. And everyone who has left houses or brothers or sisters or father or mother or children or fields, for my name's sake, will receive a hundredfold and will inherit eternal life."

- "What is in it for us?" asks the pragmatic Peter. Not the most pious of questions, but Jesus gives a full answer: a hundredfold here below, followed by eternal life.
- There are times when I need that light at the end of what seems a tunnel.

july 12–18

Something to think and pray about each day this week:

The Story of God's Family

For most of the human race our feeling of personal security grows within the family, which is normally a safe place, able to absorb hurts and heal them without judging. The Bible is a book about the family, God's family. It is not about getting it right all the time and being upstanding and perfect, but about forgiving and being a base to which members return, a secure setting in which they can rebel, relax, and find their own identity. Each generation is a new phenomenon, unlike its predecessor, and usually a worry to parents. The people of God do not create an oasis of perfect living, but rather a real home, the one place that all can come back to without fear of rejection. Jesus' strongest metaphor for God was as father of the prodigal son, trying to hold the law-abiding big brother and the crazy prodigal together in the one household.

The Presence of God
What is present to me is what has a hold on my becoming.
I reflect on the presence of God always there in love,
amidst the many things that have a hold on me.
I pause and pray that I may let God
affect my becoming in this precise moment.

Freedom
There are very few people
who realize what God would make of them
if they abandoned themselves into his hands,
and let themselves be formed by his grace. (St Ignatius)
I ask for the grace to trust myself totally to God's love.

Consciousness
In the presence of my loving Creator,
I look honestly at my feelings over the last day,
the highs, the lows, and the level ground.
Can I see where the Lord has been present?

The Word
God speaks to each one of us individually. I need to listen to what he is saying to me. (Please turn to your scripture on the following pages. Inspiration points are there should you need them. When you are ready, return here to continue.)

Conversation
What is stirring in me as I pray?
Am I consoled, troubled, left cold?
I imagine Jesus himself standing or sitting at my side
and share my feelings with him.

Conclusion
Glory be to the Father, and to the Son, and to the Holy Spirit,
As it was in the beginning, is now and ever shall be,
World without end. Amen

Sunday 12th July,
Fifteenth Sunday in Ordinary Time **Mark 6:7–13**

Jesus called the twelve and began to send them out two by two and gave them authority over the unclean spirits. He ordered them to take nothing for their journey except a staff; no bread, no bag, no money in their belts; but to wear sandals and not to put on two tunics. He said to them, "Wherever you enter a house, stay there until you leave the place. If any place will not welcome you and they refuse to hear you, as you leave, shake off the dust that is on your feet as a testimony against them." So they went out and proclaimed that all should repent. They cast out many demons and anointed with oil many who were sick and cured them.

- Lord, you warned the twelve against carrying anything they did not need. They were to be counter-witnesses to possessiveness, retail therapy, and the consumerism to which advertisements propel us. The more we have, the less we are.
- The greatest treasure that the twelve carried with them was the good news of Jesus.

Monday 13th July **Matthew 10:34–39**

Jesus said to his disciples, "Do not think that I have come to bring peace to the earth; I have not come to bring peace, but a sword. For I have come to set a man against his father, and a daughter against her mother, and a daughter-in-law against her mother-in-law; and one's foes will be members of one's own household. Whoever loves father or mother more than me is not worthy of me; and whoever loves son or daughter more than me is not worthy of me; and whoever does not take up the cross and follow me is not worthy of me. Those who find their life will lose it, and those who lose their life for my sake will find it."

- This fills me with dread. I hate to think of my Christianity dividing me from my family. Yet I can see that there are times when a stark choice is called for.
- Am I ready for it? Give me wisdom and strength, Lord.

Tuesday 14th July **Matthew 11:20–21**

Then Jesus began to reproach the cities in which most of his deeds of power had been done, because they did not repent. "Woe to you, Chorazin! Woe to you, Bethsaida! For if the deeds of power done in you had been done in Tyre and Sidon, they would have repented long ago in sackcloth and ashes."

- Let me hear the tone of your voice here, Lord. Your word for "woe" is not one of anger so much as of heartbroken sorrow and pity that your people had disregarded their opportunity. I need this model as I see the tragedies in my world and the apparent triumph of evil in some places.
- Can I keep my heart open, as you did, to suffering rather than anger?

Wednesday 15th July **Matthew 11:25–27**

At that time Jesus said, "I thank you, Father, Lord of heaven and earth, because you have hidden these things from the wise and the intelligent and have revealed them to infants; yes, Father, for such was your gracious will. All things have been handed over to me by my Father; and no one knows the Son except the Father, and no one knows the Father except the Son and anyone to whom the Son chooses to reveal him."

- Lord, it is not cleverness that you excluded—you were the cleverest—but intellectual pride that excludes the simple heart from decisions. The heart, not the head, is the home of the gospel.
- Is my heart simple enough to accept the revelation of your goodness?

Thursday 16th July **Matthew 11:28–30**

Jesus said, "Come to me, all you that are weary and are carrying heavy burdens, and I will give you rest. Take my yoke upon you, and learn from me; for I am gentle and humble in heart, and you will find rest for your souls. For my yoke is easy, and my burden is light."

- "Can one reach God by toil?" asked Yeats. "He gives himself to the pure in heart. He asks nothing but our attention."
- Do I feel your yoke as easy and well-fitting, Lord? If I feel it as a burden, then it is not your yoke I am carrying.

Friday 17th July **Matthew 12:1–8**

At that time Jesus went through the grainfields on the sabbath; his disciples were hungry, and they began to pluck heads of grain and to eat. When the Pharisees saw it, they said to him, "Look, your disciples are doing what is not lawful to do on the sabbath." He said to them, "Have you not read what David did when he and his companions were hungry? He entered the house of God and ate the bread of the Presence, which it was not lawful for him or his companions to eat, but only for the priests. Or have you not read in the law that on the sabbath the priests in the temple break the sabbath and yet are guiltless? I tell you, something greater than the temple is here. But if you had known what this means, 'I desire mercy and not sacrifice,' you would not have condemned the guiltless. For the Son of Man is lord of the sabbath."

- Mark, recounting this same incident, quotes Jesus, "The sabbath was made for man, not man for the sabbath."
- Lord, the danger with me is that I forget what the sabbath is for, forget what it means to keep it holy, forget the joy of resting on

the seventh day. The sabbath was made for us as a bonus, not a burden.

Saturday 18th July **Matthew 12:14–21**

But the Pharisees went out and conspired against him, how to destroy him. When Jesus became aware of this, he departed. Many crowds followed him, and he cured all of them, and he ordered them not to make him known. This was to fulfill what had been spoken through the prophet Isaiah: "Here is my servant, whom I have chosen, my beloved, with whom my soul is well pleased. I will put my Spirit upon him, and he will proclaim justice to the Gentiles. He will not wrangle or cry aloud, nor will anyone hear his voice in the streets. He will not break a bruised reed or quench a smoldering wick until he brings justice to victory. And in his name the Gentiles will hope."

- Have I anything of your spirit, Lord? You bid me be persistent in my pursuit of justice, yet not noisy, or contentious, or violent. That is the sort of spirit that inspires hope in others.

july 19–25

Something to think and pray about each day this week:

Revolutionary Freedom

The adult Christ is hardly intelligible to children before adolescence. But for teenagers he incarnates the highest values of all: freedom and love. As he appears in the gospel he is the freest of people: unpredictable and alarming the respectable; a shocking, revolutionary figure whom society eventually found too dangerous and had to put away; a tender and compassionate figure, reacting warmly and spontaneously to all he met; a strong and frightening figure, contemptuous of petty regulations, but open to everything living, ready to change the world. Above all, he was a man of supreme interior freedom, not driven by unconscious needs, pressures or anxieties, but doing what he wanted to do, his Father's business. He was the only person who realized fully all that a parent can mean to a child: not merely Law, but the model and the promise of an independent free existence.

The Presence of God
Jesus waits silent and unseen to come into my heart.
I will respond to His call.
He comes with His infinite power and love.
May I be filled with joy in His presence.

Freedom
A thick and shapeless tree-trunk would never believe
that it could become a statue, admired as a miracle of sculpture,
and would never submit itself to the chisel of the sculptor,
who sees by her genius what she can make of it. (St Ignatius)
I ask for the grace to let myself be shaped by my loving Creator.

Consciousness
Knowing that God loves me unconditionally,
I look honestly over the last day, its events and my feelings.
Do I have something to be grateful for? Then I give thanks.
Is there something I am sorry for? Then I ask forgiveness.

The Word
I read the Word of God slowly a few times over, and I listen to what God is saying to me. (Please turn to your scripture on the following pages. Inspiration points are there should you need them. When you are ready, return here to continue.)

Conversation
Do I notice myself reacting as I pray with the Word of God?
Do I feel challenged, comforted, angry?
Imagining Jesus sitting or standing by me
I speak out my feelings as one trusted friend to another.

Conclusion
Glory be to the Father, and to the Son, and to the Holy Spirit,
As it was in the beginning, is now and ever shall be,
World without end. Amen

Sunday 19th July,
Sixteenth Sunday in Ordinary Time **Mark 6:30–34**

The apostles gathered around Jesus, and told him all that they had done and taught. He said to them, "Come away to a deserted place all by yourselves and rest a while." For many were coming and going, and they had no leisure even to eat. And they went away in the boat to a deserted place by themselves. Now many saw them going and recognized them, and they hurried there on foot from all the towns and arrived ahead of them. As he went ashore, he saw a great crowd; and he had compassion for them, because they were like sheep without a shepherd; and he began to teach them many things.

- As you open this page or click into *Sacred Space* online, you are answering Jesus' invitation to come away to a deserted place and rest a while.
- Do not be afraid of being alone. Fear rather the opposite: as Pascal wrote, "The sole cause of man's unhappiness is that he does not know how to stay quietly in his room."
- Jesus allowed the crowds to surround him and draw comfort from him; but to refresh his own strength, he retreated alone into communion with his heavenly Father.

Monday 20th July **Matthew 12:38–42**

Then some of the scribes and Pharisees said to him, "Teacher, we wish to see a sign from you." But he answered them, "An evil and adulterous generation asks for a sign, but no sign will be given to it except the sign of the prophet Jonah. For just as Jonah was three days and three nights in the belly of the sea monster, so for three days and three nights the Son of Man will be in the heart of the earth. The people of Nineveh will rise up at the judgment with this generation and condemn it because they repented at the proclamation of Jonah, and see, something greater than Jonah is here! The queen of the South will rise up at the judgment with this generation and condemn it because she came from the ends of the earth to listen to the wisdom of Solomon, and see, something greater than Solomon is here!

- If I were a Pharisee and I met this wandering healer-prophet, perhaps I would ask for a sign too. Many Christians look for signs: miracles, voices from heaven, Mary's image on rose petals, a bleeding stigmata. Jesus points us away from spectacular signs.
- It is our faith in the person of Jesus that keeps us going. He points these Jewish men to the faith and perceptiveness of women and Gentiles.

Tuesday 21st July **Matthew 12:46–50**

While he was still speaking to the crowds, his mother and his brothers were standing outside, wanting to speak to him. Someone told him, "Look, your mother and your brothers are standing outside, wanting to speak to you." But to the one who had told him this, Jesus replied, "Who is my mother, and who are my brothers?" And pointing to his disciples, he said, "Here are my mother and my brothers! For whoever does the will of my Father in heaven is my brother and sister and mother."

- Am I one of your family, Lord? Would you include me in your gesture, as one who does the will of our Father in heaven and thus is your sister or brother?

Wednesday 22nd July, St. Mary Magdalene **John 20:11–18**

But Mary stood weeping outside the tomb. As she wept, she bent over to look into the tomb; and she saw two angels in white, sitting where the body of Jesus had been lying, one at the head and the other at the feet. They said to her, "Woman, why are you weeping?" She said to them, "They have taken away my Lord, and I do not know where they have laid him." When she had said this, she turned around and saw Jesus standing there, but she did not know that it was Jesus. Jesus said to her, "Woman, why are you weeping? Whom are you looking for?" Supposing him to be the gardener, she said to him, "Sir, if you have carried him away, tell me where you have laid him, and I will take him away." Jesus said to her, "Mary!" She turned and said to him in Hebrew, "Rabbouni!" (which means Teacher). Jesus said to her, "Do not hold on to me, because I have not yet ascended to the Father. But go to my brothers and say to them, 'I am ascending to my Father and your Father, to my God and your God.'" Mary Magdalene went and announced to the disciples, "I have seen the Lord"; and she told them that he had said these things to her.

- Mary was entrusted with the joyful news of Jesus' resurrection; she went and announced, "I have seen the Lord." She was the first to proclaim the risen Christ.
- Do I hold to myself the good news of Jesus? How do I proclaim the risen Christ?

Thursday 23rd July, St. Bridget **John 15:1–8**

"I am the true vine, and my Father is the vine-grower. He removes every branch in me that bears no fruit. Every branch that bears fruit he prunes to make it bear more fruit. You have already been cleansed by the word that I have spoken to you. Abide in me as I abide in you. Just as the branch cannot bear fruit by itself unless it abides in the vine, neither can you unless you abide in me. I am the vine, you are the branches. Those who abide in me and I in them bear much fruit, because apart from me you can do nothing. Whoever does not abide in me is thrown away like a branch and withers; such branches are gathered, thrown into the fire, and burned. If you abide in me, and my words abide in you, ask for whatever you wish, and it will be done for you. My Father is glorified by this, that you bear much fruit and become my disciples."

- How do I abide in the Lord?
- It is above all by prayer and by raising my heart and mind to God each morning. There is a worldwide community that uses *Sacred Space* as a way of abiding in Jesus and drawing strength from him.

Friday 24th July **Matthew 13:18–23**

"Hear then the parable of the sower. When anyone hears the word of the kingdom and does not understand it, the evil one comes and snatches away what is sown in the heart; this is what was sown on the path. As for what was sown on rocky ground, this is the one who hears the word and immediately receives it with joy; yet such a person has no root, but endures only for a while, and when trouble or persecution arises on account of the word, that person immediately falls away. As for what was sown among thorns, this is the one who hears the word, but the cares of the world and the lure of wealth choke the word, and it yields nothing. But as for what was sown on good soil, this is the one who hears the word and understands it, who indeed bears fruit and yields, in one case a hundredfold, in another sixty, and in another thirty."

- Teachers have been compared to springtime workers, sweating to harrow the ground and sow the seed, but seldom seeing the harvest; most of the time made to feel they are unprofitable servants.
- If this is true of teachers, it is true of much of the good that we do. Thank you, Lord, for this consoling parable. It is God, not me, that makes the seed grow; enough for me to labor and be patient.

Saturday 25th July,
St. James, Apostle **2 Corinthians 4:11–15**

For while we live, we are always being given up to death for Jesus' sake, so that the life of Jesus may be made visible in our mortal flesh. So death is at work in us, but life in you. But just as we have the same spirit of faith that is in accordance with scripture—"I believed, and so I spoke"—we also believe, and so we speak, because we know that the one who raised the Lord Jesus will raise us also with Jesus, and will bring us with you into his presence. Yes, everything is for your sake, so that grace, as it extends to more and more people, may increase thanksgiving, to the glory of God.

- Paul writes with great, sustaining optimism that his suffering is rooted in faith, faith in his own resurrection and that of those who follow Jesus—"Because we know that the one who raised the Lord Jesus will raise us also."
- Lord, teach me to give thanks for this gift of optimism.

july 26–august 1

Something to think and pray about each day this week:

God's Pupil

Ignatius Loyola spent the best of his energies on teaching people to pray. Before his conversion, his idea of prayer was reciting Our Fathers and Hail Marys. When he started to read the scriptures, he found that God was talking to him, especially through the stories about Jesus. He wrote about it later, "God taught me like a schoolboy." As the years passed, his prayer became more wordless—so does the prayer of many Christians as they mature in their spiritual life. Ignatius had such an appetite for prayer—such heart-wrenching delight in it—that he had to ration himself because the tears of joy were affecting his sight. God was for him not a word but a touch. One of his friends recalled his going up to the roof of his house at night. "He would sit there quietly, absolutely quietly. He would take off his hat and look up for a long time at the sky . . . and the tears would begin to flow down his cheeks like a stream, but so quietly and so gently that you heard not a sob nor a sigh nor the least possible movement of his body."

The Presence of God
As I sit here, the beating of my heart,
the ebb and flow of my breathing, the movements of my mind
are all signs of God's ongoing creation of me.
I pause for a moment and become aware
of this presence of God within me.

Freedom
I ask for the grace
to let go of my own concerns
and be open to what God is asking of me,
to let myself be guided and formed by my loving Creator.

Consciousness
How do I find myself today?
Where am I with God? With others?
Do I have something to be grateful for? Then I give thanks.
Is there something I am sorry for? Then I ask forgiveness.

The Word
I take my time to read the Word of God slowly a few times, allowing myself to dwell on anything that strikes me. (Please turn to your scripture on the following pages. Inspiration points are there should you need them. When you are ready, return here to continue.)

Conversation
Remembering that I am still in God's presence,
I imagine Jesus himself standing or sitting beside me
and say whatever is on my mind, whatever is in my heart,
speaking as one friend to another.

Conclusion
Glory be to the Father, and to the Son, and to the Holy Spirit,
As it was in the beginning, is now and ever shall be,
World without end. Amen

Sunday 26th July,
Seventeenth Sunday in Ordinary Time **John 6:5–13**

When Jesus looked up and saw a large crowd coming toward him, he said to Philip, "Where are we to buy bread for these people to eat?" He said this to test him, for he himself knew what he was going to do. Philip answered him, "Six months' wages would not buy enough bread for each of them to get a little." One of his disciples, Andrew, Simon Peter's brother, said to him, "There is a boy here who has five barley loaves and two fish. But what are they among so many people?" Jesus said, "Make the people sit down." Now there was a great deal of grass in the place; so they sat down, about five thousand in all. Then Jesus took the loaves, and when he had given thanks, he distributed them to those who were seated; so also the fish, as much as they wanted. When they were satisfied, he told his disciples, "Gather up the fragments left over so that nothing may be lost." So they gathered them up, and from the fragments of the five barley loaves left by those who had eaten, they filled twelve baskets.

- The boy might well have stayed quiet about his little store of food, but he let Andrew know about it. What happened next touches me deeply. Jesus Christ needs what we can bring him; we may not have much to bring, but he needs what we have.
- If we hoard what we have, who knows what miracles may be stopped from happening?

Monday 27th July **Matthew 13:31–35**

Jesus put before them another parable: "The kingdom of heaven is like a mustard seed that someone took and sowed in his field; it is the smallest of all the seeds, but when it has grown it is the greatest of shrubs and becomes a tree so that the birds of the air come and make nests in its branches." He told them another parable: "The kingdom of heaven is like yeast that a woman took and mixed in with three measures of flour until all of it was leavened." Jesus told the crowds all these things in parables; without a parable he told them nothing. This was to fulfill what had been spoken through the prophet: "I will open my mouth to speak in parables; I will proclaim what has been hidden from the foundation of the world."

- These are the most comforting of parables because they show the kingdom of heaven as organic, with its own life-force: growing by trickling increment beyond all our expectations, inviting all sorts of birds onto its branches, and growing secretly like yeast in a loaf.

Tuesday 28th July **Matthew 13:36–43**

His disciples approached Jesus, saying, "Explain to us the parable of the weeds of the field." He answered, "The one who sows the good seed is the Son of Man; the field is the world, and the good seed are the children of the kingdom; the weeds are the children of the evil one, and the enemy who sowed them is the devil; the harvest is the end of the age, and the reapers are angels. Just as the weeds are collected and burned up with fire, so will it be at the end of the age. The Son of Man will send his angels, and they will collect out of his kingdom all causes of sin and all evildoers, and they will throw them into the furnace of fire, where there will be weeping and gnashing of teeth. Then the righteous will shine like the sun in the kingdom of their Father. Let anyone with ears listen!"

- The force of this parable, of the wheat and the weeds, hits us every day. It is about having patience with the persistence of evil in the world.

- We may face malicious vandalism, like the enemy who sowed weeds in his neighbor's field. In their early stages, the weeds looked like wheat, and you could not root up weeds without taking some wheat as well. So too some of the evils we face are dressed up to look respectable. We have to fight evil, but we need not give ourselves ulcers if we find that society remains far from perfect. The final judgment lies with God.

Wednesday 29th July, St. Martha **John 11:19–27**

Many of the Jews had come to Martha and Mary to console them about their brother. When Martha heard that Jesus was coming, she went and met him, while Mary stayed at home. Martha said to Jesus, "Lord, if you had been here, my brother would not have died. But even now I know that God will give you whatever you ask of him." Jesus said to her, "Your brother will rise again." Martha said to him, "I know that he will rise again in the resurrection on the last day." Jesus said to her, "I am the resurrection and the life. Those who believe in me, even though they die, will live, and everyone who lives and believes in me will never die. Do you believe this?" She said to him, "Yes, Lord, I believe that you are the Messiah, the Son of God, the one coming into the world."

- The Book of Common Prayer reminds us, "In the midst of life we are in death."
- Let me reflect on the words of the Welsh poet Dylan Thomas: "Though they sink through the sea they shall rise again; Though lovers be lost love shall not; Death shall have no dominion."

Thursday 30th July **Matthew 13:52**

Jesus said to them, "Therefore every scribe who has been trained for the kingdom of heaven is like the master of a household who brings out of his treasure what is new and what is old."

- This raises my heart, Lord: to bring out of my treasure new things and old. I do not have to abandon or reject the parts of my life that seem to have nothing to do with you, the people I have loved and lost, the seemingly irrelevant skills that were half-learned.
- All my past belongs in that treasure. It includes even the moments that seem sordid or horrible or selfish; these too have played their part in bringing me to where I am with you.

Friday 31st July, St. Ignatius Loyola **Luke 9:23–25**

Then Jesus said to the disciples, "If any want to become my followers, let them deny themselves and take up their cross daily and follow me. For those who want to save their life will lose it, and those who lose their life for my sake will save it. What does it profit them if they gain the whole world, but lose or forfeit themselves?"

- To deny myself—to reach a point where my self is no longer the most important thing in the world; to be able to take a back seat comfortably; to be happy to listen; to accept without resentment the diminishments that come to me through time or circumstances; to see your hand, Lord, in both the bright and dark places of my life.

Saturday 1st August **Matthew 14:1–12**

At that time Herod the ruler heard reports about Jesus; and he said to his servants, "This is John the Baptist; he has been raised from the dead, and for this reason these powers are at work in him." For Herod had arrested John, bound him, and put him in prison on account of Herodias, his brother Philip's wife, because John had been telling him, "It is not lawful for you to have her." Though Herod wanted to put him to death, he feared the crowd, because they regarded him as a prophet. But when Herod's birthday came, the daughter of Herodias danced before the company, and she pleased Herod so much that he promised on oath to grant her whatever she might ask. Prompted by her mother, she said, "Give me the head of John the Baptist here on a platter." The king was grieved, yet out of regard for his oaths and for the guests, he commanded it to be given; he sent and had John beheaded in the prison. The head was brought on a platter and given to the girl, who brought it to her mother. His disciples came and took the body and buried it; then they went and told Jesus.

- There are times when I am called to say something unpopular, even prophetic: to stand against a bully or intervene in malicious gossip. It will not bring me love. But it will show that I am salt that has not lost its savor.
- Give me courage when I need it, Lord.

august 2–8

Something to think and pray about each day this week:

Food for the Journey

In the Eucharist, we are obeying Jesus' command, "Do this in memory of me." While we are remembering the Last Supper, we think also of the last meal which we had with our family: the food and faces around the table, as well as the unplanned interruptions. Jesus looked with love at his friends around the table: "With desire I have desired to eat this meal with you before I suffer." Ask God to look on us with love, to accept us as we are with all our faults, just as we try to accept and love those who share our table.

The Presence of God
I pause for a moment
and reflect on God's life-giving presence
in every part of my body, in everything around me,
in the whole of my life.

Freedom
I ask for the grace to believe
in what I could be and do
if I only allowed God, my loving Creator,
to continue to create me, guide me, and shape me.

Consciousness
In God's loving presence I unwind the past day,
starting from now and looking back, moment by moment.
I gather in all the goodness and light, in gratitude.
I attend to the shadows and what they say to me,
seeking healing, courage, forgiveness.

The Word
God speaks to each one of us individually. I need to listen to what he is saying to me. (Please turn to your scripture on the following pages. Inspiration points are there should you need them. When you are ready, return here to continue.)

Conversation
How has God's Word moved me? Has it left me cold?
Has it consoled me or moved me to act in a new way?
I imagine Jesus standing or sitting beside me,
I turn and share my feelings with him.

Conclusion
Glory be to the Father, and to the Son, and to the Holy Spirit,
As it was in the beginning, is now and ever shall be,
World without end. Amen

Sunday 2nd August,
Eighteenth Sunday in Ordinary Time **John 6:26–34**

Jesus said to the crowd, "Very truly, I tell you, you are looking for me, not because you saw signs, but because you ate your fill of the loaves. Do not work for the food that perishes, but for the food that endures for eternal life, which the Son of Man will give you. For it is on him that God the Father has set his seal." Then they said to him, "What must we do to perform the works of God?" Jesus answered them, "This is the work of God, that you believe in him whom he has sent." So they said to him, "What sign are you going to give us then, so that we may see it and believe you? What work are you performing? Our ancestors ate the manna in the wilderness; as it is written, 'He gave them bread from heaven to eat.'" Then Jesus said to them, "Very truly, I tell you, it was not Moses who gave you the bread from heaven, but it is my Father who gives you the true bread from heaven. For the bread of God is that which comes down from heaven and gives life to the world." They said to him, "Sir, give us this bread always."

- "What sign are you going to give us then, so that we may see it and believe you?" The crowd wants to know what it will gain by believing in this new teacher. Does he give good value? How, for example, do his signs rate against the signs Moses gave?
- Their faith is at a beginning stage; the focus is on their needs. Jesus wants to lead them further, gently.
- Can I move on from this first stage, to a deeper faith, to a greater love?

Monday 3rd August **Matthew 14:15–21**

When it was evening, the disciples came to him and said, "This is a deserted place, and the hour is now late; send the crowds away so that they may go into the villages and buy food for themselves." Jesus said to them, "They need not go away; you give them something to eat." They replied, "We have nothing here but five loaves and two fish." And he said, "Bring them here to me." Then he ordered the crowds to sit down on the grass. Taking the five loaves and the two fish, he looked up to heaven, and blessed and broke the loaves, and gave them to the disciples, and the disciples gave them to the crowds. And all ate and were filled; and they took up what was left over of the broken pieces, twelve baskets full. And those who ate were about five thousand men, besides women and children.

- Here, as throughout the gospels, Jesus is happy to host a meal, to eat with his friends. In his blessing and actions we have a glimpse of the Eucharistic meal in which he gives himself to us.
- Lord, teach me to value what I have to offer though it seems so small. Use me in the service of others, an extension of your compassion.

Tuesday 4th August **Matthew 14:22–27**

Jesus made the disciples get into the boat and go on ahead to the other side, while he dismissed the crowds. And after he had dismissed the crowds, he went up the mountain by himself to pray. When evening came, he was there alone, but by this time the boat, battered by the waves, was far from the land, for the wind was against them. And early in the morning he came walking toward them on the sea. But when the disciples saw him walking on the sea, they were terrified, saying, "It is a ghost!" And they cried out in fear. But immediately Jesus spoke to them and said, "Take heart, it is I; do not be afraid."

- We are rowing hard; the wind is fierce and relentless. If we let up for a moment, we move backwards. As the boat's timbers creak, we feel exhaustion and desperation.
- It is at these moments that I need you most, Lord. Even the sense of your presence changes me: "Take heart, it is I; do not be afraid."

Wednesday 5th August **Matthew 15:21–28**

Jesus left that place and went away to the district of Tyre and Sidon. Just then a Canaanite woman from that region came out and started shouting, "Have mercy on me, Lord, Son of David; my daughter is tormented by a demon." But he did not answer her at all. And his disciples came and urged him, saying, "Send her away, for she keeps shouting after us." He answered, "I was sent only to the lost sheep of the house of Israel." But she came and knelt before him, saying, "Lord, help me." He answered, "It is not fair to take the children's food and throw it to the dogs." She said, "Yes, Lord, yet even the dogs eat the crumbs that fall from their masters' table." Then Jesus answered her, "Woman, great is your faith! Let it be done for you as you wish." And her daughter was healed instantly.

- Here, Lord, for the first and only time, I see you in Gentile territory. I imagine myself in that woman's skin, desperate for my daughter's health, hoping to reach the ear of this wonder-worker, even though he is a Jew.
- At first he ignores me, then seems to insult me as though we are only dogs around the children's table. I answer him back, sensing something—is it Jewish humor?—in his eyes.
- Suddenly he softens; he hears my prayer.

Thursday 6th August,
Transfiguration of the Lord **Mark 9:2–8**

Six days later, Jesus took with him Peter and James and John, and led them up a high mountain apart, by themselves. And he was transfigured before them, and his clothes became dazzling white, such as no one on earth could bleach them. And there appeared to them Elijah with Moses, who were talking with Jesus. Then Peter said to Jesus, "Rabbi, it is good for us to be here; let us make three dwellings, one for you, one for Moses, and one for Elijah." He did not know what to say, for they were terrified. Then a cloud overshadowed them, and from the cloud there came a voice, "This is my Son, the Beloved; listen to him!" Suddenly when they looked around, they saw no one with them any more, but only Jesus.

- Jesus is working on the ups and downs of human existence: preparing his three leaders for the trials of the Passion by giving them something to remember, a moment of glory. Peter wants it to go on forever, to settle down there where it felt so good.
- Instead, Jesus brings them down the mountain, bracing them for the bad times ahead. The journey still lies ahead. Guide me, Lord.

Friday 7th August **Matthew 16:24–28**

Then Jesus told his disciples, "If any want to become my followers, let them deny themselves and take up their cross and follow me. For those who want to save their life will lose it, and those who lose their life for my sake will find it. For what will it profit them if they gain the whole world but forfeit their life? Or what will they give in return for their life? "For the Son of Man is to come with his angels in the glory of his Father, and then he will repay everyone for what has been done. Truly I tell you, there are some standing here who will not taste death before they see the Son of Man coming in his kingdom."

- Jesus' words capture the identity of the Christian so neatly—denying oneself, taking up the cross, and following Him.
- Have I really begun this journey, or are my personal concerns still centerstage for me?

Saturday 8th August **Matthew 17:14–20**

When they came to the crowd, a man came to Jesus, knelt before him, and said, "Lord, have mercy on my son, for he is an epileptic and he suffers terribly; he often falls into the fire and often into the water. And I brought him to your disciples, but they could not cure him." Jesus answered, "You faithless and perverse generation, how much longer must I be with you? How much longer must I put up with you? Bring him here to me." And Jesus rebuked the demon, and it came out of him, and the boy was cured instantly. Then the disciples came to Jesus privately and said, "Why could we not cast it out?" He said to them, "Because of your little faith. For truly I tell you, if you have faith the size of a mustard seed, you will say to this mountain, 'Move from here to there,' and it will move; and nothing will be impossible for you."

- Lord, I look and listen as you speak of the faith that moves mountains. I wonder why I am so far from that. The disciples felt the same.
- St. Mark, reporting this incident, quotes the wonderful prayer of this epileptic boy's father, "Lord, I believe, help my unbelief."

august 9–15

Something to think and pray about each day this week:

Mary's Prayer

Religious art often shows Mary carrying a rosary in her hands. But it would not make sense for Mary to be saying "Hail Mary"—Our Lady never said the rosary—but it does make sense as her gift, something that prayerful people have developed over the centuries as a simple way of praying. The fingers can find comfort in passing the blessed beads through them. The rhythm of repetitive prayers releases the mind, and it can go in all sorts of directions: to designing clothes, to focusing on the needs of children, or of sick friends, or of some overwhelming concern, and asking God to hear our prayer; to reflecting on the mysteries of Jesus' life, as linked with the different decades; or to reflecting on joyful or sorrowful times in our own lives, trying to see how God was there, when at the time he may have seemed far away.

Even when our prayer becomes more silent and wordless, as we grow older, the rosary can still help. It still releases our mind because the telling of the beads becomes quite automatic. There are people who move from the reciting of the beads into a sort of prayer that no longer needs any thought or language. It has been called the prayer of simple regard, or the prayer of stupidity, or mystical prayer. Names do not matter. Prayer is, as the catechism used to define it, a lifting of the mind and heart to God, and for that the rosary is only a springboard. It is Mary's gift, to be used as it helps us.

The Presence of God

The world is charged with the grandeur of God (Gerard Manley Hopkins).
I dwell for a moment on the presence of God
around me, in every part of my body,
and deep within my being.

Freedom

In these days, God taught me
as a schoolteacher teaches a pupil (St. Ignatius).
I remind myself that there are things God has to teach me yet
and ask for the grace to hear them and let them change me.

Consciousness

Help me, Lord, to be more conscious of your presence.
Teach me to recognize your presence in others.
Fill my heart with gratitude for the times your love
has been shown to me through the care of others.

The Word

I read the Word of God slowly a few times over, and I listen to what God is saying to me. (Please turn to your scripture on the following pages. Inspirations points are there should you need them. When you are ready, return here to continue.)

Conversation

What feelings are rising in me
as I pray and reflect on God's Word?
I imagine Jesus himself sitting or standing beside me
and open my heart to him.

Conclusion

Glory be to the Father, and to the Son, and to the Holy Spirit,
As it was in the beginning, is now and ever shall be,
World without end. Amen

Sunday 9th August,
Nineteenth Sunday in Ordinary Time **John 6:47–51**

Jesus said to the crowd, "Very truly, I tell you, whoever believes has eternal life. I am the bread of life. Your ancestors ate the manna in the wilderness, and they died. This is the bread that comes down from heaven, so that one may eat of it and not die. I am the living bread that came down from heaven. Whoever eats of this bread will live forever; and the bread that I will give for the life of the world is my flesh."

- This sixth chapter of St. John lifts us with the thought of the Lord's Supper, the meal of thanksgiving, "Eucharist." Here is Jesus sharing his life with us.
- The Eucharist nourishes us, strengthens us for the struggles that fill our day, nurtures a life that will not end with death.

Monday 10th August, St. Lawrence **John 12:24–26**

"Very truly, I tell you, unless a grain of wheat falls into the earth and dies, it remains just a single grain; but if it dies, it bears much fruit. Those who love their life lose it, and those who hate their life in this world will keep it for eternal life. Whoever serves me must follow me, and where I am, there will my servant be also. Whoever serves me, the Father will honor."

- In witnessing to Jesus, the martyrs like Lawrence faced that horrific choice, to cling to mortal life or opt for eternal life.
- Lord, you sometimes ask us to face the death to our own desires and ego in the daily contradictions and rebuffs of a long lifetime. There, too, the sacrifice of the ego enables us to bear much fruit.

Tuesday 11th August **Matthew 18:1–5**

At that time the disciples came to Jesus and asked, "Who is the greatest in the kingdom of heaven?" He called a child, whom he put among them, and said, "Truly I tell you, unless you change and become like children, you will never enter the kingdom of heaven. Whoever becomes humble like this child is the greatest in the kingdom of heaven. Whoever welcomes one such child in my name welcomes me.

- The question showed how little they had grasped of the kingdom: "Who is the greatest, the celebrity, the boss?"
- I love your answer, "Unless you change and become like children"; no longer wanting to be talked about or to be the center of attention; instead enjoying the world with innocence, savoring its freshness.
- Help me to change in this way, Lord.

Wednesday 12th August **Matthew 18:15–16**

Jesus said to the disciples, "If another member of the church sins against you, go and point out the fault when the two of you are alone. If the member listens to you, you have regained that one. But if you are not listened to, take one or two others along with you, so that every word may be confirmed by the evidence of two or three witnesses."

- Lord, you challenge me with your words. This is a minefield for me, but you start slowly, privately, personally. Rejection does not deter you.
- How do I respond if I receive correction from one who has the courage to offer it to me? Do I reject their words, or do I listen quietly without seeking the shelter of self-pity? Lord, guide me.

Thursday 13th August **Matthew 18:21–22**

Then Peter came and said to him, "Lord, if another member of the church sins against me, how often should I forgive?

As many as seven times?" Jesus said to him, "Not seven times, but, I tell you, seventy-seven times."

- Lord, you are not talking figures but feelings. If lovers quarrel, they quickly run up dozens of remarks and actions that call for pardon. If I start to count and itemize the apologies, I am lost.
- The only way for grace to enter is your way, Lord: I must put the past behind me, forget it, exact no recompense, leave a space for love.

Friday 14th August **Matthew 19:3–12**

Some Pharisees came to him, and to test him they asked, "Is it lawful for a man to divorce his wife for any cause?" He answered, "Have you not read that the one who made them at the beginning 'made them male and female,' and said, 'For this reason a man shall leave his father and mother and be joined to his wife, and the two shall become one flesh'? So they are no longer two, but one flesh. Therefore what God has joined together, let no one separate." They said to him, "Why then did Moses command us to give a certificate of dismissal and to divorce her?" He said to them, "It was because you were so hard-hearted that Moses allowed you to divorce your wives, but at the beginning it was not so. And I say to you, whoever divorces his wife, except for unchastity, and marries another commits adultery." His disciples said to him, "If such is the case of a man with his wife, it is better not to marry." But he said to them, "Not everyone can accept this teaching, but only those to whom it is given. For there are eunuchs who have been so from birth, and there are eunuchs who have been made eunuchs by others, and there are eunuchs who have made themselves eunuchs for the sake of the kingdom of heaven. Let anyone accept this who can."

- So many who love you, Lord, agonize over these words. The disciples found your ideal of marriage so demanding that it seemed safer not to marry at all. But you were speaking of a calling to love that would be safe against the one-sided possibility of divorce—a man could divorce his wife, but not vice versa.

- As I ponder your words, Lord, I pray for my friends whose marriages are mired in complications. Keep love burning in their hearts and in mine.

Saturday 15th August, The Assumption of the Blessed Virgin Mary **Luke 1:39–47**

In those days Mary set out and went with haste to a Judean town in the hill country, where she entered the house of Zechariah and greeted Elizabeth. When Elizabeth heard Mary's greeting, the child leaped in her womb. And Elizabeth was filled with the Holy Spirit and exclaimed with a loud cry, "Blessed are you among women, and blessed is the fruit of your womb. And why has this happened to me, that the mother of my Lord comes to me? For as soon as I heard the sound of your greeting, the child in my womb leaped for joy. And blessed is she who believed that there would be a fulfillment of what was spoken to her by the Lord." And Mary said, "My soul magnifies the Lord, and my spirit rejoices in God my Savior."

- When Jesus took his mother, body and soul, into heaven, he did honor to the poor clay of which our human bodies are fashioned: a first step toward making all things new.
- "The whole of nature groans in a common travail all the while. And not only do we see that, but we ourselves do the same; we ourselves, although we have already begun to reap our spiritual harvest, groan in our hearts, waiting for that adoption which is the ransoming of our bodies from their slavery." (Rom 8: 22–23)

august 16–22

Something to think and pray about each day this week:

Reflections

In front of a mirror, light a candle and regard yourself. Who is that? Do you like her, him? There are no marks for hating yourself, only for loving. Then see Jesus at your side, also looking at you in the mirror. How does he see you? His eyes are tender, happy in your company. Not because of your looks or poverty or power or friends, but because you are his sister, brother, child of God. At the end thank God for that love, which is not earned by anything we do, but because God is our father and faithful, and we are God's children; like a loving mother, God has more joy at what we are than vexation at what we are not.

The Presence of God

As I sit here, God is present,
breathing life into me and into everything around me.
For a few moments, I sit silently
and become aware of God's loving presence.

Freedom

If God were trying to tell me something, would I know?
If God were reassuring me or challenging me, would I notice?
I ask for the grace to be free of my own preoccupations
and open to what God may be saying to me.

Consciousness

How am I really feeling? Light-hearted? Heavy-hearted?
I may be very much at peace, happy to be here.
Equally, I may be frustrated, worried, or angry.
I acknowledge how I really am. It is the real me that the Lord loves.

The Word

I take my time to read the Word of God, slowly, a few times, allowing myself to dwell on anything that strikes me. (Please turn to your scripture on the following pages. Inspiration points are there should you need them. When you are ready, return here to continue.)

Conversation

What is stirring in me as I pray?
Am I consoled, troubled, left cold?
I imagine Jesus himself standing or sitting at my side
and share my feelings with him.

Conclusion

Glory be to the Father, and to the Son, and to the Holy Spirit,
As it was in the beginning, is now and ever shall be,
World without end. Amen

Sunday 16th August,
Twentieth Sunday in Ordinary Time Ephesians 5:17–20

Do not be foolish, but understand what the will of the Lord is. Do not get drunk with wine, for that is debauchery; but be filled with the Spirit, as you sing psalms and hymns and spiritual songs among yourselves, singing and making melody to the Lord in your hearts, giving thanks to God the Father at all times and for everything in the name of our Lord Jesus Christ.

- This is strong stuff, Lord. You warn me against the illusion of happiness that alcohol inspires, but urge me to make melody in my heart.
- Thank you. As Nietzsche observed, without music, life would be a mistake.

Monday 17th August Matthew 19:16–22

Then someone came to Jesus and said, "Teacher, what good deed must I do to have eternal life?" And he said to him, "Why do you ask me about what is good? There is only one who is good. If you wish to enter into life, keep the commandments." He said to him, "Which ones?" And Jesus said, "You shall not murder; You shall not commit adultery; You shall not steal; You shall not bear false witness; Honor your father and mother; also, You shall love your neighbor as yourself." The young man said to him, "I have kept all these; what do I still lack?" Jesus said to him, "If you wish to be perfect, go, sell your possessions, and give the money to the poor, and you will have treasure in heaven; then come, follow me." When the young man heard this word, he went away grieving, for he had many possessions.

- Lord, you push me too. I seem to keep the commandments and keep my self-image intact: I am a good person. But you question my enmeshment in possessions. You ask if I can hear the cry of the poor, or if I suffer from the weariness of too many demands on my compassion.

- I do not want a life shrouded in guilt, but I want to follow you.

Tuesday 18th August **Matthew 19:27–30**

Peter asked Jesus, "Look, we have left everything and followed you. What then will we have?" Jesus said to them, "Truly I tell you, at the renewal of all things, when the Son of Man is seated on the throne of his glory, you who have followed me will also sit on twelve thrones, judging the twelve tribes of Israel. And everyone who has left houses or brothers or sisters or father or mother or children or fields, for my name's sake, will receive a hundredfold, and will inherit eternal life. But many who are first will be last, and the last will be first."

- Peter had indeed left his boat and family on the shore of the lake to follow Jesus, so his question was not just self-regarding, but came from a huge love.
- Lord, I feel your eyes on me as I ask the same question. You welcome me into fellowship that spans continents and millennia, into a hundredfold that I have already begun to taste.

Wednesday 19th August **Psalm 22(23):1–4**

The Lord is my shepherd, I shall not want. He makes me lie down in green pastures; he leads me beside still waters; he restores my soul. He leads me in right paths for his name's sake. Even though I walk through the darkest valley, I fear no evil; for you are with me; your rod and your staff—they comfort me.

- These holy words have been made even more holy by their constant repetition over thousands of years. Can I sit with them, mull over them, and allow their freshness to touch me?

Thursday 20th August **Matthew 22:1–2, 11–14**

Once more Jesus spoke to them in parables, saying: "The kingdom of heaven may be compared to a king who gave a wedding banquet for his son. But when the king came in to see the guests, he noticed a man there who was not wearing a wedding robe, and he said to him, 'Friend, how did you get in here without a wedding robe?' And he was speechless. Then the king said to the attendants, 'Bind him hand and foot, and throw him into the outer darkness, where there will be weeping and gnashing of teeth.' For many are called, but few are chosen."

- Lord, you are saying something practical here, about how people respond to your invitation. If I go to a party and take no trouble about what I wear or when I turn up, just fitting the party into my day somehow, I imply that it does not matter much.
- But meeting you, whether in prayer or in church, is important, and deserves preparation. I need to ready my mind and heart for the encounter.

Friday 21st August **Matthew 22:34–40**

When the Pharisees heard that Jesus had silenced the Sadducees, they gathered together, and one of them, a lawyer, asked him a question to test him. "Teacher, which commandment in the law is the greatest?" He said to him, "'You shall love the Lord your God with all your heart, and with all your soul, and with all your mind.' This is the greatest and first commandment. And a second is like it: 'You shall love your neighbor as yourself.' On these two commandments hang all the law and the prophets."

- "You shall love your neighbor as yourself." With this second but equal commandment, Jesus took the lawyer well beyond the Jewish law he was steeped in. Love of God and neighbor begins with a proper love of self. It requires self-esteem and self-love.

- Can I sit and think about this, about the profoundly intimate link between my self, my neighbor, and our love for God?

Saturday 22nd August **Matthew 23:1–12**

Then Jesus said to the crowds and to his disciples, "The scribes and the Pharisees sit on Moses' seat; therefore, do whatever they teach you and follow it; but do not do as they do, for they do not practice what they teach. They tie up heavy burdens, hard to bear, and lay them on the shoulders of others; but they themselves are unwilling to lift a finger to move them. They do all their deeds to be seen by others; for they make their phylacteries broad and their fringes long. They love to have the place of honor at banquets and the best seats in the synagogues, and to be greeted with respect in the marketplaces, and to have people call them rabbi. But you are not to be called rabbi, for you have one teacher, and you are all students. And call no one your father on earth, for you have one Father—the one in heaven. Nor are you to be called instructors, for you have one instructor, the Messiah. The greatest among you will be your servant. All who exalt themselves will be humbled, and all who humble themselves will be exalted."

- The Pharisees showed off their religion, flaunted its trappings in phylacteries and fringes, and practiced their virtues to be seen by others.
- You push me back to the heart, Lord. I have no idea how others stand before God. The best of them may seem the least godly to an observer.
- Lord, it is not public notice I look for, but your gaze.

august 23–29

Something to think and pray about each day this week:

Jesus' Wisdom

St. Luke pictures Jesus at the dinner table of Simon the Pharisee, and the sinner is at his feet. "Shock! Horror!" cry the tabloids, "Preacher accepts public caresses of notorious prostitute!" Simon says to himself: "If this man was a prophet he would know what sort of woman this is, what a bad name she has." Simon lives in the categories of clean and unclean, of insiders and outsiders. The social fabric is threatened by accepting the presence of such a person at his table.

For Jesus there are no outsiders. He does not take issue with the accusation of being a glutton and drunkard. He sees food and drink not as a mark of who is holy, but as a means of uniting himself with all, clean and unclean alike. "Wisdom is justified in all her children," says Jesus. Wisdom does not consist in knowing the rules and passing judgment, but in befriending all her children, men and women, like the sinner. That is his good news.

The Presence of God
As I sit here with my book, God is here.
Around me, in my sensations, in my thoughts and deep within me.
I pause for a moment and become aware
of God's life-giving presence.

Freedom
I need to close out the noise, to rise above the noise;
The noise that interrupts, that separates,
The noise that isolates.
I need to listen to God again.

Consciousness
Knowing that God loves me unconditionally,
I can afford to be honest about how I am.
How has the last day been, and how do I feel now?
I share my feelings openly with the Lord.

The Word
God speaks to each one of us individually. I need to listen to what he is saying to me. (Please turn to your scripture on the following pages. Inspiration points are there should you need them. When you are ready, return here to continue.)

Conversation
Do I notice myself reacting as I pray with the Word of God?
Do I feel challenged, comforted, angry?
Imagining Jesus sitting or standing by me,
I speak out my feelings, as one trusted friend to another.

Conclusion
Glory be to the Father, and to the Son, and to the Holy Spirit,
As it was in the beginning, is now and ever shall be,
World without end. Amen

Sunday 23rd August,
Twenty-first Sunday in Ordinary Time **John 6:64–69**

Jesus said to the disciples, "But among you there are some who do not believe." For he knew from the first who were the ones that did not believe, and who was the one that would betray him. And he said, "For this reason I have told you that no one can come to me unless it is granted by the Father." Because of this many of his disciples turned back and no longer went about with him. So Jesus asked the twelve, "Do you also wish to go away?" Simon Peter answered him, "Lord, to whom can we go? You have the words of eternal life. We have come to believe and know that you are the Holy One of God."

- Jesus' question respects the disciples' freedom. "Do you wish to go away?" I can sense that dramatic moment of uncertainty. There is movement in the group. Some are taking themselves off, not in confrontation, but in sadness.
- Peter stands firm and articulates what Jesus means to him: "Lord, to whom can we go? You have the words of eternal life." A wonderful answer, one that I savor.

Monday 24th August,
St. Bartholomew, Apostle **John 1:45–51**

Philip found Nathanael and said to him, "We have found him about whom Moses in the law and also the prophets wrote, Jesus son of Joseph from Nazareth." Nathanael said to him, "Can anything good come out of Nazareth?" Philip said to him, "Come and see." When Jesus saw Nathanael coming towards him, he said of him, "Here is truly an Israelite in whom there is no deceit!" Nathanael asked him, "Where did you come to know me?" Jesus answered, "I saw you under the fig tree before Philip called you." Nathanael replied, "Rabbi, you are the Son of

God! You are the King of Israel!" Jesus answered, "Do you believe because I told you that I saw you under the fig tree? You will see greater things than these." And he said to him, "Very truly, I tell you, you will see heaven opened and the angels of God ascending and descending upon the Son of Man."

- Wise Philip! Nathanael does not want to hear about a Messiah, especially one from the rival country town of Nazareth.
- Philip does not argue—arguments do not bring people to God—but says, "Come and see."
- If I can help others to meet you and know you, Lord, it will be more effective than any argument.

Tuesday 25th August **Matthew 23:23–26**

Jesus said, "Woe to you, scribes and Pharisees, hypocrites! For you tithe mint, dill, and cummin, and have neglected the weightier matters of the law: justice and mercy and faith. It is these you ought to have practiced without neglecting the others. You blind guides! You strain out a gnat but swallow a camel! "Woe to you, scribes and Pharisees, hypocrites! For you clean the outside of the cup and of the plate, but inside they are full of greed and self-indulgence. You blind Pharisee! First clean the inside of the cup so that the outside also may become clean."

- The kingdom of God is not complicated. I do not have to master lists of rules, as though preparing to take a driving test. But I need to stay alert to the weightier things: justice, mercy, faith.
- Lord, help me to keep my eyes on the inside of the cup.

Wednesday 26th August **1 Thessalonians 2:9–13**

You remember our labor and toil, brothers and sisters; we worked night and day so that we might not burden any of you while we proclaimed to you the gospel of God. You are witnesses, and God also, how pure, upright, and blameless our conduct was toward you believers. As you know, we dealt with each one of you like a father with his children, urging and encouraging you and pleading that you should lead a life worthy of God, who calls you into his own kingdom and glory. We also constantly give thanks to God for this, that when you received the word of God that you heard from us, you accepted it not as a human word but as what it really is, God's word, which is also at work in you believers.

- Paul worked his passage when he lived with the new Christian communities. Work is a gift from God; it is useful, and it brings dignity to people so that they can be fully human.
- Is my work, however humble, a way of serving others, a way of contributing to society? How do I encounter God there?

Thursday 27th August **Matthew 24:42–47**

"Keep awake therefore, for you do not know on what day your Lord is coming. But understand this: if the owner of the house had known in what part of the night the thief was coming, he would have stayed awake and would not have let his house be broken into. Therefore you also must be ready, for the Son of Man is coming at an unexpected hour. Who then is the faithful and wise slave, whom his master has put in charge of his household, to give the other slaves their allowance of food at the proper time? Blessed is that slave whom his master will find at work when he arrives. Truly I tell you, he will put that one in charge of all his possessions."

- Lord, as I get older, I have a problem with keeping awake and being alert moment by moment. I can see what sense it makes to live in the present moment and to recognize your presence in the now.

- Take me as I am, Lord, not a particularly faithful or wise servant, but one who is still looking forward to the encounter with you.

Friday 28th August **Matthew 25:1–13**

Jesus said to his disciples, "Then the kingdom of heaven will be like this. Ten bridesmaids took their lamps and went to meet the bridegroom. Five of them were foolish, and five were wise. When the foolish took their lamps, they took no oil with them; but the wise took flasks of oil with their lamps. As the bridegroom was delayed, all of them became drowsy and slept. But at midnight there was a shout, 'Look! Here is the bridegroom! Come out to meet him.' Then all those bridesmaids got up and trimmed their lamps. The foolish said to the wise, 'Give us some of your oil, for our lamps are going out.' But the wise replied, 'No! there will not be enough for you and for us; you had better go to the dealers and buy some for yourselves.' And while they went to buy it, the bridegroom came, and those who were ready went with him into the wedding banquet; and the door was shut. Later the other bridesmaids came also, saying, 'Lord, lord, open to us.' But he replied, 'Truly I tell you, I do not know you.' Keep awake therefore, for you know neither the day nor the hour."

- What can I take from this story? That I need my own oil so as to enter the kingdom under my own steam, that the Lord is waiting for me today and at this very hour—not so much waiting to summon me from life, but rather to reach my heart where I am at this moment.

Saturday 29th August **Matthew 25:14–30**

Jesus said to his disciples, "A man, going on a journey, summoned his slaves and entrusted his property to them; to one he gave five talents, to another two, to another one, to each according to his ability. Then he went away. The one who had received the five talents went off at once and traded with them, and made five more talents. In the same way, the one who had the two talents made two more talents. But the one who had received the one talent went off and dug a hole in the ground and hid his master's money. After a long time the master of those slaves came and settled accounts with them. Then the one who had received the five talents came forward, bringing five more talents, saying, 'Master, you handed over to me five talents; see, I have made five more talents.' His master said to him, 'Well done, good and trustworthy slave; you have been trustworthy in a few things, I will put you in charge of many things; enter into the joy of your master.' And the one with the two talents also came forward, saying, 'Master, you handed over to me two talents; see, I have made two more talents.' His master said to him, 'Well done, good and trustworthy slave; you have been trustworthy in a few things, I will put you in charge of many things; enter into the joy of your master.' Then the one who had received the one talent also came forward, saying, 'Master, I knew that you were a harsh man, reaping where you did not sow, and gathering where you did not scatter seed; so I was afraid, and I went and hid your talent in the ground. Here you have what is yours.' But his master replied, 'You wicked and lazy slave! You knew, did you, that I reap where I did not sow, and gather where I did not scatter? Then you ought to have invested my money with the bankers, and on my return I would have received what was my own with interest. So take the talent from him, and give it to the one with the ten talents.'"

- This is a sharp lesson, Lord: that there can be no religion without adventure and risk—you have no use for the shut mind.
- You do not ask that we all follow the same pattern or aim for the same achievements, but rather that we use what gifts we have in the situation in which we are placed.

august 30–september 5

Something to think and pray about each day this week:

The Power of the Leaven

When Jesus speaks about care for "the little ones," he includes in their number his own followers. In many parts of the world the Church is indeed a small presence, inconspicuous and barely noticed. Jesus does not want his missionaries, including the bishops and pope, to concern themselves with honor and respect. They too are "little ones." Do I have misgivings about this? Do I feel the Church should aim to be a strong presence and a powerbroker, able to have its way in public matters? History shows instances of many attempts to coerce people into virtuous behavior in the name of religion.

How does that square with Jesus' words about our being a leaven in the world, germinating quietly while remaining true to our own flavor, like salt that keeps its savor? This is not a simple matter. We want to profess the Lord before people and make our voice heard. But when we strive for a public voice the way advertisers do, we risk compromising the word, and adapting to values other than Christ's.

Lord, what do you ask of me, to be a light or a leaven, to shine in public, or to work invisibly? Make me easy in the role you assign me. Guide me, Lord, in this difficult balance between being the light of the world and the unseen leaven.

The Presence of God

I pause for a moment, aware that God is here.
I think of how everything around me,
the air I breathe, my whole body
is tingling with the presence of God.

Freedom

I will ask God's help,
to be free from my own preoccupations,
to be open to God in this time of prayer,
to come to love and serve him more.

Consciousness

In the presence of my loving Creator,
I look honestly at my feelings over the last day,
the highs, the lows, and the level ground.
Can I see where the Lord has been present?

The Word

I read the Word of God slowly a few times over, and I listen to what God is saying to me. (Please turn to your scripture on the following pages. Inspiration points are there should you need them. When you are ready, return here to continue.)

Conversation

Remembering that I am still in God's presence,
I imagine Jesus himself standing or sitting beside me
and say whatever is on my mind, whatever is in my heart,
speaking as one friend to another.

Conclusion

Glory be to the Father, and to the Son, and to the Holy Spirit,
As it was in the beginning, is now and ever shall be,
World without end. Amen

Sunday 30th August,
Twenty-second Sunday in Ordinary Time Mark 7:14–15

Then Jesus called the crowd again and said to them, "Listen to me, all of you, and understand: there is nothing outside a person that by going in can defile, but the things that come out are what defile."

- This was revolutionary stuff. The Maccabees had suffered torture and death rather than eat the flesh of pigs. St. Peter struggled to associate with Gentiles. Jesus was wiping out with one stroke the laws for which Jews had suffered and died.
- He pushes us to look inside. What can defile a person? The heart's evil intentions: fornication, theft, murder, adultery, avarice, wickedness, deceit, and so on. Remember Belloc? "I said to Heart, How goes it? Heart replied: Right as a Ribstone Pippin! but it lied."

Monday 31st August Luke 4:16–22

When he came to Nazareth, where he had been brought up, he went to the synagogue on the sabbath day, as was his custom. He stood up to read, and the scroll of the prophet Isaiah was given to him. He unrolled the scroll and found the place where it was written: "The Spirit of the Lord is upon me, because he has anointed me to bring good news to the poor. He has sent me to proclaim release to the captives and recovery of sight to the blind, to let the oppressed go free, to proclaim the year of the Lord's favor." And he rolled up the scroll, gave it back to the attendant, and sat down. The eyes of all in the synagogue were fixed on him. Then he began to say to them, "Today this scripture has been fulfilled in your hearing." All spoke well of him and were amazed at the gracious words that came from his mouth.

- Let me slip into the back of the synagogue to witness this. Jesus is in his hometown, a handsome young man who has already been talked about for his teaching and cures. He reads the verses of Isaiah and sits down to teach as rabbis did.

- I listen, Lord, as you start to proclaim the good news. It has a unique flavor on your lips. It is not just that you proclaim the good news. You are the good news in your person.

Tuesday 1st September **Luke 4:31–35**

He went down to Capernaum, a city in Galilee, and was teaching them on the sabbath. They were astounded at his teaching because he spoke with authority. In the synagogue there was a man who had the spirit of an unclean demon, and he cried out with a loud voice, "Let us alone! What have you to do with us, Jesus of Nazareth? Have you come to destroy us? I know who you are, the Holy One of God." But Jesus rebuked him, saying, "Be silent, and come out of him!"

- You spoke with authority, Lord. I have learned to question authority and seek evidence for what is ordered. Faced with you, I see the evidence in your person and in your power to cure.
- I am happy that you would rebuke all that is evil in me and purify me.

Wednesday 2nd September **Luke 4:38–39**

After leaving the synagogue Jesus entered Simon's house. Now Simon's mother-in-law was suffering from a high fever, and they asked him about her. Then he stood over her and rebuked the fever, and it left her. Immediately she got up and began to serve them.

- How little we know about Simon's wife or family life, but here we have Simon's mother-in-law living in his house. She is very sick with a high fever, and they ask Jesus about her.

- May I ask you, Lord, about my health? Others may be bored if I go on about it, but it concerns me, so I know it concerns you too. You touch me through my body. I want to learn to love your touch.

Thursday 3rd September **Luke 5:4–11**

When Jesus had finished speaking, he said to Simon, "Put out into the deep water and let down your nets for a catch." Simon answered, "Master, we have worked all night long but have caught nothing. Yet if you say so, I will let down the nets." When they had done this, they caught so many fish that their nets were beginning to break. So they signaled their partners in the other boat to come and help them. And they came and filled both boats, so that they began to sink. But when Simon Peter saw it, he fell down at Jesus' knees, saying, "Go away from me, Lord, for I am a sinful man!" For he and all who were with him were amazed at the catch of fish that they had taken; and so also were James and John, sons of Zebedee, who were partners with Simon. Then Jesus said to Simon, "Do not be afraid; from now on you will be catching people." When they had brought their boats to shore, they left everything and followed him.

- As Simon rowed the lake all night trying to guess the movements of the fish, he knew that fishing was a lottery: so many uncertainties, rewarded occasionally by hitting the jackpot. When he landed this undeserved prize, he was both excited and ashamed, "I do not deserve it, Lord."
- You call me too, Lord. I do not deserve it. Teach me to recognize the bounty you give me.

Friday 4th September **Luke 5:33–39**

Then the Pharisees and the scribes said to Jesus, "John's disciples, like the disciples of the Pharisees, frequently fast and pray, but your disciples eat and drink." Jesus said to them, "You cannot make wedding guests fast while the bridegroom is with them, can you? The days will come when the bridegroom will be taken away from them, and then they will fast in those days." He also told them a parable: "No one tears a piece from a new garment and sews it on an old garment; otherwise the new will be torn, and the piece from the new will not match the old. And no one puts new wine into old wineskins; otherwise the new wine will burst the skins and will be spilled, and the skins will be destroyed. But new wine must be put into fresh wineskins.'"

- Lord, I do not want to be a musty old wineskin, unable to contain new wine. May I be like you, fresh, supple, able to stretch to new ideas and habits.
- May I find joy in the company of friends as you did, especially when you ate and drank around a common table.

Saturday 5th September **Luke 6:1–5**

One sabbath while Jesus was going through the grainfields, his disciples plucked some heads of grain, rubbed them in their hands, and ate them. But some of the Pharisees said, "Why are you doing what is not lawful on the sabbath?" Jesus answered, "Have you not read what David did when he and his companions were hungry? He entered the house of God and took and ate the bread of the Presence, which it is not lawful for any but the priests to eat, and gave some to his companions?" Then he said to them, "The Son of Man is lord of the sabbath."

- It starts as a relaxed rural scene: Jesus and the twelve wandering by a field of ripe wheat and almost absent-mindedly plucking some ears, rubbing them in their hands, and eating the grain.
- It turns into a solemn assertion. When Jesus claims to be lord of the sabbath, he does not mean that he is just an arbiter in legal disputes over sabbath practices. Rather he claims to have dominion over the third commandment, and over the Law itself.

september 6–12

Something to think and pray about each day this week:

In Sickness and Health

My friend Tom, a big, bearded man in his fifties who is a support to hundreds of needy people, had blinding headaches. In hospital they found a tumor on his brain. They cut it out, gave him radiation treatment, and sent him home, no longer able to work, needing support for himself. We who live with him were not just shocked, but somehow insulted by that tumor. As we listen to our own bodies, we do so with distrust, braced for such an insult somewhere. Sickness always feels wrong. Nothing spurs us to urgent prayer more than the sickness of someone close to us. We turn to God almost with indignation, "This is wrong. You must be on our side."

God is on our side. The touch of Jesus cures the bleeding woman. He takes the little girl by the hand ("*Talitha, cumi*") and she stands up, hungry. God is on the side of life, health, and appetite. All through our life we struggle for health, in ourselves and others. We are now the hands and touch of Jesus. When we care for the sick, or use our brains to keep them and ourselves healthy, we are continuing Jesus' work. Knowing we are made for neverending life in heaven, we also strive for health and life in this world. We pray for it, and we also work for it. We pray for those who are sick, like Tom and our many friends or relatives. We pray also for those who, like Jesus, battle with mind and body against sickness and those who care for the sick.

The Presence of God

For a few moments, I think of God's veiled presence in things:
in the elements, giving them existence;
in plants, giving them life; in animals, giving them sensation;
and finally, in me, giving me all this and more,
making me a temple, a dwelling-place of the Spirit.

Freedom

God is not foreign to my freedom.
Instead the Spirit breathes life into my most intimate desires,
gently nudging me toward all that is good.
I ask for the grace to let myself be enfolded by the Spirit.

Consciousness

Knowing that God loves me unconditionally,
I look honestly over the last day, its events and my feelings.
Do I have something to be grateful for? Then I give thanks.
Is there something I am sorry for? Then I ask forgiveness.

The Word

I take my time to read the Word of God, slowly, a few times, allowing myself to dwell on anything that strikes me. (Please turn to your scripture on the following pages. Inspiration points are there should you need them. When you are ready, return here to continue.)

Conversation

How has God's Word moved me? Has it left me cold?
Has it consoled me or moved me to act in a new way?
I imagine Jesus standing or sitting beside me,
I turn and share my feelings with him.

Conclusion

Glory be to the Father, and to the Son, and to the Holy Spirit,
As it was in the beginning, is now and ever shall be,
World without end. Amen

Sunday 6th September,
Twenty-third Sunday in Ordinary Time **Mark 7:31–37**

Then he returned from the region of Tyre, and went by way of Sidon towards the Sea of Galilee, in the region of the Decapolis. They brought to him a deaf man who had an impediment in his speech; and they begged him to lay his hand on him. He took him aside in private, away from the crowd, and put his fingers into his ears, and he spat and touched his tongue. Then looking up to heaven, he sighed and said to him, "*Ephphatha,*" that is, "Be opened." And immediately his ears were opened, his tongue was released, and he spoke plainly. Then Jesus ordered them to tell no one; but the more he ordered them, the more zealously they proclaimed it. They were astounded beyond measure, saying, "He has done everything well; he even makes the deaf to hear and the mute to speak."

- This deaf, speech-impaired man stands for millions who cannot communicate, nor enter into dialogue with those who would talk with them. They cannot find the words; they are cut off.
- Jesus treats the man quietly and physically. Aside in private, he handles the deaf man with intimate gestures, even sharing his spittle, sighing, and praying.
- Lord, I can hear and I can speak; but I have much to learn about really being in touch with others. Open my ears, release my tongue, teach me to speak plainly.

Monday 7th September **Luke 6:6–11**

On another sabbath he entered the synagogue and taught, and there was a man there whose right hand was withered. The scribes and the Pharisees watched him to see whether he would cure on the sabbath, so that they might find an accusation against him. Even though he knew what they were thinking, he said to the man who had the withered hand, "Come and stand here." He got up and stood there. Then Jesus said to them, "I ask you, is it lawful to do good or to do harm on the sabbath, to save life or to destroy it?" After looking around at all of them, he said to him, "Stretch out your hand." He did so, and his hand was restored. But they were filled with fury and discussed with one another what they might do to Jesus.

- Jesus knew he was being watched, but without hesitation he acted. He was breaking the letter of the Law—do not work on the sabbath (and healing was seen as work)—but reaching for the deeper law, that it is always right to do a good thing on the sabbath.
- Lord, I stretch out my working hand for your blessing. Do good to me too.

Tuesday 8th September,
Birthday of the Blessed Virgin Mary Matthew 1:18–23

Now the birth of Jesus the Messiah took place in this way. When his mother Mary had been engaged to Joseph, but before they lived together, she was found to be with child from the Holy Spirit. Her husband Joseph, being a righteous man and unwilling to expose her to public disgrace, planned to dismiss her quietly. But just when he had resolved to do this, an angel of the Lord appeared to him in a dream and said, "Joseph, son of David, do not be afraid to take Mary as your wife, for the child conceived in her is from the Holy Spirit. She will bear a son, and you are to name him Jesus, for he will save his people from their sins." All this took place to fulfill what had been spoken by the Lord through the prophet: "Look, the virgin shall conceive and bear a son, and they shall name him Emmanuel," which means, "God is with us."

- On Mary's birthday, I warm to Belloc's *Ballade to Our Lady of Czestochowa*:

  You shall receive me when the clouds are high
  With evening, and the sheep attain the fold.
  This is the faith that I have held and hold,
  And this is that in which I mean to die.

Wednesday 9th September **Luke 6:20–23**

Then Jesus looked up at his disciples and said: "Blessed are you who are poor, for yours is the kingdom of God. Blessed are you who are hungry now, for you will be filled. Blessed are you who weep now, for you will laugh. Blessed are you when people hate you, and when they exclude you, revile you, and defame you on account of the Son of Man. Rejoice in that day and leap for joy, for surely your reward is great in heaven; for that is what their ancestors did to the prophets."

- There is something to be discovered here: that it is a blessing, a grace, to be poor, to be hungry, to be hated.
- Even if I do not seek out these states, may I be ready for that blessing if it is given to me.

Thursday 10th September **Luke 6:27–38**

Jesus said to his disciples, "But I say to you that listen, Love your enemies, do good to those who hate you, bless those who curse you, pray for those who abuse you. If anyone strikes you on the cheek, offer the other also; and from anyone who takes away your coat do not withhold even your shirt. Give to everyone who begs from you; and if anyone takes away your goods, do not ask for them again. Do to others as you would have them do to you. If you love those who love you, what credit is that to you? For even sinners love those who love them. If you do good to those who do good to you, what credit is that to you? For even sinners do the same. If you lend to those from whom you hope to receive, what credit is that to you? Even sinners lend to sinners, to receive as much again. But love your enemies, do good, and lend, expecting nothing in return. Your reward will be great, and you will be children of the Most High; for he is kind to the ungrateful and the wicked. Be merciful, just as your Father is merciful. Do not judge, and you will not be judged; do not condemn, and you will not be condemned. Forgive, and you will be forgiven; give, and it will be given to you. A good measure, pressed down, shaken together, running over, will be put into your lap; for the measure you give will be the measure you get back."

- This is the counsel of perfection, Lord. The advice is so difficult that it is dangerous even to talk about it unless one is in the position of being abused, struck, robbed.
- Then we can taste what it means to love: not so much a sentiment of the heart, but αγαπαν (agapan*)*, an attitude of wishing well, benevolence. As your executioners hammered nails into your hands and feet, you wished them well, begging God to forgive them. That is what you mean.
- "Do to others as you would have them do to you," has passed into common speech. Can I look at these words again? Can I ask the Lord to help me love my enemies?

Friday 11th September **Luke 6:39–42**

He also told them a parable: "Can a blind person guide a blind person? Will not both fall into a pit? A disciple is not above the teacher, but everyone who is fully qualified will be like the teacher. Why do you see the speck in your neighbor's eye, but do not notice the log in your own eye? Or how can you say to your neighbor, 'Friend, let me take out the speck in your eye,' when you yourself do not see the log in your own eye? You hypocrite, first take the log out of your own eye, and then you will see clearly to take the speck out of your neighbor's eye."

- Lord, when you tell me to hold off criticism until I have cleared my own slate, you are telling me not to criticize at all because I am never above criticism myself.
- In the story of the adulterous woman, when you said: "Let the one without sin cast the first stone," what happened? They went out, beginning with the eldest.
- Throwing stones, or bad-mouthing others, is an ignoble business. Taking to pieces is the trade of those who cannot construct.

Saturday 12th September **Luke 6:47–49**

Jesus said to the disciples, "I will show you what someone is like who comes to me, hears my words, and acts on them. That one is like a man building a house, who dug deeply and laid the foundation on rock; when a flood arose, the river burst against that house but could not shake it, because it had been well built. But the one who hears and does not act is like a man who built a house on the ground without a foundation. When the river burst against it, immediately it fell, and great was the ruin of that house."

- A resolution only becomes real when you start to put it into practice. There are those who speak of patriotism but withhold taxes to support their country; who expect a school to teach their children honesty but would lie in front of the same children.
- Lord, may my words and my life be of one piece.

september 13–19

Something to think and pray about each day this week:

Light in the world

Jesus uses contrasting metaphors for how we should live: light of the world, leaven hidden in dough, salt that adds savor. They apply at different times in each person's life and in the life of the Church. Sometimes we are put in the spotlight and have our fifteen minutes of fame. If, briefly, we are the light of the world, we can pray that when we are in such focus we may be worthy of our Christian vocation. Most of the time we are more like salt, or leaven, working for good even when unseen. The image of being leaven or salt may be less attractive than being light. If there is anything of the exhibitionist in us, reflecting on this image will discover it.

The Presence of God

Jesus waits silent and unseen to come into my heart.
I will respond to his call.
He comes with his infinite power and love.
May I be filled with joy in his presence.

Freedom

Everything has the potential to draw forth from me a fuller love and life.
Yet my desires are often fixed, caught, on illusions of fulfillment.
I ask that God, through my freedom, may orchestrate
my desires in a vibrant loving melody rich in harmony.

Consciousness

How do I find myself today?
Where am I with God? With others?
Do I have something to be grateful for? Then I give thanks.
Is there something I am sorry for? Then I ask forgiveness.

The Word

God speaks to each one of us individually. I need to listen to what he is saying to me. (Please turn to your scripture on the following pages. Inspiration points are there should you need them. When you are ready, return here to continue.)

Conversation

What feelings are rising in me
as I pray and reflect on God's Word?
I imagine Jesus himself sitting or standing beside me
and open my heart to him.

Conclusion

Glory be to the Father, and to the Son, and to the Holy Spirit,
As it was in the beginning, is now and ever shall be,
World without end. Amen

Sunday 13th September,
Twenty-fourth Sunday in Ordinary Time Mark 8:27–30

Jesus went on with his disciples to the villages of Caesarea Philippi; and on the way he asked his disciples, "Who do people say that I am?" And they answered him, "John the Baptist; and others, Elijah; and still others, one of the prophets." He asked them, "But who do you say that I am?" Peter answered him, "You are the Messiah." And he sternly ordered them not to tell anyone about him.

- The same question is always relevant: "Who is Jesus?" Peter said "You are the Messiah." That is, Jesus is the one sent by God to set his people free.
- Do I allow Jesus to be my Messiah and set me free? If not, what is holding me back? Can I talk to him about it?

Monday 14th September,
Triumph of the Holy Cross John 3:14–17

Jesus said, "And just as Moses lifted up the serpent in the wilderness, so must the Son of Man be lifted up, that whoever believes in him may have eternal life. For God so loved the world that he gave his only Son, so that everyone who believes in him may not perish but may have eternal life. Indeed, God did not send the Son into the world to condemn the world, but in order that the world might be saved through him."

- God loves the world. This is my faith, Lord. Sometimes it seems to go against the evidence when floods, earthquakes, droughts, and tsunamis devastate people.
- Central to my faith is the figure of Jesus, lifted on the cross, knowing what it was to be devastated and a failure, but offering himself in love for us.

Tuesday 15th September, Our Lady of Sorrows — John 19:25–27

Meanwhile, standing near the cross of Jesus were his mother, and his mother's sister, Mary the wife of Clopas, and Mary Magdalene. When Jesus saw his mother and the disciple whom he loved standing beside her, he said to his mother, "Woman, here is your son." Then he said to the disciple, "Here is your mother." And from that hour the disciple took her into his own home.

- Yeats's poem helps me to plumb the depths of Mary's thoughts on Calvary:

  What is this flesh I purchased with my pains,
  This fallen star my milk sustains,
  This love that makes my heart's blood stop
  Or strikes a sudden chill into my bones
  And makes my hair stand up?

Wednesday 16th September — Luke 7:31–35

"To what then will I compare the people of this generation, and what are they like? They are like children sitting in the marketplace and calling to one another, 'We played the flute for you, and you did not dance; we wailed, and you did not weep.' For John the Baptist has come eating no bread and drinking no wine, and you say, 'He has a demon;' the Son of Man has come eating and drinking, and you say, 'Look, a glutton and a drunkard, a friend of tax collectors and sinners!' Nevertheless, wisdom is vindicated by all her children."

- Both John the Baptist, in his austerity, and Jesus, feasting and living life to the full, are models of wisdom.
- The service of God comes in all sorts of forms, and they have this in common: They are shot through with love.

Thursday 17th September **Luke 7:36–50**

One of the Pharisees asked Jesus to eat with him, and he went into the Pharisee's house and took his place at the table. And a woman in the city, who was a sinner, having learned that he was eating in the Pharisee's house, brought an alabaster jar of ointment. She stood behind him at his feet, weeping, and began to bathe his feet with her tears and to dry them with her hair. Then she continued kissing his feet and anointing them with the ointment. Now when the Pharisee who had invited him saw it, he said to himself, "If this man were a prophet, he would have known who and what kind of woman this is who is touching him—that she is a sinner." Jesus spoke up and said to him, "Simon, I have something to say to you." "Teacher," he replied, "speak." "A certain creditor had two debtors; one owed five hundred denarii, and the other fifty. When they could not pay, he cancelled the debts for both of them. Now which of them will love him more?" Simon answered, "I suppose the one for whom he cancelled the greater debt." And Jesus said to him, "You have judged rightly." Then turning towards the woman, he said to Simon, "Do you see this woman? I entered your house; you gave me no water for my feet, but she has bathed my feet with her tears and dried them with her hair. You gave me no kiss, but from the time I came in, she has not stopped kissing my feet. You did not anoint my head with oil, but she has anointed my feet with ointment. Therefore, I tell you, her sins, which were many, have been forgiven; hence she has shown great love. But the one to whom little is forgiven, loves little." Then he said to her, "Your sins are forgiven." But those who were at the table with him began to say among themselves, "Who is this who even forgives sins?" And he said to the woman, "Your faith has saved you; go in peace."

- Imagine Jesus reclining at table in the courtyard, leaning on his left elbow, his right arm free for eating. People who heard of his presence could come in off the street to listen.
- I see the woman with her hair unbound—that in itself was scandalous—coming up behind his feet, weeping over them, drying them with her hair, and anointing them with ointment. It is an emotional, intimate encounter.
- Jesus is easy, relaxed, smiling. Simon holds his breath, in astonishment and anger. I savor each element of the scene.

Friday 18th September **Luke 8:1–3**

Soon afterwards he went on through cities and villages, proclaiming and bringing the good news of the kingdom of God. The twelve were with him, as well as some women who had been cured of evil spirits and infirmities: Mary, called Magdalene, from whom seven demons had gone out, and Joanna, the wife of Herod's steward Chuza, and Susanna, and many others, who provided for them out of their resources.

- The twelve are well remembered, but the women are often forgotten. Their inclusion would have startled the Jews. They were not just supporting Jesus, but risking their reputations.
- For a group of women, including the powerful like Joanna and the ex-prostitutes like Magdalene, to leave home and travel with a rabbi and his followers was scandalous. They showed the love and courage of great Christian women through the ages.

Saturday 19th September **Luke 8:4–5a, 11b**

When a great crowd gathered and people from town after town came to him, Jesus said in a parable: "A sower went out to sow his seed; the seed is the word of God."

- Parents and teachers have been called springtime workers. They sweat to harrow the ground and sow the seed, seldom seeing the harvest, but often made to feel they are unprofitable servants.
- How is faith formed? How are moral values passed on? Not by lectures from father, or nagging from mother, still less by sermons in church. Children watch parents, and non-believers watch Christians, more than they listen to them. The faith will grow even if we do not poke it.
- We smell, admire, and enjoy flowers. We do not constantly pull them up to see if they are growing.

september 20–26

Something to think and pray about each day this week:

The Sting of Darkness

In the northern hemisphere, this is the week of the equinox, when night and day are equally balanced. From now on, darkness is pushing down the daylight on half of the Earth—to an extreme degree in northern Norway, to a minimal degree in the tropics. The nights are now longer than the days. Some of us find it hard to endure the lengthening nights. As the year moves toward its end, we feel our own mortality. The changing seasons affect our mood, and we have to remind ourselves that winter will not last forever. Jesus spoke of the night coming when no one can work. That pulls us up sharply in the post-Edison era. Electricity, and the light and power that it brings, has taken some of the sting out of darkness. The inborn rhythms of our humanity have a place for both light and darkness. In my own life, do I respect what opportunities each presents, the day for action, the night for lying fallow and recouping my strength?

The Presence of God

I reflect for a moment on God's presence around me and in me.
Creator of the universe, the sun and the moon, the earth,
every molecule, every atom, everything that is:
God is in every beat of my heart. God is with me, now.

Freedom

There are very few people
who realize what God would make of them
if they abandoned themselves into his hands,
and let themselves be formed by his grace. (St Ignatius)
I ask for the grace to trust myself totally to God's love.

Consciousness

I remind myself that I am in the presence of the Lord.
I will take refuge in His loving heart.
He is my strength in times of weakness.
He is my comforter in times of sorrow.

The Word

I read the Word of God slowly, a few times over, and I listen to what God is saying to me. (Please turn to your scripture on the following pages. Inspiration points are there should you need them. When you are ready, return here to continue.)

Conversation

What is stirring in me as I pray?
Am I consoled, troubled, left cold?
I imagine Jesus himself standing or sitting at my side
and share my feelings with him.

Conclusion

Glory be to the Father, and to the Son, and to the Holy Spirit,
As it was in the beginning, is now and ever shall be,
World without end. Amen

Sunday 20th September,
Twenty-fifth Sunday in Ordinary Time Mark 9:33–37

Then Jesus and the disciples came to Capernaum; and when he was in the house he asked them, "What were you arguing about on the way?" But they were silent, for on the way they had argued with one another who was the greatest. He sat down, called the twelve, and said to them, "Whoever wants to be first must be last of all and servant of all." Then he took a little child and put it among them; and taking it in his arms, he said to them, "Whoever welcomes one such child in my name welcomes me, and whoever welcomes me welcomes not me but the one who sent me."

- This is a call to a life of radical humility and service, following the pattern of Jesus' own life. How do I hear his call to be "last and servant of all?" Does it challenge me? Does it leave me feeling insecure?
- Do I feel I'm at the bottom of the heap anyway? Can I hear the tender challenge of Jesus calling me to join him in his way of living?

Monday 21st September,
St. Matthew, Apostle and Evangelist Matthew 9:9–13

As Jesus was walking along, he saw a man called Matthew sitting at the tax booth; and he said to him, "Follow me." And he got up and followed him. And as he sat at dinner in the house, many tax collectors and sinners came and were sitting with him and his disciples. When the Pharisees saw this, they said to his disciples, "Why does your teacher eat with tax collectors and sinners?" But when he heard this, he said, "Those who are well have no need of a physician, but those who are sick. Go, and learn what this means, 'I desire mercy, not sacrifice.' For I have come to call not the righteous, but sinners."

- When Jesus called to himself a man who was generally hated, he was showing his faith in the possibilities of human nature. He saw in Matthew not only what he was, but also what he could be.
- Lord, look on me too in that way.

Tuesday 22nd September **Luke 8:19–21**

Then his mother and his brothers came to him, but they could not reach him because of the crowd. And he was told, "Your mother and your brothers are standing outside, wanting to see you." But he said to them, "My mother and my brothers are those who hear the word of God and do it."

- Jesus is not disowning his mother, but rather pointing to her greatest glory: that she could say to God's messenger, "Here am I, the servant of the Lord; let it be with me according to your word."

Wednesday 23rd September **Luke 9:1–6**

Jesus called the twelve together and gave them power and authority over all demons and to cure diseases, and he sent them out to proclaim the kingdom of God and to heal. He said to them, "Take nothing for your journey, no staff, nor bag, nor bread, nor money—not even an extra tunic. Whatever house you enter, stay there, and leave from there. Wherever they do not welcome you, as you are leaving that town, shake the dust off your feet as a testimony against them." They departed and went through the villages, bringing the good news and curing diseases everywhere.

- Jesus did not tell the twelve what to say; instead, his instruction was to take nothing and receive hospitality when and as it was offered. There is no mention of sermon notes.
- This passage was an inspiration to Francis of Assisi: he did not want his friars to preach salvation so much as "be" salvation.

Thursday 24th September **Luke 9:7–9**

Now Herod the ruler heard about all that had taken place, and he was perplexed, because it was said by some that John had been raised from the dead, by some that Elijah had appeared, and by others that one of the ancient prophets had arisen. Herod said, "John I beheaded; but who is this about whom I hear such things?" And he tried to see him.

- "Herod tried to see Jesus." This urge did not come from openness to God's revelation, but rather from the same idle curiosity Herod was to show during Jesus' passion. But there is also a hint of fear that he may be facing a greater power than he had reckoned.
- Lord, if my religion is just a curiosity or news item, I am better off without it. I long to see you. I desire to come close to you.

Friday 25th September **Luke 9:18–22**

Once when Jesus was praying alone, with only the disciples near him, he asked them, "Who do the crowds say that I am?" They answered, "John the Baptist; but others, Elijah; and still others, that one of the ancient prophets has arisen." He said to them, "But who do you say that I am?" Peter answered, "The Messiah of God." He sternly ordered and commanded them not to tell anyone, saying, "The Son of Man must undergo great suffering, and be rejected by the elders, chief priests, and scribes, and be killed, and on the third day be raised."

- You question me directly, Lord: 'But who do you say that I am?"
- How do I answer this? Who is this Jesus, in my life? Can I let him change my life?

Saturday 26th September **Luke 9:43–45**

And all were astounded at the greatness of God. While everyone was amazed at all that he was doing, he said to his disciples, "Let these words sink into your ears: The Son of Man is going to be betrayed into human hands." But they did not understand this saying; its meaning was concealed from them, so that they could not perceive it. And they were afraid to ask him about this saying.

- Lord, when you mentioned the cross, you found it hard to get a hearing from your own friends. They were afraid to ask you about betrayal. It was bad news and did not square with their hopes of your triumph.
- Help me to let these words sink into my ears.

september 27–october 3

Something to think and pray about each day this week:

Singing Psalms to God

We have no direct experience of God. Our limited minds and hearts cannot engage the infinite. But we believe that God works on us, and we feel that effect in our hearts. We become aware of reaching beyond ourselves, in various ways, not all of them consoling. For instance, we sense our need of God when we experience our incompetence, emptiness, failure. I cannot make myself what I should be. My heart is restless till it rests in God. This hunger, thirst, and longing is a theme that runs through the psalms: Psalm 22—I cry by day, my God, and you are silent, I cry by night and you just let me; Psalm 42—As a deer stretches out for living water, so do I reach out, God, with all my being toward you. I thirst for God, the living God; Psalm 63—God, you are my God, I am seeking you, my soul is thirsting for you, my flesh is longing for you, a land parched, weary, and waterless. I long to gaze on you in the sanctuary and to see your power and glory. I sing for joy in the shadow of your wings. My soul clings to you. Your right hand supports me.

The Presence of God

I remind myself that, as I sit here now,
God is gazing on me with love and holding me in being.
I pause for a moment and think of this.

Freedom

Lord, grant me the grace to be free from the excesses of this life.
Let me not get caught up with the desire for wealth.
Keep my heart and mind free to love and serve you.

Consciousness

How am I really feeling? Light-hearted? Heavy-hearted?
I may be very much at peace, happy to be here.
Equally, I may be frustrated, worried, or angry.
I acknowledge how I really am. It is the real me that the Lord loves.

The Word

I take my time to read the Word of God, slowly, a few times, allowing myself to dwell on anything that strikes me. (Please turn to your scripture on the following pages. Inspiration points are there should you need them. When you are ready, return here to continue.)

Conversation

Do I notice myself reacting as I pray with the Word of God?
Do I feel challenged, comforted, angry?
Imagining Jesus sitting or standing by me,
I speak out my feelings, as one trusted friend to another.

Conclusion

Glory be to the Father, and to the Son, and to the Holy Spirit,
As it was in the beginning, is now and ever shall be,
World without end. Amen

Sunday 27th September,
Twenty-sixth Sunday in Ordinary Time **Mark 9:38–41**

John said to Jesus, "Teacher, we saw someone casting out demons in your name, and we tried to stop him, because he was not following us." But Jesus said, "Do not stop him; for no one who does a deed of power in my name will be able soon afterward to speak evil of me. Whoever is not against us is for us. For truly I tell you, whoever gives you a cup of water to drink because you bear the name of Christ will by no means lose the reward."

- I need this reminder, Lord. It warns me against thinking that I, or my group, have cornered God's grace. I see others doing good or tackling evil, and just because they are "not following us," I feel a proprietary resentment.
- John Wesley deplored "that miserable bigotry that makes many so unready to believe that there is any work of God but among themselves."
- Lord, splits and jealousies are not a sign of your good spirit. Give me a generous heart.

Monday 28th September **Luke 9:46–50**

An argument arose among them as to which one of them was the greatest. But Jesus, aware of their inner thoughts, took a little child and put it by his side, and said to them, "Whoever welcomes this child in my name welcomes me, and whoever welcomes me welcomes the one who sent me; for the least among all of you is the greatest." John answered, "Master, we saw someone casting out demons in your name, and we tried to stop him, because he does not follow with us." But Jesus said to him, "Do not stop him; for whoever is not against you is for you."

- Imagine the little child in this scene, the expression on the child's face. What is he or she like? Wide-eyed? Innocent? Trusting?

- Lord, when I begin to feel secure, powerful, on top of things, you unsettle me. You ask me to emulate the powerlessness of children who cannot plan for themselves.
- I come with all my baggage, my skepticism, competitiveness, self-regard. Can I put this aside and be like the little child?

Tuesday 29th September,
Sts. Michael, Gabriel, and Raphael **John 1:47–51**

When Jesus saw Nathanael coming toward him, he said of him, "Here is truly an Israelite in whom there is no deceit!" Nathanael asked him, "Where did you get to know me?" Jesus answered, "I saw you under the fig tree before Philip called you." Nathanael replied, "Rabbi, you are the Son of God! You are the King of Israel!" Jesus answered, "Do you believe because I told you that I saw you under the fig tree? You will see greater things than these." And he said to him, "Very truly, I tell you, you will see heaven opened and the angels of God ascending and descending upon the Son of Man."

- The three angels we celebrate today are God's messengers with special functions. Gabriel, who brought the message to Mary, is the patron of telecommunications and radio. Raphael, who guided Tobias on his journey, is the patron of nurses, physicians, and the blind. Michael is venerated as the protector of Christians and especially of soldiers.
- The angels remind us that God's speaks in many ways, that God's messengers are in many guises.

Wednesday 30th September **Luke 9:57–62**

As they were going along the road, someone said to him, "I will follow you wherever you go." And Jesus said to him, "Foxes have holes, and birds of the air have nests; but the Son of Man has nowhere to lay his head." To another he said, "Follow me." But he said, "Lord, first let me go and bury my father." But Jesus said to him, "Let the dead bury their own dead; but as for you, go and proclaim the kingdom of God." Another said, "I will follow you, Lord; but let me first say farewell to those at my home." Jesus said to him, "No one who puts a hand to the plow and looks back is fit for the kingdom of God."

- Here we see three apparently generous individuals who are ready to become followers. Jesus, in each case, seems to make things more difficult for them.
- What is my reaction to this? What is Jesus up to? Does he sense a false note in their offer? If Jesus is calling his followers to give without the slightest reservation or hesitation, is he perhaps telling us something about himself?

Thursday 1st October,
St. Theresa of the Child Jesus **Isaiah 66:10–13a**

Rejoice with Jerusalem, and be glad for her, all you who love her; rejoice with her in joy, all you who mourn over her—that you may nurse and be satisfied from her consoling breast; that you may drink deeply with delight from her glorious bosom. For thus says the Lord: I will extend prosperity to her like a river, and the wealth of the nations like an overflowing stream; and you shall nurse and be carried on her arm, and dandled on her knees. As a mother comforts her child, so I will comfort you.

- This is God speaking to me.
- Can I relate to God as being like a mother who comforts her child? God is beyond gender.
- Thank you, God, for this glimpse of your tenderness.

Friday 2nd October **Luke 10:13–16**

"Woe to you, Chorazin! Woe to you, Bethsaida! For if the deeds of power done in you had been done in Tyre and Sidon, they would have repented long ago, sitting in sackcloth and ashes. But at the judgment it will be more tolerable for Tyre and Sidon than for you. And you, Capernaum, will you be exalted to heaven? No, you will be brought down to Hades. Whoever listens to you listens to me, and whoever rejects you rejects me, and whoever rejects me rejects the one who sent me.

- Lord, you have done deeds of power in my life. I did not always recognize them or use the opportunities. I take confidence in the thought of you looking for the lost sheep, forgiving again and again, loving me as I am, in my weakness.

Saturday 3rd October **Luke 10:21–24**

At that same hour Jesus rejoiced in the Holy Spirit and said, "I thank you, Father, Lord of heaven and earth, because you have hidden these things from the wise and the intelligent and have revealed them to infants; yes, Father, for such was your gracious will. All things have been handed over to me by my Father; and no one knows who the Son is except the Father, or who the Father is except the Son and anyone to whom the Son chooses to reveal him." Then turning to the disciples, Jesus said to them privately, "Blessed are the eyes that see what you see! For I tell you that many prophets and kings desired to see what you see, but did not see it, and to hear what you hear, but did not hear it."

- The theory of evolution suggests the slow climb upward of humanity from the level of the beasts.
- Jesus is the end and climax of the evolutionary process because in him humanity meets God; he is at once the perfection of manhood and the fullness of godhead.

october 4–10

Something to think and pray about each day this week:

Little Children

You remember that Jesus once took a little child, whom the apostles were shooing away, and told them: Unless you become like little children, you will not enter the kingdom of heaven. The fact is, at the end, we do become like little children. We stop achieving, lose our driving license, and depend more and more on others to do things for us. Fr. Pedro Arrupe, general of the Jesuits from 1965 to 1983, at the end of his life was felled by a stroke, which crippled and silenced him. He could neither walk nor talk, though he could still write. He sent this message to the Jesuits who gathered to elect his successor: "More than ever, I find myself in the hands of God. This is what I have wanted all my life, from my youth. And this is still the one thing I want. But now there is a difference: The initiative is entirely with God. It is indeed a profound spiritual experience to know and feel myself so totally in his hands."

The Presence of God
In the silence of my innermost being,
in the fragments of my yearned-for wholeness,
can I hear the whispers of God's presence?
Can I remember when I felt God's nearness
when we walked together and I let myself be embraced by God's love?

Freedom
I ask for the grace
to let go of my own concerns
and be open to what God is asking of me,
to let myself be guided and formed by my loving Creator.

Consciousness
I exist in a web of relationships—links to nature, people, God.
I trace out these links, giving thanks for the life that flows through them.
Some links are twisted or broken: I may feel regret, anger, disappointment.
I pray for the gift of acceptance and forgiveness.

The Word
The Word of God comes down to us through the scriptures. May the Holy Spirit enlighten my mind and my heart to respond to the gospel teachings. (Please turn to your scripture on the following pages. Inspiration points are there should you need them. When you are ready, return here to continue.)

Conversation
Remembering that I am still in God's presence,
I imagine Jesus himself standing or sitting beside me,
and say whatever is on my mind, whatever is in my heart,
speaking as one friend to another.

Conclusion
Glory be to the Father, and to the Son, and to the Holy Spirit,
As it was in the beginning, is now and ever shall be,
World without end. Amen

Sunday 4th October,
Twenty-seventh Sunday in Ordinary Time   Mark 10:13–16

People were bringing little children to Jesus in order that he might touch them; and the disciples spoke sternly to them. But when Jesus saw this, he was indignant and said to them, "Let the little children come to me; do not stop them; for it is to such as these that the kingdom of God belongs. Truly I tell you, whoever does not receive the kingdom of God as a little child will never enter it." And he took them up in his arms, laid his hands on them, and blessed them.

- This scene shows how Jesus understood children. A crowd of them interrupted his preaching, and the apostles were shooing them away. They were noisy, energetic, enjoying life, and running instinctively toward someone who also enjoyed it.
- The apostles were aggrieved: These kids are not serious; we are here to listen to Jesus, and we can't hear him properly. Jesus intervened, invited the children closer, and laid his hands on them. He gave them two precious things that cost no money: time and affection.
- The Gospel urges us to love. Can we take time today to do that?

Monday 5th October   Luke 10:30–37

Jesus replied, "A man was going down from Jerusalem to Jericho, and fell into the hands of robbers, who stripped him, beat him, and went away, leaving him half dead. Now by chance a priest was going down that road; and when he saw him, he passed by on the other side. So likewise a Levite, when he came to the place and saw him, passed by on the other side. But a Samaritan while traveling came near him; and when he saw him, he was moved with pity. He went to him and bandaged his wounds, having poured oil and wine on them. Then he put him on his own animal, brought him to an inn, and took care of him. The next day he took out two denarii, gave them to the innkeeper, and said, 'Take care of him; and when I come back, I will repay you whatever more you spend.' Which of these three, do you think, was a neighbor to the man who fell into the hands of the robbers?" He said, "The one who showed him mercy." Jesus said to him, "Go and do likewise."

- Who is my neighbor? Jesus seems to suggest that it is the person whom I view with suspicion and don't like, or who views me with suspicion and doesn't like me.
- Do I have any neighbors in this challenging sense of the word? What is Jesus trying to say to me?

Tuesday 6th October **Luke 10:38–42**

Now as they went on their way, Jesus entered a certain village, where a woman named Martha welcomed him into her home. She had a sister named Mary, who sat at the Lord's feet and listened to what he was saying. But Martha was distracted by her many tasks; so she came to him and asked, "Lord, do you not care that my sister has left me to do all the work by myself? Tell her then to help me." But the Lord answered her, "Martha, Martha, you are worried and distracted by many things; there is need of only one thing. Mary has chosen the better part, which will not be taken away from her."

- Jesus repeats Martha's name with deep affection as he chides her. She will remember the message—stop fussing. Because she learned the lesson, it is Martha, not Mary, who has a place in the calendar of saints (29 July).
- It is sometimes the things we are told in public reproof that touch us deepest and bring us close to God.

- Lord, save me from being a hyperactive fusspot, from imagining you brought me into the world to help you out of a jam. Teach me the pleasures of contemplation.

Wednesday 7th October **Luke 11:1–4**

Jesus was praying in a certain place, and after he had finished, one of his disciples said to him, "Lord, teach us to pray, as John taught his disciples." He said to them, "When you pray, say: Father, hallowed be your name. Your kingdom come. Give us each day our daily bread. And forgive us our sins, for we ourselves forgive everyone indebted to us. And do not bring us to the time of trial."

- One teacher of prayer used to advise, "Say the Lord's Prayer, and take an hour to say it."
- This prayer of Jesus has depths we never totally fathom. We can linger on every word.

Thursday 8th October **Luke 11:5–10**

And Jesus said to them, "Suppose one of you has a friend, and you go to him at midnight and say to him, 'Friend, lend me three loaves of bread; for a friend of mine has arrived, and I have nothing to set before him.' And he answers from within, 'Do not bother me; the door has already been locked, and my children are with me in bed; I cannot get up and give you anything.' I tell you, even though he will not get up and give him anything because he is his friend, at least because of his persistence he will get up and give him whatever he needs. So I say to you, Ask, and it will be given you; search, and you will find; knock, and the door will be opened for you. For everyone who asks receives, and everyone who searches finds, and for everyone who knocks, the door will be opened."

- It is often at midnight, or in the small hours, that I most feel the need of God; but then when I call, God sometimes seems to be asleep. God does not hear me.
- Lord, you tell me emphatically to persist, to keep battering at your door for myself and those I love. You tell me that prayer is not wasted. As Tennyson has it, "More things are wrought by prayer than this world dreams of."

Friday 9th October **Luke 11:23**

Whoever is not with me is against me, and whoever does not gather with me scatters.

- Lord, let me not be one of the passive ones, who contribute to the triumph of evil by staying on the fence. If I am not on the way, I am in the way.

Saturday 10th October **Luke 11:27–28**

While Jesus was speaking, a woman in the crowd raised her voice and said to him, "Blessed is the womb that bore you and the breasts that nursed you!" But he said, "Blessed rather are those who hear the word of God and obey it!"

- This woman intrigues me. Was she childless, or did she have some difficulty with a child? Her cry is so spontaneous, so charged with love and admiration for the person of Jesus, I would love to have been in her shoes.
- Jesus turns the compliment and refers in a subtle and beautiful way back to his mother, Mary, who believed God's word and made herself his handmaid.

october 11–17

Something to think and pray about each day this week:

The Rhythm of Prayer

One of the chief dead-ends in developing my spiritual life is to want to have someone else's spiritual life. If, for instance, I visit a convent one day, or see a monastery on TV, I may find myself thinking, "I wish I could pray like them." But if I am a school-teacher, or an accountant, or looking after my children all day, then that rhythm of prayer may just not be suited to me. *Pray as you can, not as you can't* is an obvious maxim, but one that is frequently overlooked, leading to a lot of unrealistic expectations and frustration.

Finding my own rhythm, a way of praying that suits me, may involve some experimentation with times and places and with different styles and approaches. At times I will need to persevere and not give up on something too easily. I also need, however, to be prepared to say, "This doesn't work for me." Finding a way of praying I can sustain is an important step in developing my relationship with God.

The Presence of God

God is with me, but more,
God is within me, giving me existence.
Let me dwell for a moment on God's life-giving presence
in my body, my mind, my heart,
and in the whole of my life.

Freedom

I ask for the grace to believe
in what I could be and do
if I only allowed God, my loving Creator,
to continue to create me, guide me, and shape me.

Consciousness

Knowing that God loves me unconditionally,
I can afford to be honest about how I am.
How has the last day been, and how do I feel now?
I share my feelings openly with the Lord.

The Word

I read the Word of God slowly, a few times over, and I listen to what God is saying to me. (Please turn to your scripture on the following pages. Inspiration points are there should you need them. When you are ready, return here to continue.)

Conversation

How has God's Word moved me? Has it left me cold?
Has it consoled me or moved me to act in a new way?
I imagine Jesus standing or sitting beside me,
I turn and share my feelings with him.

Conclusion

Glory be to the Father, and to the Son, and to the Holy Spirit,
As it was in the beginning, is now and ever shall be,
World without end. Amen

Sunday 11th October,
Twenty-eighth Sunday in Ordinary Time Mark 10:17–22

As Jesus was setting out on a journey, a man ran up and knelt before him, and asked him, "Good Teacher, what must I do to inherit eternal life?" Jesus said to him, "Why do you call me good? No one is good but God alone. You know the commandments: 'You shall not murder; You shall not commit adultery; You shall not steal; You shall not bear false witness; You shall not defraud; Honor your father and mother.'" He said to him, "Teacher, I have kept all these since my youth." Jesus, looking at him, loved him and said, "You lack one thing; go, sell what you own, and give the money to the poor, and you will have treasure in heaven; then come, follow me." When he heard this, he was shocked and went away grieving, for he had many possessions.

- An extraordinary meeting: Mark, the least poetical of the evangelists, throws in details that bring the gospel to life.
- Why does Jesus take issue with the man calling him "good"? Then, "Jesus, looking at him, loved him." Something in Jesus' gaze was unforgettable.
- Mark does not spare us the shock and grief of the man as he hears, and then rejects, Jesus' invitation, or Jesus' calm acceptance of that refusal. He will not do violence to our freedom.

Monday 12th October Luke 11:29–32

When the crowds were increasing, Jesus began to say, "This generation is an evil generation; it asks for a sign, but no sign will be given to it except the sign of Jonah. For just as Jonah became a sign to the people of Nineveh, so the Son of Man will be to this generation. The queen of the South will rise at the judgment with the people of this generation and condemn them, because she came from the ends of the earth to listen to the wisdom of Solomon, and see, something greater than Solomon is here! The people of Nineveh will rise up at the judgment with this generation and condemn it, because they repented at the proclamation of Jonah, and see, something greater than Jonah is here!"

- Jonah was remembered as the prophet who warned his people to repent, and all of them, including the king, heard and heeded him. They seized their opportunity and were ready to be jolted out of their routine.
- Lord, you come to me in unexpected and sometimes unwelcome forms. The Jews who gathered around Jesus failed to recognize the truth he spoke. May I be ready, not merely to listen to your words, but to shape my life by them.

Tuesday 13th October **Luke 11:37–41**

While Jesus was speaking, a Pharisee invited him to dine with him; so he went in and took his place at the table. The Pharisee was amazed to see that he did not first wash before dinner. Then the Lord said to him, "Now you Pharisees clean the outside of the cup and of the dish, but inside you are full of greed and wickedness. You fools! Did not the one who made the outside make the inside also? So give for alms those things that are within; and see, everything will be clean for you."

- How much energy and care I spend on my outside, Lord! Not just my appearance, but taking trouble about the way others see me. Bart Simpson used to cry, "I didn't do it! Nobody saw me! You can't prove it!" There is still some of that child in me.
- You read my heart, Lord. You know the movements and deviances under the surface of my behavior. Teach me to live first of all in your presence, free from seeking human respect.

Wednesday 14th October **Luke 11:42–46**

"But woe to you Pharisees! For you tithe mint and rue and herbs of all kinds, and neglect justice and the love of God; it is these you ought to have practiced, without neglecting the others. Woe to you Pharisees! For you love to have the seat of honor in the synagogues and to be greeted with respect in the marketplaces. Woe to you! For you are like unmarked graves, and people walk over them without realizing it." One of the lawyers answered him, "Teacher, when you say these things, you insult us too." And he said, "Woe also to you lawyers! For you load people with burdens hard to bear, and you yourselves do not lift a finger to ease them."

- Jesus did not blame the Pharisees for multiplying rules about tithing mint and rue. But he denounced them for neglecting the deeper commandments, justice and the love of God.
- Every community, including churches, tends to have its "in-group," those with influence, those treated with respect.
- Lord, save me from that fate. Let me be content to be overlooked and forgotten.

Thursday 15th October,
St. Teresa of Avila **Romans 8:26–27**

The Spirit helps us in our weakness; for we do not know how to pray as we ought, but that very Spirit intercedes with sighs too deep for words. And God, who searches the heart, knows what is the mind of the Spirit, because the Spirit intercedes for the saints according to the will of God.

- Lord, you search me and you know me. When I am sick, distracted, or in other ways unable to pray, the Holy Spirit, more intimate to me than my own self, links me with you, and prays for me with sighs too deep for words.

- Your Spirit is active in me. Thank you.

Friday 16th October **Luke 12:6–7**

"Are not five sparrows sold for two pennies? Yet not one of them is forgotten in God's sight. But even the hairs of your head are all counted. Do not be afraid; you are of more value than many sparrows."

- The Jews used to say that every blade of grass has its own guardian angel. God has an eye for the details, for the monsters as well as the molecules.
- We mortals are born and die in our millions, many of us forgotten. Yet the Lord cherishes each of us personally. Without that faith, I would despair. So I come back to this verse. In God's eyes each of us is precious.

Saturday 17th October **Luke 12:8–12**

"And I tell you, everyone who acknowledges me before others, the Son of Man also will acknowledge before the angels of God; but whoever denies me before others will be denied before the angels of God. And everyone who speaks a word against the Son of Man will be forgiven; but whoever blasphemes against the Holy Spirit will not be forgiven. When they bring you before the synagogues, the rulers, and the authorities, do not worry about how you are to defend yourselves or what you are to say; for the Holy Spirit will teach you at that very hour what you ought to say."

- Luke is writing for Christians who encounter conflict and persecution as followers of Jesus. The words of Jesus at once challenge and console. They challenge us to remain loyal to him, to acknowledge him as Lord, no matter what suffering or derision that entails for us. They reassure us that we do not need to be clever or quick-witted in the face of persecutors.

- We can trust the Holy Spirit to give us either the right words or, as in Jesus' passion, the eloquent silence that will bear witness to him.

october 18–24

Something to think and pray about each day this week:

Securing Our Treasure

In one of the gospel parables, the rich man is mulling over his treasures and plans to build even bigger barns to store all his crops. He relishes his security: My soul, you have plenty of good things laid by for many years to come. Jesus reflects: A man's life is not made secure by what he owns. As we grow quiet in prayer, our hearts can be invaded in the same way by false securities. In the measure that my heart is in past treasures, I am fossilized and dead, for life is only in the present. So to each of these past treasures I am grateful, yet I say goodbye, explaining that, grateful though I am that it came into my life, it must move out, or my heart will never learn to love the present.

The Presence of God

To be present is to arrive as one is and open up to the other.
At this instant, as I arrive here, God is present waiting for me.
God always arrives before me, desiring to connect with me
even more than my most intimate friend.
I take a moment and greet my loving God.

Freedom

In these days, God taught me
as a schoolteacher teaches a pupil (St Ignatius).
I remind myself that there are things God has to teach me yet
and ask for the grace to hear them and let them change me.

Consciousness

In the presence of my loving Creator,
I look honestly at my feelings over the last day,
the highs, the lows, and the level ground.
Can I see where the Lord has been present?

The Word

I take my time to read the Word of God slowly a few times, allowing myself to dwell on anything that strikes me. (Please turn to your scripture on the following pages. Inspiration points are there should you need them. When you are ready, return here to continue.)

Conversation

What feelings are rising in me
as I pray and reflect on God's Word?
I imagine Jesus himself sitting or standing beside me
and open my heart to him.

Conclusion

Glory be to the Father, and to the Son, and to the Holy Spirit,
As it was in the beginning, is now and ever shall be,
World without end. Amen

Sunday 18th October,
Twenty-ninth Sunday in Ordinary Time **Mark 10:35–45**

James and John, the sons of Zebedee, came forward to him and said to him, "Teacher, we want you to do for us whatever we ask of you." And he said to them, "What is it you want me to do for you?" And they said to him, "Grant us to sit, one at your right hand and one at your left, in your glory." But Jesus said to them, "You do not know what you are asking. Are you able to drink the cup that I drink, or be baptized with the baptism that I am baptized with?" They replied, "We are able." Then Jesus said to them, "The cup that I drink you will drink; and with the baptism with which I am baptized, you will be baptized; but to sit at my right hand or at my left is not mine to grant, but it is for those for whom it has been prepared." When the ten heard this, they began to be angry with James and John. So Jesus called them and said to them, "You know that among the Gentiles those whom they recognize as their rulers lord it over them, and their great ones are tyrants over them. But it is not so among you; but whoever wishes to become great among you must be your servant, and whoever wishes to be first among you must be slave of all. For the Son of Man came not to be served, but to serve, and to give his life a ransom for many."

- This lovely dialogue leads us deep into Jesus' way of teaching. It starts with the sort of untamed desire that lies behind many of our prayers. Jesus leads James and John into the implications of what they are asking. He does not throw suffering at them, but invites them to share his cup.
- Invite me too, Lord. I would prefer to serve with you than to sit on a throne.

Monday 19th October **Luke 12:15–21**

Jesus said to them, "Take care! Be on your guard against all kinds of greed; for one's life does not consist in the abundance of possessions." Then he told them a parable: "The land of a rich man produced abundantly. And he thought to himself, 'What should I do, for I have no place to store my crops?' Then he said, 'I will do this: I will pull down my barns and build larger ones, and there I will store all my grain and my goods.' And I will say to my soul, 'Soul, you have ample goods laid up for many years; relax, eat, drink, be merry.' But God said to him, 'You fool! This very night your life is being demanded of you. And the things you have prepared, whose will they be?' So it is with those who store up treasures for themselves but are not rich toward God."

- That rich man was talking to himself, not to friends; and his talk was all "I" and "my." His horizon was bounded by his plans and pleasures. He was a Scrooge chasing a phantom of happiness.
- Where is my security? Is a pension plan, a bank balance, or peace of soul based on a bond with God?

Tuesday 20th October **Luke 12:35–38**

Jesus said to his disciples, "Be dressed for action and have your lamps lit; be like those who are waiting for their master to return from the wedding banquet, so that they may open the door for him as soon as he comes and knocks. Blessed are those slaves whom the master finds alert when he comes; truly I tell you, he will fasten his belt and have them sit down to eat, and he will come and serve them. If he comes during the middle of the night, or near dawn, and finds them so, blessed are those slaves."

- It was Cardinal Newman who wrote, "Fear not that your life will come to an end; fear rather that it will never come to a beginning."

- Do I treasure the present moment, the only time that available to me to respond to God's gifts, to prove myself?
- How do I stay alert to the Lord's presence?

Wednesday 21st October **Luke 12:39–44, 48b**

Jesus said, "But know this: if the owner of the house had known at what hour the thief was coming, he would not have let his house be broken into. You also must be ready, for the Son of Man is coming at an unexpected hour." Peter said, "Lord, are you telling this parable for us or for everyone?" And the Lord said, "Who then is the faithful and prudent manager whom his master will put in charge of his slaves, to give them their allowance of food at the proper time? Blessed is that slave whom his master will find at work when he arrives. Truly I tell you, he will put that one in charge of all his possessions." "From everyone to whom much has been given, much will be required; and from the one to whom much has been entrusted, even more will be demanded."

- Jesus, you tell me to be ready for the hour when you unexpectedly come into my life. When that hour comes, may I be at peace with myself, loving myself as you love me.
- May I be able to answer with St. Vincent de Paul, who was asked on his death-bed if he forgave his enemies: "I have no enemies."

Thursday 22nd October **Luke 12:49–51**

"I came to bring fire to the earth, and how I wish it were already kindled! I have a baptism with which to be baptized, and what stress I am under until it is completed! Do you think that I have come to bring peace to the earth? No, I tell you, but rather division!"

- "What stress I am under," says Jesus. It stems from his mission. He is sent by the Father to purify and to distinguish what is genuine from dross. Life according to the beatitudes has its share of conflict.

- For those who hunger and thirst for justice, this world is not a comfortable place. As Simeon prophesied to Mary, Jesus was "destined to be a sign that is rejected" (Lk 2:35).
- What about me? Do I merge seamlessly and comfortably with the values of this world? Do I hunger and thirst for anything?

Friday 23rd October **Luke 12:54–57**

He also said to the crowds, "When you see a cloud rising in the west, you immediately say, 'It is going to rain'; and so it happens. And when you see the south wind blowing, you say, 'There will be scorching heat'; and it happens. You hypocrites! You know how to interpret the appearance of earth and sky, but why do you not know how to interpret the present time? And why do you not judge for yourselves what is right?"

- Lord, you are shaking my complacency. You ask me to judge the signs of the times, to recognize what is evil and greedy and perverse —to take sides for justice and mercy.
- Teach me to interpret the present time with your eyes.

Saturday 24th October **Luke 13:6–9**

Jesus told this parable: "A man had a fig tree planted in his vineyard; and he came looking for fruit on it and found none. So he said to the gardener, 'See here! For three years I have come looking for fruit on this fig tree, and still I find none. Cut it down! Why should it be wasting the soil?' He replied, 'Sir, let it alone for one more year, until I dig round it and put manure on it. If it bears fruit next year, well and good; but if not, you can cut it down.'"

- As with so many of Jesus' words, this must be set in its context. He is speaking to his own people, using an image from the prophets: Israel as the Lord's vineyard. He is begging his people to wake up to their opportunity, to bear fruit.
- You speak to me too, Lord. You look to me for fruit, for signs of love in my life. I do not want to be wasting my opportunities, but I rely on you to have patience and help me. Dig around me and nourish me, even if it hurts.
- You alone know how to make something good of my life.

october 25–31

Something to think and pray about each day this week:

Coming Closer

Late October in the northern hemisphere brings a sense of the year declining, of mortality and gathering darkness. Even in these moments of unsettlement, or even in worse moments like we leaving home, losing friends or job, we may feel the closeness of God. We bring Psalm 90 to mind: "Lord you have been our refuge from age to age, before the mountains were born, before the earth or the world came to birth, you were God, from all eternity and for ever. Teach us to count how few days we have, and so gain wisdom of heart. Let us wake in the morning filled with your love. Let your servants see what you can do for them."

Presence of God
What is present to me is what has a hold on my becoming.
I reflect on the presence of God always there in love,
amidst the many things that have a hold on me.
I pause and pray that I may let God
affect my becoming in this precise moment.

Freedom
If God were trying to tell me something, would I know?
If God were reassuring me or challenging me, would I notice?
I ask for the grace to be free of my own preoccupations
and open to what God may be saying to me.

Consciousness
Knowing that God loves me unconditionally,
I look honestly over the last day, its events and my feelings.
Do I have something to be grateful for? Then I give thanks.
Is there something I am sorry for? Then I ask forgiveness.

The Word
God speaks to each one of us individually. I need to listen to what he is saying to me. (Please turn to your scripture on the following pages. Inspiration points are there should you need them. When you are ready, return here to continue.)

Conversation
What is stirring in me as I pray?
Am I consoled, troubled, left cold?
I imagine Jesus himself standing or sitting at my side
and share my feelings with him.

Conclusion
Glory be to the Father, and to the Son, and to the Holy Spirit,
As it was in the beginning, is now and ever shall be,
World without end. Amen

Sunday 25th October,
Thirtieth Sunday in Ordinary Time **Mark 10:46–52**

They came to Jericho. As he and his disciples and a large crowd were leaving Jericho, Bartimaeus son of Timaeus, a blind beggar, was sitting by the roadside. When he heard that it was Jesus of Nazareth, he began to shout out and say, "Jesus, Son of David, have mercy on me!" Many sternly ordered him to be quiet, but he cried out even more loudly, "Son of David, have mercy on me!" Jesus stood still and said, "Call him here." And they called the blind man, saying to him, "Take heart; get up, he is calling you." So throwing off his cloak, he sprang up and came to Jesus. Then Jesus said to him, "What do you want me to do for you?" The blind man said to him, "My teacher, let me see again." Jesus said to him, "Go; your faith has made you well." Immediately he regained his sight and followed him on the way.

- Mark has heard this story from St. Peter, whom he accompanied, so the scene is vivid. I imagine the margin of the dirt road on which Jesus is walking. There sits the blind beggar Bartimaeus, a symbol of all the marginalized.
- Some of the bystanders scold him for making a fuss. Others pick up the quick response of Jesus and encourage Bartimaeus: "Take heart, get up, he is calling you."
- What are my reactions? What do I want Jesus to do for me?

Monday 26th October **Luke 13:10–17**

Now Jesus was teaching in one of the synagogues on the sabbath. And just then there appeared a woman with a spirit that had crippled her for eighteen years. She was bent over and was quite unable to stand up straight. When Jesus saw her, he called her over and said, "Woman, you are set free from your ailment." When he laid his hands on her, immediately she stood up straight and began praising God. But the leader of the synagogue, indignant because Jesus had cured on the sabbath, kept saying to the crowd, "There are six days on which work ought to be done; come on those days and be cured, and not on the sabbath day." But the Lord answered him and said, "You hypocrites! Does not each of you on the sabbath untie his ox or his donkey from the manger, and lead it away to give it water? And ought not this woman, a daughter of Abraham, whom Satan bound for eighteen long years, be set free from this bondage on the sabbath day?" When he said this, all his opponents were put to shame; and the entire crowd was rejoicing at all the wonderful things that he was doing.

- Release from bondage is the key theme in this story. Jesus is the liberator, enabling us to stand straight, freeing us from what bows our heads so that we see only the earth in front of us.
- The synagogue leader is afraid to take on Jesus; instead he rebukes the crowd for seeking a cure on the sabbath. There is cowardice here, as well as hypocrisy.
- We can feel the joy of the crowd who sense that God is on the side of freedom and health. Lord, give me the spirit of freedom and give me the energy and health to serve you.

Tuesday 27th October **Luke 13:18–21**

He said therefore, "What is the kingdom of God like? And to what should I compare it? It is like a mustard seed that someone took and sowed in the garden; it grew and became a tree, and the birds of the air made nests in its branches." And again he said, "To what should I compare the kingdom of God? It is like yeast that a woman took and mixed in with three measures of flour until all of it was leavened."

- To the crowds who expected the kingdom of God to come with fanfare and the beating of drums, Jesus offers two wonderful images of organic growth. The mustard seed grows slowly, but as a tree it has room for all sorts of birds in its branches. Now, as in its first centuries, the Church has room for all races, colors, and cultures. We are not clones, but hugely diverse.
- Another image of the kingdom: yeast in the dough, working for good even when unseen. Lord, I feel safer as yeast, working invisibly and unnoticed. I do not look to see results, just to know that I am an active part of your kingdom.

Wednesday 28th October,
Sts. Simon and Jude, Apostles **Ephesians 2:19-22**

So then you are no longer strangers and aliens, but you are citizens with the saints and also members of the household of God, built upon the foundation of the apostles and prophets, with Christ Jesus himself as the cornerstone. In him the whole structure is joined together and grows into a holy temple in the Lord; in whom you also are built together spiritually into a dwelling place for God.

- The image of the Church as a building merges with the human image to create a picture for us of a building made of living stones, centered on Jesus.
- How do I work to build this community, the "members of the household of God"?
- Am I constructive in this household? How do my actions give life to the people of God?

Thursday 29th October **Romans 8:31b–35**

If God is for us, who is against us? He who did not withhold his own Son, but gave him up for all of us, will he not with him also give us everything else? Who will bring any charge against

God's elect? It is God who justifies. Who is to condemn? It is Christ Jesus, who died, yes, who was raised, who is at the right hand of God, who indeed intercedes for us. Who will separate us from the love of Christ? Will hardship, or distress, or persecution, or famine, or nakedness, or peril, or sword?

- This is Paul at his lyrical best in one of the most magnificent statements in the scriptures, a symphony to the all-powerful love of God.
- The love of God, made clear in the life of Christ Jesus, is the basis of Christian life and hope, and it is unshakeable.

Friday 30th October **Luke 14:1–6**

On one occasion when Jesus was going to the house of a leader of the Pharisees to eat a meal on the sabbath, they were watching him closely. Just then, in front of him, there was a man who had dropsy. And Jesus asked the lawyers and Pharisees, "Is it lawful to cure people on the sabbath, or not?" But they were silent. So Jesus took him and healed him, and sent him away. Then he said to them, "If one of you has a child or an ox that has fallen into a well, will you not immediately pull it out on a sabbath day?" And they could not reply to this.

- I imagine this scene. The powerful lawyers and Pharisees are growing increasingly angry. Here is their guest whom they want to entrap; instead, without any words, he responds to the simple, deep faith of the man with dropsy by curing him. Then the man is gone.
- Do I have such compassion? Do I have such courage?

Saturday 31st October **Luke 14:1, 7–11**

On one occasion when Jesus was going to the house of a leader of the Pharisees to eat a meal on the sabbath, they were watching him closely. When he noticed how the guests chose the places of honor, he told them a parable. "When you are invited by someone to a wedding banquet, do not sit down at the place of honor, in case someone more distinguished than you has been invited by your host; and the host who invited both of you may come and say to you, 'Give this person your place,' and then in disgrace you would start to take the lowest place. But when you are invited, go and sit down at the lowest place, so that when your host comes, he may say to you, 'Friend, move up higher'; then you will be honored in the presence of all who sit at the table with you. For all who exalt themselves will be humbled, and those who humble themselves will be exalted."

- Celebrities give us much entertainment, but we may need to be careful not to exaggerate their importance. Do I ever envy them the red carpet or the spotlight?
- Humility does not mean groveling, but being real, being of service.

november 1–7

Something to think and pray about each day this week:

New Saints

In the New Testament the word "saint" is applied to Christians generally. Being a Christian at all was extraordinary. Christians stood out sharply from their environment, regarded as something strange if not hostile. To the Christian the gospel really was a revelation; something unlooked for, something hitherto unknown. The life of Jesus had made us aware of how God is minded toward us, and the experience was life-changing, "all things had become new."

In modern times, being a Christian is resuming its old distinctive character: To be moved by God's revelation is increasingly felt as something extraordinary, as it truly is—as grace, happiness, responsibility, something great, and, at the same time, dangerous.

The Presence of God
God is with me, but more, God is within me.
Let me dwell for a moment on God's life-giving presence
in my body, in my mind, in my heart,
as I sit here, right now.

Freedom
I need to close out the noise, to rise above the noise;
The noise that interrupts, that separates,
The noise that isolates.
I need to listen to God again.

Consciousness
I remind myself that I am in the presence of the Lord.
I will take refuge in His loving heart.
He is my strength in times of weakness.
He is my comforter in times of sorrow.

The Word
I read the Word of God slowly a few times over, and I listen to what God is saying to me. (Please turn to your scripture on the following pages. Inspiration points are there should you need them. When you are ready, return here to continue.)

Conversation
Do I notice myself reacting as I pray with the Word of God?
Do I feel challenged, comforted, angry?
Imagining Jesus sitting or standing by me,
I speak out my feelings, as one trusted friend to another.

Conclusion
Glory be to the Father, and to the Son, and to the Holy Spirit,
As it was in the beginning, is now and ever shall be,
World without end. Amen

Sunday 1st November,
Feast of All Saints **Matthew 5:2–12**

He began to speak, and taught them, saying: "Blessed are the poor in spirit, for theirs is the kingdom of heaven. Blessed are those who mourn, for they will be comforted. Blessed are the meek, for they will inherit the earth. Blessed are those who hunger and thirst for righteousness, for they will be filled. Blessed are the merciful, for they will receive mercy. Blessed are the pure in heart, for they will see God. Blessed are the peacemakers, for they will be called children of God. Blessed are those who are persecuted for righteousness' sake, for theirs is the kingdom of heaven. Blessed are you when people revile you and persecute you and utter all kinds of evil against you falsely on my account. Rejoice and be glad, for your reward is great in heaven, for in the same way they persecuted the prophets who were before you."

- The beatitudes offer a glimpse of Jesus' interior landscape, of the sources of his happiness. They are not legislation, but an interior vision, fired by a hunger for justice in this world and by confidence in a future when the mourners will be comforted, the poor will be enriched, and the meek will inherit the earth.
- We know that the love of riches can lead to neglect of God and of the poor. The Christian community has always tried to make the care of the poor its priority, as it is God's priority. Is it mine?

Monday 2nd November,
Feast of All Souls **Matthew 25:31–40**

"When the Son of Man comes in his glory, and all the angels with him, then he will sit on the throne of his glory. All the nations will be gathered before him, and he will separate people one from another as a shepherd separates the sheep from the goats, and he will put the sheep at his right hand

and the goats at the left. Then the king will say to those at his right hand, 'Come, you that are blessed by my Father, inherit the kingdom prepared for you from the foundation of the world; for I was hungry and you gave me food, I was thirsty and you gave me something to drink, I was a stranger and you welcomed me, I was naked and you gave me clothing, I was sick and you took care of me, I was in prison and you visited me.' Then the righteous will answer him, 'Lord, when was it that we saw you hungry and gave you food, or thirsty and gave you something to drink? And when was it that we saw you a stranger and welcomed you, or naked and gave you clothing? And when was it that we saw you sick or in prison and visited you?' And the king will answer them, 'Truly I tell you, just as you did it to one of the least of these who are members of my family, you did it to me.'"

- Can I be identified as a Christian by my words and actions?
- Can I take some time to sit and think about what I can do today?

Tuesday 3rd November **Romans 12:5–7**

We, who are many, are one body in Christ, and individually we are members one of another. We have gifts that differ according to the grace given to us: prophecy, in proportion to faith; ministry, in ministering; the teacher, in teaching; the exhorter, in exhortation; the giver, in generosity; the leader, in diligence; the compassionate, in cheerfulness.

- "According to the grace given to us." We are each given this grace, this gift, but differently. Can I sit with that phrase for a while?
- Does this challenge me? Do I focus on the gifts that others have, but not my own? Do I give thanks to God?
- I note that gifts are in no way passive, but expressed in action, by teachers teaching and givers giving. How do I celebrate my gifts?

Wednesday 4th November,
St. Charles Borromeo **John 10:11–16**

Jesus said to the Pharisees, "I am the good shepherd. The good shepherd lays down his life for the sheep. The hired hand, who is not the shepherd and does not own the sheep, sees the wolf coming and leaves the sheep and runs away–and the wolf snatches them and scatters them. The hired hand runs away because a hired hand does not care for the sheep. I am the good shepherd. I know my own, and my own know me, just as the Father knows me and I know the Father. And I lay down my life for the sheep. I have other sheep that do not belong to this fold. I must bring them also, and they will listen to my voice. So there will be one flock, one shepherd."

- "I know my own, and my own know me." This is not a simple friendship Jesus talks about, but a deeply personal and intimate relationship—"just as the Father knows me and I know the Father." This is a life journey, to reach such intimacy.
- Lord, do I know you?

Thursday 5th November **Luke 15:1–10**

Now all the tax collectors and sinners were coming near to listen to him. And the Pharisees and the scribes were grumbling and saying, "This fellow welcomes sinners and eats with them." So he told them this parable: "Which one of you, having a hundred sheep and losing one of them, does not leave the ninety-nine in the wilderness and go after the one that is lost until he finds it? When he has found it, he lays it on his shoulders and rejoices. And when he comes home, he calls together his friends and neighbors, saying to them, 'Rejoice with me, for I have found my sheep that was lost.' Just so, I tell you, there will be more joy in heaven over one sinner who repents than over ninety-nine righteous persons who need no repentance. Or what woman having ten silver coins, if she loses one of them, does not light a lamp, sweep the house, and search carefully until she finds it? When she has found it, she calls together her friends and neighbors, saying, 'Rejoice with me, for I have found the coin that I had lost.' Just so, I tell you, there is joy in the presence of the angels of God over one sinner who repents."

- Who are today's sinners, reviled by the media? Whenever I see a finger-pointing headline in the news denouncing someone who has been caught, I will think like you, Lord.
- Instead of letting my anger be harnessed against them, let me feel some compassion, realizing that, but for the grace of God, I could be in those shoes.

Friday 6th November **Luke 16:1–8**

Then Jesus said to the disciples, "There was a rich man who had a manager, and charges were brought to him that this man was squandering his property. So he summoned him and said to him, 'What is this that I hear about you? Give me an accounting of your management, because you cannot be my manager any longer.' Then the manager said to himself, 'What will I do, now that my master is taking the position away from me? I am not strong enough to dig, and I am ashamed to beg. I have decided what to do so that, when I am dismissed as manager, people may welcome me into their homes.' So, summoning his master's debtors one by one, he asked the first, 'How much do you owe my master?' He answered, 'A hundred jugs of olive oil.' He said to him, 'Take your bill, sit down quickly, and make it fifty.' Then he asked another, 'And how much do you owe?' He replied, 'A hundred containers of wheat.' He said to him, 'Take your bill and make it eighty.' And his master commended the dishonest manager because he had acted shrewdly; for the children of this age are more shrewd in dealing with their own generation than are the children of light."

- Lord, you are telling me to be astute, to use wisely what wealth I have. Having money is a responsibility. I can use it selfishly or to help family and the needy. God gave us temporal things to use.
- My wealth consists not in what I keep, but what I give away. You judge me by how I use the things of which I am only a steward.

Saturday 7th November **Luke 16:9–15**

Jesus said to the disciples, "And I tell you, make friends for yourselves by means of dishonest wealth so that when it is gone, they may welcome you into the eternal homes. Whoever is faithful in a very little is faithful also in much; and whoever is dishonest in a very little is dishonest also in much. If then you have not been faithful with the dishonest wealth, who will entrust to you the true riches? And if you have not been faithful with what belongs to another, who will give you what is your own? No slave can serve two masters; for a slave will either hate the one and love the other, or be devoted to the one and despise the other. You cannot serve God and wealth." The Pharisees, who were lovers of money, heard all this, and they ridiculed him. So he said to them, "You are those who justify yourselves in the sight of others; but God knows your hearts; for what is prized by human beings is an abomination in the sight of God."

- To be faithful in small things is the flower of love. When I prepare a gift for the one I love, every detail counts, and I do it with joy. A gentleman excused his lack of religious practice to St. Catherine of Siena, saying he was busy with temporal affairs. She answered, "It is you who make them temporal."

- Lord, let this be my way to you, to do the small things well out of love for you so that they become significant for eternity.

november 8–14

Something to think and pray about each day this week:

On the Way

When the apostles asked Jesus, "Teach us to pray," he taught them the Our Father. That is the beginning for all of us. There is no word or phrase in the Our Father that does not repay if you mine it for meaning and savor it. Even the opening word "our"—not just "my" father, for I share you with the human race. Is there anyone whom I felt uneasy to claim as a sister or brother? Take the prayer slowly, breathing slowly as you relish it and are led into its depths. It sets the scene: each of us as a temple of the Holy Spirit reaching out to the Father through his Son.

Many of you who read this have gone beyond words to a sort of quiet presence. When Jean Vianney, the Curé of Ars, noticed an old peasant sitting for hours in his church, he asked him what he was doing. "I look at the good God, and the good God looks at me." That old man was well on his way.

The Presence of God
As I sit here, the beating of my heart,
the ebb and flow of my breathing, the movements of my mind
are all signs of God's ongoing creation of me.
I pause for a moment, and become aware
of this presence of God within me.

Freedom
Lord, grant me the grace to be free from the excesses of this life.
Let me not get caught up with the desire for wealth.
Keep my heart and mind free to love and serve you.

Consciousness
In God's loving presence I unwind the past day,
starting from now and looking back, moment by moment.
I gather in all the goodness and light, in gratitude.
I attend to the shadows and what they say to me,
seeking healing, courage, forgiveness.

The Word
I take my time to read the Word of God slowly, a few times, allowing myself to dwell on anything that strikes me. (Please turn to your scripture on the following pages. Inspiration points are there should you need them. When you are ready, return here to continue.)

Conversation
Remembering that I am still in God's presence,
I imagine Jesus himself standing or sitting beside me
and say whatever is on my mind, whatever is in my heart,
speaking as one friend to another.

Conclusion
Glory be to the Father, and to the Son, and to the Holy Spirit,
As it was in the beginning, is now and ever shall be,
World without end. Amen

Sunday 8th November,
Thirty-second Sunday in Ordinary Time Mark 12:38–44

As Jesus taught in the temple, he said, "Beware of the scribes, who like to walk around in long robes, and to be greeted with respect in the marketplaces, and to have the best seats in the synagogues and places of honor at banquets! They devour widows' houses and for the sake of appearance say long prayers. They will receive the greater condemnation." He sat down opposite the treasury, and watched the crowd putting money into the treasury. Many rich people put in large sums. A poor widow came and put in two small copper coins, which are worth a penny. Then he called his disciples and said to them, "Truly I tell you, this poor widow has put in more than all those who are contributing to the treasury. For all of them have contributed out of their abundance; but she out of her poverty has put in everything she had, all she had to live on."

- The big givers may see their name in lights; but for you, Lord, the big giver is the one who gives from the heart. You do not count the coins, but the generosity.
- Yet I need some help in my generosity. The appeals are endless as we learn more of the world's poverty. Perhaps the hardest thing for me to give is my time and energy.

Monday 9th November,
Dedication of the Lateran Basilica John 2:13–22

The Passover of the Jews was near, and Jesus went up to Jerusalem. In the temple he found people selling cattle, sheep, and doves, and the money changers seated at their tables. Making a whip of cords, he drove all of them out of the temple, both the sheep and the cattle. He also poured out the coins of the money changers and overturned their tables. He told those who were selling the doves, "Take these things out of here! Stop making my Father's house a marketplace!" His disciples remembered that it was written, "Zeal for your house will consume me." The Jews then said to him, "What sign can you show us for doing this?" Jesus answered them, "Destroy this temple, and in three days I will raise it up." The Jews then said, "This temple has been under construction for forty-six years, and will you raise it up in three days?" But he was speaking of the temple of his body. After he was raised from the dead, his disciples remembered that he had said this; and they believed the scripture and the word that Jesus had spoken.

- I imagine myself visiting the Temple when Jesus enters. I am accustomed to the moneychangers and to the hucksters who trade with worshippers by selling cattle, sheep, and doves for the ritual sacrifices.
- The fury of Jesus startles me, upsets me, makes me think. Surely these guys are making an honest few dollars?
- But this is the house of God. When money creeps in, it tends to take over. Can God get a hearing amid the clatter of coins?

Tuesday 10th November **Wisdom 2:23, 3:1–3**

God created us for incorruption, and made us in the image of his own eternity. The souls of the righteous are in the hand of God, and no torment will ever touch them.

In the eyes of the foolish they seemed to have died, and their departure was thought to be a disaster, and their going from us to be their destruction; but they are at peace.

- Am I made in the image of your nature, Lord? Like Hopkins, I marvel at your work:

I am all at once what Christ is, since he was what I am, and this Jack, joke, poor potsherd, patch, matchwood, immortal diamond.

Wednesday 11th November **Luke 17:11–19**

On the way to Jerusalem, Jesus was going through the region between Samaria and Galilee. As he entered a village, ten lepers approached him. Keeping their distance, they called out, saying, "Jesus, Master, have mercy on us!" When he saw them, he said to them, "Go, and show yourselves to the priests." And as they went, they were made clean. Then one of them, when he saw that he was healed, turned back, praising God with a loud voice. He prostrated himself at Jesus' feet and thanked him. And he was a Samaritan. Then Jesus asked, "Were not ten made clean? But the other nine, where are they? Was none of them found to return and give praise to God except this foreigner?" Then he said to him, "Get up, and go on your way; your faith has made you well."

- Lord, all through my life I have known kindnesses; there have been people whom I thanked after a big favor, using inflated language—that I would never forget them. But my gratitude grows cold.
- Let me count my blessings, never take them for granted.

Thursday 12th November **Luke 17:20–25**

Once Jesus was asked by the Pharisees when the kingdom of God was coming, and he answered, "The kingdom of God is not coming with things that can be observed; nor will they say, 'Look, here it is!' or 'There it is!' For, in fact, the kingdom of God is among you." Then he said to the disciples, "The days are coming when you will long to see one of the days of the Son of Man, and you will not see it. They will say to you, 'Look there!' or 'Look here!' Do not go, do not set off in pursuit. For as the lightning flashes and lights up the sky from one side to the other, so will the Son of Man be in his day. But first he must endure much suffering and be rejected by this generation."

- Talk of the Second Coming excited the early Christians but leaves us cold. We have heard too many false prophets telling us the end is nigh. The prophets are dead, and the end is still far off. "The kingdom of God is among you," Jesus says. It's in the now, not in an indefinite future.
- Are there echoes of the same thing in my life? What am I waiting for before I will acknowledge the kingdom of God around me? Am I waiting for someone to say, "There it is"?

Friday 13th November **Luke 17:26–37**

"Just as it was in the days of Noah, so too it will be in the days of the Son of Man. They were eating and drinking, and marrying and being given in marriage, until the day Noah entered the ark, and the flood came and destroyed all of them. Likewise, just as it was in the days of Lot: they were eating and drinking, buying and selling, planting and building, but on the day that Lot left Sodom, it rained fire and sulfur from heaven and destroyed all of them—it will be like that on the day that the Son of Man is revealed. On that day, anyone on the housetop who has belongings in the house must not come down to take them away; and likewise anyone in the field must not turn back. Remember Lot's wife. Those who try to make their life secure will lose it, but those who lose their life will keep it. I tell you, on that night there will be two in one bed; one will be taken and the other left. There will be two women grinding meal together; one will be taken and the other left."

- Three apocalyptic visions weave in and out of one another in these chapters of Luke: Jesus' sense of his own forthcoming passion and death; his warning of the destruction of Jerusalem by the Romans; and the second coming of Jesus at the end of time.

- Jesus is on his way to Jerusalem to die. He does not have much time left. He knows that he faces the ultimate choice soon. Is that why he speaks so vehemently about the need to choose now and about the insecurity of this life?

Saturday 14th November **Luke 18:1–8**

Then Jesus told them a parable about their need to pray always and not to lose heart. He said, "In a certain city there was a judge who neither feared God nor had respect for people. In that city there was a widow who kept coming to him and saying, 'Grant me justice against my opponent.' For a while he refused; but later he said to himself, 'Though I have no fear of God and no respect for anyone, yet because this widow keeps bothering me, I will grant her justice, so that she may not wear me out by continually coming.'" And the Lord said, "Listen to what the unjust judge says. And will not God grant justice to his chosen ones who cry to him day and night? Will he delay long in helping them? I tell you, he will quickly grant justice to them. And yet, when the Son of Man comes, will he find faith on earth?"

- In this story Jesus piles up the odds against the widow. She is a woman in a male-dominated society, therefore at a disadvantage. More than that, she has no husband to back her. More than that, the judge is unjust and notoriously ruthless. But she gets a hearing by making a nuisance of herself.
- Jesus tells us to do the same with God, who wants to be good to us. Pray always, and do not lose heart. God's answer may be as hard to fathom as his answer to Jesus' prayer in Gethsemane, "Let this chalice pass from me—but your will be done."

november 15–21

Something to think and pray about each day this week:

Being Together in Prayer

When Ignatius Loyola went to the University of Paris, a group of young men gathered around him. What did he do? He taught them to pray, in the shape that came to be known as the *Spiritual Exercises*. Because Ignatius had been a remarkable soldier, people sometimes think of the Jesuits he founded as a sort of army. In fact, what united them was not any sort of military discipline, but a shared experience of the *Spiritual Exercises*.

Many other unexpected Christians shared that experience. Richard Baxter, a Puritan contemporary of Cromwell, said he was converted by reading and praying his way through a dog-eared copy of the *Exercises*. In the 1800s, Russian Orthodox Christians made the same discovery. In the 1900s, it was an Anglican who produced one of the best editions of the book.

When we turn to God in personal prayer centered on Jesus, the walls that divide the Christian churches melt away. We find that we can pray together. The secret history of the Church is not in the councils, doctrines, crusades, or bishops, still less in churches or cathedrals, but in the body of Christians who pray to the Father through Jesus Christ his son: what you might call the contemplative tradition, where men and women share a sacred space.

The Presence of God
As I sit here, the beating of my heart,
the ebb and flow of my breathing, the movements of my mind
are all signs of God's ongoing creation of me.
I pause for a moment, and become aware
of this presence of God within me.

Freedom
I will ask God's help,
to be free from my own preoccupations,
to be open to God in this time of prayer,
to come to love and serve him more.

Consciousness
Help me, Lord, to be more conscious of your presence.
Teach me to recognize your presence in others.
Fill my heart with gratitude for the times your love
has been shown to me through the care of others.

The Word
I take my time to read the Word of God slowly, a few times, allowing myself to dwell on anything that strikes me. (Please turn to your scripture on the following pages. Inspiration points are there should you need them. When you are ready, return here to continue.)

Conversation
Remembering that I am still in God's presence,
I imagine Jesus himself standing or sitting beside me
and say whatever is on my mind, whatever is in my heart,
speaking as one friend to another.

Conclusion
Glory be to the Father, and to the Son, and to the Holy Spirit,
As it was in the beginning, is now and ever shall be,
World without end. Amen

Sunday 15th November,
Thirty-third Sunday in Ordinary Time Mark 13:28–32

Jesus said to Peter, James, John, and Andrew, "From the fig tree learn its lesson: as soon as its branch becomes tender and puts forth its leaves, you know that summer is near. So also, when you see these things taking place, you know that he is near, at the very gates. Truly I tell you, this generation will not pass away until all these things have taken place. Heaven and earth will pass away, but my words will not pass away. But about that day or hour no one knows, neither the angels in heaven, nor the Son, but only the Father."

- Lord, I do not know about the end of the world, but there have been times when I felt I was facing the end of my world: when I lost a job, or faced the death of someone dear to me. Yet I lived on and found unsuspected resources.
- In all the losses and catastrophes that threaten, I know that you are with me.

Monday 16th November Luke 18:35–43

As he approached Jericho, a blind man was sitting by the roadside begging. When he heard a crowd going by, he asked what was happening. They told him, "Jesus of Nazareth is passing by." Then he shouted, "Jesus, Son of David, have mercy on me!" Those who were in front sternly ordered him to be quiet; but he shouted even more loudly, "Son of David, have mercy on me!" Jesus stood still and ordered the man to be brought to him; and when he came near, he asked him, "What do you want me to do for you?" He said, "Lord, let me see again." Jesus said to him, "Receive your sight; your faith has saved you." Immediately he regained his sight and followed him, glorifying God; and all the people, when they saw it, praised God.

- Jesus does not cure unbidden; He waits to be asked. What may seem from the outside as a desperate need (the man who is blind needing sight) could be such a habitual state for the sightless that they could not imagine themselves otherwise. So Jesus checks first: "What do you want me to do for you?"
- Lord, there is a sort of sight I ask from you: to use my eyes fully, to relish every nuance of color that surrounds me, to pick up the life and feeling in others' faces and bodies, to see what you want me to see and not just what I want to see.

Tuesday 17th November **Luke 19:1–10**

Jesus entered Jericho and was passing through it. A man was there named Zacchaeus; he was a chief tax-collector and was rich. He was trying to see who Jesus was, but on account of the crowd he could not, because he was short in stature. So he ran ahead and climbed a sycamore tree to see him, because he was going to pass that way. When Jesus came to the place, he looked up and said to him, "Zacchaeus, hurry and come down; for I must stay at your house today." So he hurried down and was happy to welcome him. All who saw it began to grumble and said, "He has gone to be the guest of one who is a sinner." Zacchaeus stood there and said to the Lord, "Look, half of my possessions, Lord, I will give to the poor; and if I have defrauded anyone of anything, I will pay back four times as much." Then Jesus said to him, "Today salvation has come to this house, because he too is a son of Abraham. For the Son of Man came to seek out and to save the lost."

- "He was trying to see who Jesus was." That is my search too. You lived two millennia ago, Lord. I wish I knew what you would be like today.

- But when I turn to the gospels and seek your face, I find that you have been waiting for me, as you were looking for Zacchaeus. You call me by my name as you called him.

Wednesday 18th November **Psalm 16(17):1, 6, 8, 15**

I call upon you, for you will answer me, O God; incline your ear to me, hear my words. Guard me as the apple of your eye; hide me in the shadow of your wings, As for me, I shall behold your face in righteousness; when I awake I shall be satisfied, beholding your likeness.

- Lord, I need to feel I am the apple of your eye as I cope with what each day brings. More than that, I look forward to that for which I was born.
- "When I awake I shall be satisfied with the sight of your glory." My heart is restless till it rests in you.

Thursday 19th November **Luke 19:41–44**

As he came near and saw the city, he wept over it, saying, "If you, even you, had only recognized on this day the things that make for peace! But now they are hidden from your eyes. Indeed, the days will come upon you, when your enemies will set up ramparts around you and surround you, and hem you in on every side. They will crush you to the ground, you and your children within you, and they will not leave within you one stone upon another; because you did not recognize the time of your visitation from God."

- You did not force the hand of your people, Lord. You gave them their opportunity and wept when they were too blind to take it. So in my life you do not force me into goodness. I have the freedom to seize opportunities or to let them slip.

- St. Augustine warned us: "Fear the Lord Jesus when he passes by, for he will not pass this way again." The Greeks saw opportunity as "*kairos*," a fleet-footed boy who flashes past. We must be alert if we are to catch him.

Friday 20th November **Luke 19:45–48**

Then Jesus entered the temple and began to drive out those who were selling things there; and he said, "It is written, 'My house shall be a house of prayer'; but you have made it a den of robbers." Every day he was teaching in the temple. The chief priests, the scribes, and the leaders of the people kept looking for a way to kill him; but they did not find anything they could do, for all the people were spellbound by what they heard.

- Commerce tends to grow and grow when it finds a market, so the Temple, the place of prayer, degenerated into a sort of marketplace. Jesus needed to challenge the drift and reassert its holiness.
- Does it happen in my life, Lord? You desire to dwell in this temple that is my body, but first the pressure to survive, and then the appetite for more money, can so possess me that I find little space for you. Please make my soul a place of prayer.

Saturday 21st November,
Presentation of Our Lady **Matthew 12:46–50**

While he was still speaking to the crowds, his mother and his brothers were standing outside, wanting to speak to him. Someone told him, "Look, your mother and your brothers are standing outside, wanting to speak to you." But to the one who had told him this, Jesus replied, "Who is my mother, and who are my brothers?" And pointing to his disciples, he said, "Here are my mother and my brothers! For whoever does the will of my Father in heaven is my brother and sister and mother."

- Can I imagine this scene? Jesus' beloved family comes by as he is preaching. He seizes the chance to widen that fortunate group. He is not denying family ties, but extending them with a gesture that is like an ordination.
- When he points to the group of disciples, can I imagine that I am standing among them?

november 22–28

Something to think and pray about each day this week:

Reaching for God

My friend Roisín was married to an ambassador and had to go to endless dinners where she would sit beside bankers, industrialists, diplomats, and the like from every country and culture in the world, of every religion and none. There were times when Roisín would interrupt the chit-chat about politics, holidays, and domestic arrangements, and turn to the person beside her, from Japan, India, Algeria, Germany, Rwanda, or wherever, and ask: "Tell me, how do you pray?"

There would be a stunned silence. It was not a politically correct question for a diplomatic dinner. But Roisín was so interested that she would persist until she got an answer. She told me that she always reached some answer. These men and women were astonished to be asked something so personal. But whether they were Muslims, Buddhists, Confucians, ex-Christians, agnostics, or whatever, they all reached for God in some shape, at some time. When we seek a language that will bring the good news to other cultures, we will find that language not in books of theology, but in our own experience of God.

The Presence of God
I pause for a moment
and reflect on God's life-giving presence
in every part of my body, in everything around me,
in the whole of my life.

Freedom
God is not foreign to my freedom.
Instead the Spirit breathes life into my most intimate desires,
gently nudging me toward all that is good.
I ask for the grace to let myself be enfolded by the Spirit.

Consciousness
I exist in a web of relationships—links to nature, people, God.
I trace out these links, giving thanks for the life that flows through them.
Some links are twisted or broken: I may feel regret, anger, disappointment.
I pray for the gift of acceptance and forgiveness.

The Word
God speaks to each one of us individually. I need to listen to what he is saying to me. (Please turn to your scripture on the following pages. Inspiration points are there should you need them. When you are ready, return here to continue.)

Conversation
How has God's Word moved me? Has it left me cold?
Has it consoled me or moved me to act in a new way?
I imagine Jesus standing or sitting beside me,
I turn and share my feelings with him.

Conclusion
Glory be to the Father, and to the Son, and to the Holy Spirit,
As it was in the beginning, is now and ever shall be,
World without end. Amen

Sunday 22nd November,
Feast of Christ the King **John 18:33–37**

Then Pilate entered the headquarters again, summoned Jesus, and asked him, "Are you the King of the Jews?" Jesus answered, "Do you ask this on your own, or did others tell you about me?" Pilate replied, "I am not a Jew, am I? Your own nation and the chief priests have handed you over to me. What have you done?" Jesus answered, "My kingdom is not from this world. If my kingdom were from this world, my followers would be fighting to keep me from being handed over to the Jews. But as it is, my kingdom is not from here." Pilate asked him, "So you are a king?" Jesus answered, "You say that I am a king. For this I was born, and for this I came into the world, to testify to the truth. Everyone who belongs to the truth listens to my voice."

- Lord, that is a strange question you asked Pilate: "Do you ask this on your own?" It pushes me back to my own piety: Is it springing from the needs of my own heart, or is it second-hand, asking questions and taking answers out of books and sermons?
- Let me belong to the truth, listen to your voice, and answer you not with borrowed thoughts or emotions, but with the seeking, however ill-formed, in my own heart.

Monday 23rd November **Luke 21:1–4**

Jesus looked up and saw rich people putting their gifts into the treasury; he also saw a poor widow put in two small copper coins. He said, "Truly I tell you, this poor widow has put in more than all of them; for all of them have contributed out of their abundance, but she out of her poverty has put in all she had to live on."

- Generosity is all relative, of course. Solomon prayed, "Keep me from sacrifices that cost me nothing."

- Teach me true large-heartedness like that of the poor widow, a generosity that gives in secret, and that gives until it hurts.

Tuesday 24th November **Luke 21:5–11**

When some were speaking about the temple, how it was adorned with beautiful stones and gifts dedicated to God, Jesus said, "As for these things that you see, the days will come when not one stone will be left upon another; all will be thrown down." They asked him, "Teacher, when will this be, and what will be the sign that this is about to take place?" And he said, "Beware that you are not led astray; for many will come in my name and say, 'I am he!' and, 'The time is near!' Do not go after them. When you hear of wars and insurrections, do not be terrified; for these things must take place first, but the end will not follow immediately." Then he said to them, "Nation will rise against nation, and kingdom against kingdom; there will be great earthquakes, and in various places famines and plagues; and there will be dreadful portents and great signs from heaven."

- In these last days of the Church's year, we hear Jesus, in Jerusalem, as he faces his own death and foretells crises and great upset facing his followers.
- Jesus does not minimize or water down the difficulties. He himself went on to face the ultimate in crisis and upset. The crisis was not the last word.

Wednesday 25th November **Luke 21:12–19**

Jesus said to his disciples, "But before all this occurs, they will arrest you and persecute you; they will hand you over to synagogues and prisons, and you will be brought before kings and governors because of my name. This will give you an opportunity to testify. So make up your minds not to prepare your defense in advance; for I will give you words and a wisdom that none of your opponents will be able to withstand or contradict. You will be betrayed even by parents and brothers, by relatives and friends; and they will put some of you to death. You will be hated by all because of my name. But not a hair of your head will perish. By your endurance you will gain your souls."

- This picture of arrest and persecution seems remote from our experience: something hard to imagine happening to us.
- However, most of us have known betrayal and unjust treatment at some point of our lives. Whether at school, or in the family, or at work, or with acquaintances, we have tasted hatred at some stage.
- If Jesus could face it, so can we. He tells us that, whatever happens, it is not the end. You will survive. But do not let the experience quench your love or your faith.

Thursday 26th November **Luke 21:20–28**

Jesus said to the disciples, "When you see Jerusalem surrounded by armies, then know that its desolation has come near. Then those in Judea must flee to the mountains, and those inside the city must leave it, and those out in the country must not enter it; for these are days of vengeance, as a fulfillment of all that is written. Woe to those who are pregnant and to those who are nursing infants in those days! For there will be great distress on the earth and wrath against this people; they will fall by the edge of the sword and be taken away as captives among all nations; and Jerusalem will be trampled on by the Gentiles, until the times of the Gentiles are fulfilled. There will be signs in the sun, the moon, and the stars, and on the earth distress among nations confused by the roaring of the sea and the waves. People will faint from fear and foreboding of what is coming upon the world, for the powers of the heavens will be shaken. Then they will see 'the Son of Man coming in a cloud' with power and great glory. Now when these things begin to take place, stand up and raise your heads, because your redemption is drawing near."

- The readers of Luke's Gospel knew these words referred to two distinct prophecies of Jesus, concerning the destruction of Jerusalem and the Second Coming of Christ in their lifetime.
- Our perspective is different, but the theme of distress and desolation still strikes a chord with us. We commend to God in prayer the thousands who live in desolation and foreboding, the victims of war and famine.
- Lord, in your kingdom look with pity on the suffering people of Iraq, Sudan, and other places of misery. For many of them, regardless of their faith, you are their only secure refuge.

Friday 27th November **Luke 21:29–31**

Then Jesus told them a parable: "Look at the fig tree and all the trees; as soon as they sprout leaves you can see for yourselves and know that summer is already near. So also, when you see these things taking place, you know that the kingdom of God is near."

- Let me take time off to step back and to look at the signs of the times: not the immediate concerns of today, but what I see and remember from my own lifetime.
- We have moved a little forward perhaps—from world wars to relative peace for many, from rampant nationalism to some structures of common concern, in the United Nations, the European Union, and the like.
- There is less hunger, disease, and infant mortality, better communication and mutual help. The kingdom of God has quite a distance to go, but perhaps it is getting nearer.

Saturday 28th November **Luke 21:34–36**

Jesus said to his disciples, "Be on guard so that your hearts are not weighed down with dissipation and drunkenness and the worries of this life, and that day catch you unexpectedly, like a trap. For it will come upon all who live on the face of the whole earth. Be alert at all times, praying that you may have the strength to escape all these things that will take place, and to stand before the Son of Man."

- Dissipation: While it may be sold as fun, by the morning after most would agree with Nietzsche that "the mother of dissipation is not joy, but joylessness."
- Joy and moderation go hand in hand. When our hearts are happy, our own skins are a good place to be; we do not need to be blown out of our minds by alcohol or other drugs.